PRAISE FOR
THE SKIES BELONG TO US

A *Boston Globe* Top Nonfiction Book of the Year

A *San Francisco Chronicle* Recommended Book of the Year

An *Outside* Best Adventure Book of the Year

A *Slate* Staff Pick of the Year

A Google Play Best Book of the Year

A KQED Best Book of the Year

"This material, naturally a great yarn, is handled exceedingly well. . . . Koerner has a rare empathy, and by acknowledging the fullness of their strange story, he suggests a deeper truth about the nature of extremism."
—*New York Times Book Review*

"The free-wheeling, hijacking-crazy days of the 1960s and early '70s come to life vividly in Brendan I. Koerner's evocative new page-turner."
—*Los Angeles Times*

"Thrums with the revolutionary, paranoid energy of the era."
—*Boston Globe*

"Brilliantly evoking the atmosphere of the era with its bubbling racial tensions, Vietnam War disillusionment, and marijuana fug, *The Skies Belong to Us* weaves a vivid retelling of America's longest-distance hijacking and its globe-spanning, stranger-than-fiction aftermath with the history of this most mediagenic of crimes. . . . As *The Skies Belong to Us* so entertainingly and insightfully demonstrates, even a recent historical era can seem not merely like a different time, but like a different planet."
—*The Daily Beast*

"Koerner's book is original and riveting, relying on extensive information derived from Freedom of Information Act requests, newspaper reports, and original interviews. . . . These descriptions, which form the bedrock of the book, are amazing."

—*Bookforum*

"The ratio of astonishing facts to words per page makes this book a terrifically fun summer read."

—Kathryn Schulz, *New York* magazine

"Koerner captures the emotional arcs of Holder and Kerkow, a ragged process of accelerated maturation, with humor, understanding and pathos in a book that is impossible to put down. History, writ large and small, has never been so engaging."

—Rick Kleffel, KQED.org

"Both a fascinating look into the psychology of America and a detailed portrait of the lives of two of the era's key players, Koerner has put together a brilliant piece of narrative nonfiction that often reads like an exciting caper."

—*RVANews*

"The level of detail in *The Skies Belong to Us* is outstanding, and it's these quirky pieces that make the book so mesmerizing. . . . Essential reading for anyone interested in aviation or the cultural history of the '60s and '70s, but honestly I don't know how anyone could read this book and not find it enthralling."

—*Metro Pulse*

"Arresting from its opening, with a cinematic attention to the details of how two ordinary kids from the suburbs got wrapped up in everything from the Black Panthers to Parisian art circles to Angela Davis to the evening news . . . Where *Skies* hit me wasn't merely in its text, but in the profound implications of its story on our contemporary issues."

—Anil Dash, Dashes.com

"Hard not to like . . . Koerner captures the kinetic energy of the criminals on the lam and the syrup-slow lifestyles they lead after the engines are shut off and everyone is led off the plane."

—BoingBoing.net

"A thrill-ride . . . Koerner's chronicle of these events is exhaustively researched and staggering to behold."

—AskthePilot.com

"One of the most intriguing pieces of nonfiction I've read this year . . . It's a riveting story of a single, climactic hijacking, but it's also a meditation on the short span of political and policy memory."

—Alyssa Rosenberg, ThinkProgress.org

"Brendan I. Koerner has meticulously reconstructed one of the maddest and most fascinating crime stories in American history. The result is a riveting and illuminating book that will hold you in its spell."

—David Grann, author of *The Lost City of Z*

"*The Skies Belong to Us* is one of the most exciting and fascinating books that I've read this year. It recreates a time when American skyjackings were so common—and casual—that they occurred every week and brings you into the thrilling heart of one of the most audacious hijackings in history. I couldn't stop reading, and what's most amazing is that it's all true."

—Charles Duhigg, author of *The Power of Habit*

"Brendan I. Koerner has turned an odd, nearly forgotten aerial-hijacking episode into an astonishing, hilarious, and unputdownable true-crime narrative. I had no idea that any story could connect the Eldridge Cleaver of the sixties with the TSA miseries of today's air travel, but *The Skies Belong to Us* does that and much more. This is a marvelously entertaining, instructive, and humane book."

—James Fallows, national correspondent for *The Atlantic* and author of *China Airborne*

"Besides being a can't-put-it-down page-turner and an evocative recollection of a forgotten slice of history, *The Skies Belong To Us* feels uncannily relevant today in its depiction of how political forces can impede rational solutions to criminal violence."

—Benjamin Wallace, author of *The Billionaire's Vinegar*

"A thrill ride through the turbulent times when airline hijackings were a weekly occurrence, *The Skies Belong to Us* is true-crime writing at its best. Fast-paced and hard to put down, Brendan I. Koerner's historical page-turner artfully reconstructs one of the most astonishing skyjackings of the Vietnam War era while telling a larger story of politics, money, and how air travel became what it is today."

—Nick Turse, author of *Kill Anything That Moves*

THE SKIES BELONG TO US

ALSO BY BRENDAN I. KOERNER

NOW THE HELL WILL START
One Soldier's Flight from the Greatest Manhunt of World War II

THE SKIES BELONG TO US

Love and Terror in the Golden Age of Hijacking

BRENDAN I. KOERNER

B\D\W\Y BROADWAY BOOKS | NEW YORK

Published in the United States by Broadway Books,
an imprint of the Crown Publishing Group,
a division of Random House LLC, a Penguin Random House
Company, New York.
www.crownpublishing.com

Broadway Books and its logo, B \ D \ W \ Y,
are trademarks of Random House LLC.

Originally published in hardcover in the United States by
Crown Publishers, an imprint of the Crown Publishing Group,
a division of Random House LLC, New York, in 2013.

Library of Congress Cataloging-in-Publication Data
Koerner, Brendan I.
The skies belong to us : love and terror in the golden age
of hijacking / Brendan I. Koerner.—First edition.
pages cm
Includes bibliographical references and index.
1. Hijacking of aircraft—United States—Case studies. I. Title.
HE9803.Z7H545 2013
364.15'52—dc23
2012043203

ISBN 978-0-307-88611-8
eBook ISBN 978-0-307-88612-5

Printed in the United States of America

Book design by Barbara Sturman
Cover design by Darren Haggar
Cover photographs: AP Images

2 4 6 8 10 9 7 5 3

First Paperback Edition

For Maceo and Ciel

Figures can't calculate . . .

My son, from whence this madness, this neglect
Of my commands, and those whom I protect?
Why this unmanly rage? Recall to mind
Whom you forsake, what pledges leave behind.

—VIRGIL, *The Aeneid*

I shoulda stayed in Job Corps,
but now I'm an outlaw . . .

—GHOSTFACE KILLAH

Contents

THE SKIES BELONG TO US

PRELUDE

The man in the black sunglasses tells the waitress he's fine with just coffee. One of his two lunchmates, a dapper Mexican gentleman he knows only as Dave, implores him to eat something—a shrimp cocktail, perhaps, or a half-dozen oysters. But the man insists he has no interest in food.

It is a typically gorgeous afternoon along the San Diego Bay. Sunlight filters through palm fronds into the Brigantine Seafood Restaurant's brick-walled dining room. The sunglassed man and his two companions sit in a semicircular black-leather booth, beneath yellowing nautical charts and kitschy photographs of old yachts. They have come here to discuss a delicate matter.

It is Dave who breaks the ice. He says that he has reviewed a diagram of the man's proposed project, which he praises for its sophistication. He is confident that his associates in Tijuana will have no problem supplying the materials necessary to transform the man's vision into a reality. The only issue to discuss now is money.

The sunglassed man is wary of getting fleeced. "I want to look around," he says as he fiddles with the handle of his coffee mug. "See what else is on the market."

But Dave is keen to strike a deal. He says that he would be happy to accept a small deposit now, then wait for the balance until after the project is complete. He swears that none of his competitors would ever dream of offering such a generous payment plan.

The sunglassed man concurs. He asks Dave if a deposit of $100 will be enough to get things moving.

Dave seems pleased. He is curious about just one thing.

"Now, tell me—what is it that you want to blow up?"

1

"KEEP SMILING"

MAJESTIC MOUNT RAINIER slowly sharpened into view alongside Western Airlines Flight 701, its cratered peak coated with snow and ice that glistened in the strong June sun. Curious passengers craned their necks left to catch a glimpse of the dormant volcano, while the flight's more nonchalant travelers kept their noses buried in newspapers, reading up on President Richard Nixon's trip to Moscow and the carpet-bombing of Huế. Stewardesses clad in peach-hued minidresses roamed the narrow aisle, clearing empty plates and champagne flutes in preparation for landing. They would be on the ground in Seattle in twenty-five minutes.

Once they finished cleaning up, the three stewardesses assigned to coach class packed into the aft galley, where a few leftover meals awaited. The women had been working nonstop since seven a.m., flying down to Los Angeles before returning to Seattle, so they were plenty famished as Flight 701 neared its end. To preserve the illusion that its stewardesses were paragons of female daintiness, Western forbade its shapely "girls" to let passengers see them eat. The women made sure to shut the galley's red curtain before tearing into their lunches. Safe from prying eyes, they shoveled forkfuls of sirloin steak and steamed broccoli into their brightly lipsticked mouths, taking care to avoid dripping gravy onto their polka-dot scarves.

Gina Cutcher stood closest to the galley's curtain, her back to the cabin as she ate and gabbed with her two colleagues, Carol Clymer and Marla Smith. Midway through their hurried meal, Cutcher was startled to hear the *tchk-tchk-tchk* of sliding curtain rings. She turned and found herself toe to toe with the passenger from seat 18D, the handsome black man in the crisply pressed Army dress uniform bedecked with ribbons. He peered down at her through wire-rimmed glasses fitted with amber lenses.

Oh no, she thought. *The voucher. I forgot about his voucher.*

Earlier in the flight, as Cutcher had been serving this man a drink, a bump of turbulence had caused her to spill some bourbon on the lapels of his olive-green jacket. He had been a real sport about the accident, just laughing it off—"Don't worry about it at all," he had told her. "No damage done." But in keeping with Western's customer service policy, Cutcher had insisted on bringing him a dry cleaning voucher. Now she realized that she had never made good on that promise.

An apology was on the tip of her tongue when the man spoke up. "I need to show you something," he said politely, placing two sheets of three-by-five notepaper on the galley's countertop. "Read these."

The puzzled Cutcher began to read as Smith and Clymer peered over her shoulder. The first sheet contained a neatly handwritten message, marred by numerous capitalization and spelling quirks. But there was no mistaking its meaning:

Success through Death

Everyone, Except the Captain will leave the Cabin.
There are four of us and two bombs. Do as you're told and No Shooting will take place.

1) *Your Co-pilot and Navigator are to leave the Cabin (four paces apart.) Take seats to the rear of the Aircraft.*

2) Place Aircraft on Audio-pilot, Place your hands on top of your Head. leave the Cabin door open.

Weatherman
S.D.S. of California
You have 2 mins, Sir.

The other sheet was filled with a diagram of what appeared to be a briefcase. Several rectangles of varying size, each labeled with a number from one to four, were sketched inside the drawing. A column of text to the left of the diagram explained the briefcase's contents:

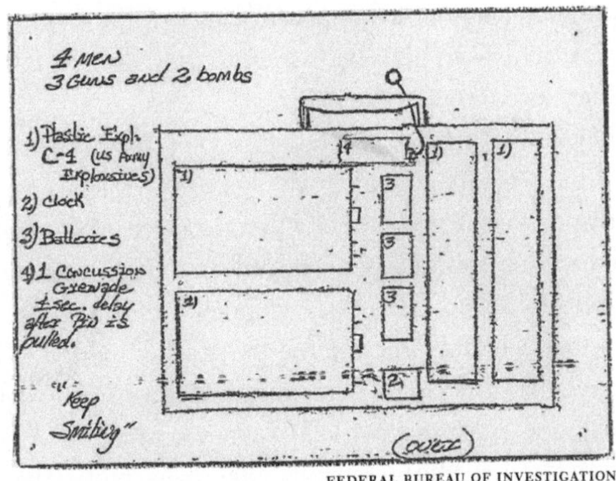

FEDERAL BUREAU OF INVESTIGATION

4 Men
3 Guns and 2 bombs

1) Plastic Explo C-4 (US Army Explosives)
2) Clock
3) Batteries
4) 1 Concussion Grenade 1 sec. delay after Pin is pulled.

"Keep Smiling"
(over)

Cutcher turned the note over. There was just one more sentence:

"To the Captain, and don't stop!"

The man raised his left hand so the stewardesses could see that he was holding a black Samsonite briefcase. A thin piece of copper wire snaked from its top, right by the handle. It was connected to a metal ring draped around the man's left index finger. He made a show of rhythmically tapping the briefcase with his right hand, as if to say, *In here.*

The man elbowed his way past Cutcher and stepped into the galley. He leaned against the countertop, pushed his glasses up to the bridge of his nose, and locked eyes with Cutcher. Every trace of kindness was now gone from his gaze.

"You have two minutes," he said.

Cutcher did not hesitate to obey the notes' final instruction: she headed for the cockpit.

Smith and Clymer stood there, frozen in place, as the man stared at his immaculately shined shoes. The only sound in the galley was the dull buzz of the Boeing 727's three engines. Smith furtively glanced over at Clymer, who was still holding the bowl of red Jell-O that she had been eating for dessert. Clymer's mouth was slightly agape, her hands shaking so much that her Jell-O cubes wobbled.

After an eternal thirty seconds, the man broke the silence. "Should've blown it up," he mumbled without looking up from his shoes. "On takeoff, blown it up. We're all gonna die anyway."

Clymer's red Jell-O wobbled even more.

Cutcher, meanwhile, was racing toward the front of the plane, the two notes flapping in her hand. When she reached the first-class section, she spotted the flight's lead stewardess, Donna Jones, stowing glasses into a cabinet. "It's happening to us!" Cutcher exclaimed. "Open the door, open the door! We have two minutes!"

Jones led Cutcher to the cockpit and rang the entrance bell twice—the signal for an urgent matter. The door opened, and the two women entered the cramped compartment. Jerome Juergens, Flight 701's captain, sensed right away that Cutcher was on the verge of panic.

Cutcher thrust the notes forward. "Captain," she said, "before you go on descending, please, you—you need to read these!"

Juergens zipped through the poorly spelled list of instructions, but he lingered over the diagram for several moments, looking for some flaw in the bomb's design. Juergens was a decorated ex-Marine, a man who had learned a thing or two about explosives while flying A-1 Skyraiders in Korea. He hoped the drawing might betray its artist as a bluffer, someone unfamiliar with the intricacies of detonating C-4. But the diagram was obviously the handiwork of a man who knew what he was doing.

Juergens passed the notes to his co-pilot, Edward Richardson, and calmly gave Cutcher his orders: "Go back and tell this man we'll comply with anything he wants us to do."

As Cutcher left to fetch the man from the aft galley, Richardson could only marvel at his dreadful luck: this was the second time he had been hijacked in less than a month.

ONLY THE MOST seasoned travelers can recall the days when flying was an ethereal pleasure rather than a grind. Decades have passed since coach-class passengers enjoyed luxuries that have since become inconceivable: lumps of Alaskan crabmeat served atop monogrammed china, generous pours of free liquor, leggy stewardesses who performed their duties with geisha-like courtesy. Even on short-haul flights between minor cities, the customer was truly king.

Yet what seems most archaic about that bygone age is not the pampering that passengers received while aloft, but how easily they moved while on the ground. It was once possible to pass through an entire airport, from curbside to gate, without encountering a single inconvenience—no X-ray machines, no metal detectors, no uniformed security personnel with grabby hands and bitter dispositions. Anyone could stroll onto a tarmac and queue for boarding without holding a ticket or presenting identification. Some flights even permitted passengers to pay their fares after takeoff, as if jets were merely commuter trains with wings.

A generation of skyjackers exploited this naïveté. Between 1961, when the first plane was seized in American airspace, and 1972, the year Flight 701 was waylaid en route to Seattle, 159 commercial flights were hijacked in the United States. All but a fraction of those hijackings took place during the last five years of that frenetic era, often at a clip of one or more per week. There were, in fact, many days when two planes were hijacked simultaneously, strictly by coincidence.* Few other crime waves in American history have stoked such widespread paranoia: every time a plane's public address system crackled to life, passengers could not help but think that a stranger's voice was about to intone, "Ladies and gentlemen, I am now in charge . . ."

In struggling to make sense of this madness, pundits and politicians often invoked the term *epidemic* to describe the skyjacking crisis. They spoke more truly than they knew, for one of the best ways to understand the Golden Age of Hijacking is through the lens of public health. The phenomenon spread in strict accordance with the laws of epidemiology: skyjackings always occurred in clusters that traced back to a single incident that had turned contagious. These outbreaks grew more and more devastating over time, as the impulse to hijack jumped from host to host like any organic pathogen. This "virus" traveled via mass media, especially television newscasts; the networks' stately anchormen were forever narrating clips of hijacked planes and the tearful families of hostages. Rather than empathize with the victims, some viewers were titillated by the skyjackers' ability to create spectacles that held the whole country in thrall.

Those viewers were susceptible to the skyjacking virus because they had lost all faith in America's promise. It is no accident that the

---

*In 1970, a University of Chicago statistician devised a procedure for assessing the probability of these so-called double hijackings. He was inspired to tackle the project after noticing that three double hijackings had taken place in a four-month span, beginning in November 1968.

epidemic began to crest as the last vestiges of 1960s idealism were being extinguished. Large segments of the population were aggrieved that words and placards had failed to end the war in Vietnam, or cement the gains of a civil rights movement that was decimated by assassinations. That disappointment quickly mutated into a more pervasive sense of hopelessness, a feeling that no amount of civic engagement could ever salvage a system that had been rigged to serve a selfish elite. Some of the frustrated drifted into hedonism, papering over their disillusionment with sexual excess or cheap brown heroin. But others sought increasingly radical ways in which to articulate their vague yet all-consuming rage.

Airplanes were ideal targets for these troubled souls. On a practical level, skyjackers could use planes to flee to distant lands, where they presumed they would be celebrated for their audacity. But there was also a strong psychological component to skyjacking's allure, one that stemmed from America's love affair with flight. Even as commercial air travel became accessible to the masses during the 1960s, it retained an aura of wonder and privilege—pilots were debonair heroes, the planes themselves marvels of technological might. By seizing a jet as it hurtled across the nation's most exotic frontier, a lone skyjacker could instantly command an audience of millions. There was no more spectacular way for the marginalized to feel the rush of power.

Though all skyjackers shared a common hunger for respect, their individual narratives were bewilderingly varied. When I first became fascinated by the Golden Age of Hijacking, after reading about a Puerto Rican nationalist who spent forty-one years in exile after diverting a Boeing 707 to Cuba,* I was awed by the sheer range of characters who had commandeered the era's planes. Their ranks included frazzled veterans, chronic fabulists, compulsive gamblers, bankrupt businessmen, thwarted academics, career felons, and even lovesick

*That skyjacker, Luis Armando Peña Soltren, voluntarily returned to the United States in October 2009, so that he could reunite with his family. He was arrested upon leaving his plane in New York and eventually pleaded guilty to conspiracy to commit air piracy. In January 2011 he was sentenced to fifteen years in prison.

teens. Each had an intensely personal, if sadly deluded, rationale for believing they could skyjack their way to better lives.

The more I immersed myself in the annals of American skyjacking, the more I fixated on the epidemic's final, most frenzied phase: the great outbreak of 1972. The skyjackers that year were bold and foolish beyond measure, prone to taking risks that smacked of lunacy. Middle-aged men parachuted from jets while clutching six-figure ransoms to their chests; manic extremists demanded passage to war zones a hemisphere away; young mothers brandished pistols while feeding formula to their infants. The FBI's burgeoning zeal for violent intervention did little to dissuade these adventurers, who were far beyond caring whether they died in pursuit of their grandiose goals. By the end of 1972, the skyjackers had become so reckless, so dismissive of human life, that the airlines and the federal government had no choice but to turn every airport into a miniature police state.

There is an absorbing tale to tell about each of the forty American skyjackers who made 1972 such a perilous year to fly. But none is as captivating as that of Willie Roger Holder and Catherine Marie Kerkow, the young couple who took control of Western Airlines Flight 701 as it soared past Mount Rainier.

Holder and Kerkow were ordinary skyjackers in many ways. He was a traumatized ex-soldier motivated by a hazy mix of outrage and despair; she was a mischievous party girl who longed for a more meaningful future. Neither was a master criminal, as evidenced by the utter zaniness of their hijacking plan.

Yet through a combination of savvy and dumb luck, Holder and Kerkow pulled off the longest-distance skyjacking in American history, a feat that made them notorious around the globe. Their success set them apart from their peers: by the end of 1972, virtually all of the year's other skyjackers were either dead or in jail. In its annual "The Year in Pictures" issue that December, *Life* ran a rogues' gallery of a dozen skyjackers who had already been convicted of air piracy, along with captions detailing their stiff sentences: twenty years, thirty years, forty years, forty-five years, life without parole. Holder and Kerkow were notably absent from that catalog of failures.

But Holder and Kerkow's story was far from over once they managed their escape. In the months and years that followed, they would take up with revolutionaries, melt into an international underground, and mingle with aristocrats and movie stars who lauded them as icons. But when their fame inevitably began to fade and their love dissolved, Holder and Kerkow were forced to learn that reinventing oneself, that most American of aspirations, is never without its sorrows.

2

COOS BAY

THE KNOCK ON the door came at an inopportune moment for Cathy Kerkow, right as she was working a gob of shampoo through her long brown hair. Though she wasn't expecting any visitors that January afternoon in 1972, she was far too genial a soul to ignore the caller. She wrapped a kimono-style bathrobe around her slender body and hurried from the shower, leaving a trail of soapy water in her wake.

Kerkow opened the door to discover an exceptionally tall, rail-thin black man with close-cropped hair and manicured sideburns. A pair of tortoiseshell sunglasses shielded his sleepy eyes from San Diego's midday glare. He grinned at the lovely sight before him, a scantily clad twenty-year-old girl with rivulets of water sluicing down her cleavage. Kerkow flashed back a coy smile, pleased to know that her abundant charms were working their standard magic.

The man asked if he had the right apartment for an acquaintance of his, a young lady by the name of Beth Newhouse. Kerkow replied that Beth was her roommate, and that he could probably find her shopping at the local drugstore. The man promptly left without saying goodbye; Kerkow stood in the doorway and watched him speed off in a yellow Pontiac Firebird. As the car vanished around the Murray Street bend, she thought, *I know him from somewhere.*

Twenty minutes later the man and Newhouse returned to the

apartment together. Apologizing for his prior rudeness, the man now introduced himself to Kerkow as Roger Holder. He explained that he had once been Newhouse's downstairs neighbor, back when she lived near Ocean Beach. They had recently bumped into each other on Broadway near 4th Avenue, down among the saloons of San Diego's red-light district, and Newhouse had passed along her current address in suburban El Cajon. With time to kill that afternoon, Holder had decided to pop by for a visit.

Newhouse was less than thrilled to see Holder again. She had always considered him something of a creep—not least of all because he had used a different name, Linton Charles White, when they had first met the year before. She had given him her address only after much cajoling, and now she was eager to get rid of her unwelcome guest without causing a scene. So Newhouse remarked that her boyfriend would be arriving soon, and that he was the insanely jealous type; if Holder didn't split, there could be trouble.

But Kerkow didn't want Holder to leave just yet—not while she was still trying to piece together why he looked so darn familiar. To delay his departure, she suggested they all share a quick joint; the girls were small-time marijuana dealers who never lacked for pungent grass. Holder readily accepted the offer.

As the joint circulated around the trio, Kerkow and Holder kept making eyes at each other, lobbing signals back and forth. They both pined to take a roll on Kerkow's queen-size waterbed—the only piece of furniture she owned—but the circumstances weren't right. Before he left, though, Holder asked the two women if he could repay their kindness by treating them to breakfast that coming Saturday. Newhouse declined, but Kerkow said yes to the morning date.

Two days later Holder picked her up in his Firebird and took her to a diner on University Avenue. As they spooned sugar into their coffees, Holder made a confession: he had been driving himself crazy trying to figure out where he and Kerkow had met before. He had the strangest sense this wasn't the first time their paths had crossed. But try as he might, the memory of their previous encounter was eluding him.

Kerkow admitted that she, too, had felt a powerful twinge of recognition upon seeing Holder at her apartment door. But how could that be? She had been in San Diego for only five months, scarcely enough time to forget such a memorable face. Prior to that she had spent virtually her whole life in Coos Bay, a logging town on Oregon's southern coast. Surely there was no way Holder had ever passed through such an isolated place.

Holder set down his coffee and leaned back in the booth. He rubbed his chin and mouth in thought, then filled his lungs with soothing Pall Mall smoke.

Coos Bay. Yes, he said, he knew Coos Bay. He knew it very well.

WHEN CATHERINE MARIE Kerkow was born in October 1951, Coos Bay was in the midst of a splendid postwar boom. Located on a thickly forested peninsula dotted with scenic lakes, the town was blessed with a harbor deep enough to accommodate the world's largest timber ships, which hauled off Oregon's precious firs and cedars by the millions. A never-ending stream of logging trucks jammed the coastal roads, rumbling past the enormous waterfront sawmill that draped the town in the scent of fresh-cut wood.

The timber trade produced vast fortunes for Coos Bay's leading families, who resided in chandeliered homes overlooking the harbor and the verdant hills beyond. Yet the town's middle class thrived, too, as the logging money trickled down to saw operators, shopkeepers, and civil servants. Families grateful for their prosperity packed the church pews every Sunday to hear sermons about the virtues of hard work and the perils of sin. Their children were Boy Scouts and Campfire Girls who spent their allowances on double features at the Egyptian Theater, the town's Art Deco centerpiece.

Newlyweds Bruce and Patricia Kerkow seemed to be on track for just such a pleasant future when Cathy became their firstborn child. The couple wasted little time rounding out their family: by the time she was six, Cathy had been joined by three younger brothers. Though he loved his children dearly, Bruce was also frustrated by fatherhood's demands. A driver for a dredging company by trade, he yearned to make his living as a jazz organist instead. But there was no way to carve out such an offbeat career while stuck in Coos Bay with a sizable family. As Bruce's dream became more remote with the birth of each child, he turned morose: at the Kiwanis Club meetings and church potlucks that were the linchpins of Coos Bay's social life, rumors swirled that the Kerkows' marriage might be on the rocks.

In the summer of 1959, however, the town's gossipmongers began to chatter about news far more salacious than the Kerkows' marital woes. A year earlier the Navy had opened a sonar station on Coos Head, a bluff overlooking the bay, in order to track Soviet submarine activity in the Pacific Ocean. Now the installation had taken on a new chief cook, a fifteen-year Navy veteran who had recently returned from duty in the Taiwan Strait. To the horror of Coos Bay's more provincial inhabitants, this cook was also black. His name was Seavenes Holder.

A North Carolina native whose hobby was penning gospel lyrics,* Seavenes had joined the Navy shortly before D-day. He served aboard the USS *Beale* during the invasion of Okinawa, then sailed into Nagasaki right after the city had been flattened by the "Fat Man" atomic bomb. These historic adventures convinced Seavenes to become a Navy lifer. He was stationed in Norfolk, Virginia, when his second son, Willie Roger Holder, was born on June 14, 1949—Flag Day, as proud and patriotic Seavenes was fond of pointing out.

In the mid-1950s the growing Holder family relocated from Virginia to Alameda, California, home to one of the nation's foremost naval bases. Seavenes was gone for months at a time on the USS *Rogers*, a destroyer that prowled the waters of the western Pacific. With four young children now taxing the patience of his wife, Marie, he longed for an assignment that would let him come home each night.

---

*Seavenes Holder once hired a Chicago-based publishing company, Richard Brothers, to create music to accompany a song he had written, titled "Begin the Day with Jesus." There is no evidence that the song was ever recorded.

When the job at Coos Head opened up, the opportunity seemed like a blessing from above.

In August 1959 the Holders piled into the family's Ford Crown Victoria and headed north up Highway 101, thrilled to be starting life anew in southwestern Oregon. Seavenes was in a jolly mood during the ride, talking up all the hunting and fishing trips he had planned for the kids. Ten-year-old Roger was most excited about the fact that his father had rented a four-bedroom house, a major upgrade over their cramped Alameda bungalow. He would finally have a room all to himself.

But when Seavenes showed up at the real estate office to collect the house keys, he was told that the property was no longer available and that his mailed deposit would be refunded. Seavenes knew exactly what that meant: the agent with whom he had arranged the lease over the phone hadn't realized that the Holders were black.

The family camped out in a hotel room while Seavenes scrambled to find more permanent accommodations. He was rejected by several landlords who made little effort to conceal their bias: Coos Bay had just a single black family at the time, headed by the proprietor of a downtown shoeshine stand, and many residents were dead set against darkening the town's collective pigmentation any further.

The Holders eventually settled into a house in the blue-collar Empire neighborhood, on the peninsula's western side. The landlord, an eccentric older woman who drove a tractor and smoked cigars, provided Seavenes with a shotgun, advising him that he might need it to fend off intruders. Her warning quickly proved correct: two nights after the Holders moved in, a pickup truck full of rowdy men pulled into the family's driveway at two a.m. "Niggers go home!" the trespassers yelled as they waved flashlights through the Holders' windows and pelted the door with rocks. From that point on, such menacing late-night visits became routine.

The family's tormentors operated in the daytime, too. When Marie went shopping for groceries on Newmark Avenue, housewives would spit in her face as she walked the aisles, or hiss that she'd better not touch the vegetables with her unclean hands. The children were taunted whenever they dared play in the local park; the oldest child, eleven-year-old Seavenes Jr., started carrying a small hatchet in order to protect himself.

The elder Seavenes pleaded with his family to turn the other cheek, assuring them that the bigots would soon tire of their bullying. And so on September 9, Roger and his younger brother, Danny, were packed off to Madison Elementary School to begin the fall semester. The very next day several older boys cornered seven-year-old Danny on the school's playground. The leader of the pack knocked him to the ground, then kicked his prone body at least a dozen times. The beating was severe enough to land Danny in the hospital, where doctors briefly feared that the boy might lose a testicle.

The petrified Danny initially refused to identify his attacker. The police eventually coaxed him into fingering the culprit, but the boy was never arrested. When news of the assault started to make the rounds, Coos Bay's progressive residents declared themselves aghast at their racist neighbors' campaign of terror. An emergency meeting of the Madison Parent Teacher Association was called to discuss the matter, and a local weekly paper chimed in with a soul-searching editorial on its front page:

> Why and how could such a thing happen, and what can be done, is the question everyone is asking.
>
> Although it could have been just a schoolyard fight, many who have tried to analyze the situation do not believe it to be only that. The viciousness of the attack indicates strong feelings, such as those instilled by an adult or by an older person the boy looked up to. Children can be little tyrants when meting out punishment for others their own age. This was not the case.

A majority of the school's parents banded together to beg the Holders to send Danny back to Madison, promising Seavenes and

Marie that no more harm would come to their youngest son. And the embarrassed police vowed to protect the family against further racial harassment.

But the spirit of reconciliation did not last. Embittered by Danny's beating, Seavenes filed suit against the State of Oregon for failing to protect his family's civil rights. When his superiors caught wind of the case, they ordered him to drop the matter and report back to Alameda at once. The Navy did not want to risk antagonizing Coos Bay any further.

As their distraught parents packed up the house, Seavenes Jr. and Roger spent an unseasonably warm October day exploring the woods around Empire Lakes, a popular recreation area. They came to a secluded stretch of shoreline, where they spotted a boy and girl dipping jars into the water. Fuming over his family's humiliation, Seavenes Jr. whispered to Roger that they should avenge poor Danny by beating up the two kids. But Roger nixed that plan—he just wanted to see what the kids were doing with their jars.

The Holder boys approached the water's edge. Roger saw that the girl was around eight years old; the boy appeared to be her little brother. She was pale and slight, with prominent ears and oversize glasses. Roger asked what she and her brother were doing.

"Catching salamanders," the girl replied.

Roger peered at the muddy water inside the girl's jar and laughed. "Those ain't salamanders," he said. "Those are tadpoles, see? Tadpoles—baby frogs."

The girl reached into her jar and pulled out one of the minuscule creatures by its tail. She dangled it right in front of Roger's face, so he could inspect its frilly gills and nascent limbs. "I know a baby salamander when I see one," she snapped. When Roger could say nothing in reply, the girl broke into a wide grin; she was obviously pleased to have won the argument.

The girl's brother tugged at her sleeve—he wanted to head back to the picnic area, where Mom and Dad were waiting. "Well, next time I see you, I hope you've learned more about salamanders," the grinning girl said to Roger while screwing a brass lid onto her jar. "Bye-bye."

"Good luck with them salamanders!" Roger Holder shouted after Cathy Kerkow as she and her brother disappeared into the woods. He was certain that she heard him, though she never did look back.

Four days later the Holders' Crown Victoria headed south down Highway 101. The family had been run out of Oregon after less than three months.

As Cathy Kerkow entered junior high, her parents' shaky marriage finally fell apart. Bruce moved north to Seattle to pursue his music, leaving Patricia to care for their four children all by herself. The split was a minor scandal in conservative Coos Bay, where *divorce* was still a dirty word; the consensus was that only the lowest of scoundrels would abandon their kids to chase bohemian dreams. The town rallied behind the much-loved Patricia, who took a full-time secretarial job at Southwestern Oregon Community College (SWOCC) to make ends meet.

Because of her demanding work schedule, Patricia relied on Cathy to help run the household. Though barely more than a child herself, Cathy was expected to mend clothes, prepare roasts, and make sure her three younger brothers were dressed for school or church on time. While her friends from the neighborhood were outside on South 10th Street, running footraces between the lampposts or playing games of Truth or Dare, Cathy was often stuck inside her family's second-floor flat, tending to chores. The sweet and quiet girl never complained about her responsibilities as assistant mom, nor voiced any sadness over her father's departure. But there was pain beneath her placid surface.

When she entered Marshfield High School in 1965, Kerkow was going through an awkward phase. The shy and gangly girl threw herself into the sorts of extracurriculars that proper young Coos Bay ladies were supposed to enjoy: chorus, the Latin club, and a Christian group that provided meals to elderly shut-ins. She made straight B's and became close friends with one of her fellow sopranos, Beth Newhouse, the daughter of the town's leading attorney.

As Kerkow progressed through Marshfield, though, she shed her gawkiness and blossomed into a talented athlete. She took up running, which had long been the biggest sport in Coos Bay—the town's temperate climate allowed for year-round training, and the surrounding hills were ideal for strengthening young legs. The Marshfield track team was a powerhouse in the late 1960s, led by the best schoolboy miler in the United States, a scrappy carpenter's son named Steve Prefontaine. Kerkow made the varsity squad as a junior and set a school record in the eighty-yard hurdles, an achievement that earned her special mention in Marshfield's yearbook alongside her friend and classmate Prefontaine.

Junior year was also when Kerkow began to take full advantage of her newfound ability to set male hearts aflutter. Endowed with a cherubic smile and lithe curves, the sixteen-year-old Kerkow had matured into the sort of intimidating beauty whom boys often lack the courage to approach. She started going steady with a handsome jock named Dennis Krummel, a baseball star who had grown up in her neighborhood. They made the rounds at Coos Bay's teenage hotspots, cruising past the Egyptian Theater and feasting on hamburgers at Dairy Queen.

Intoxicated by her first taste of adolescent freedom, Kerkow began to display a rebellious streak that she had long suppressed, one rooted in the trauma of her family's dissolution several years before. The once-dutiful daughter now quarreled with her mother and retreated from the more wholesome aspects of high school life. She quit the track team, broke up with Krummel, and started to date a surfer who was in his early twenties. Kerkow would watch him ride the chilly waves off Bastendorff Beach, where scruffy types smoked grass and drank Rainier beer at all-night crab boils. The couple tooled around Coos Bay in his wood-paneled station wagon, with Kerkow's well-toned legs dangling from the passenger-side window. The Marshfield boys would

Cathy Kerkow in the Marshfield High School yearbook, 1969.
COOS HISTORICAL & MARITIME MUSEUM

sigh whenever the woodie passed, chagrined to realize that fair Cathy was now well outside their league.

Kerkow was so busy enjoying the perks of her feminine wiles that she never paused to contemplate her future. And so when she received her Marshfield diploma in June 1969, she had only the vaguest notion of what to do next. Much like her absent father, she harbored pie-in-the-sky dreams of becoming a professional singer. But her main ambition at the age of seventeen was more mundane: she wanted to hang out with cool boys who would take her to the coolest parties.

The next two years of Kerkow's life were a blur of fleeting romances and halfhearted attempts at adulthood. After spending the summer of 1969 working at a sawmill in Prineville, she returned to Coos Bay and enrolled at SWOCC to study oceanography. But she was a lackadaisical student, accumulating just a bare minimum of credits. She also worked a succession of menial jobs, all of which she lost in short order. She was fired from a Rexall drugstore, for example, amid accusations that she had stolen amphetamines for her surfer friends; she lasted less than three weeks at a Payless drugstore after her boss deemed her too lazy to operate the cash register. Kerkow was eventually reduced to taking seasonal positions to fund her leisure: stocking shelves at a housewares store during the holidays, picking shrimp in the spring. She supplemented her meager income by shoplifting; she loved to give the salesclerks a cordial nod as she walked out the door, lipstick and stockings stuffed in her purse.

As she floundered in Coos Bay, Kerkow tried on a range of different identities, looking for ways to define herself as something more than just another aimless college kid. In October 1970 she traveled two hours northeast to Eugene, a city that many in Coos Bay considered a latter-day Gomorrah, to attend a symposium featuring high-ranking members of the Black Panther Party. Kerkow cared nothing for the Panthers' radical politics, but she swooned over their style and attitude: the black leather jackets, the berets perched atop Afros, the fiery speeches about the system's rot. Above all, she knew the Panthers were feared and reviled in Coos Bay; to embrace them, however superficially, would make her dangerously hip.

A few months later she bumped into her ex-boyfriend Dennis Krummel on the campus of SWOCC, where he was also a student. Krummel was wearing an Air Force Reserve Officer Training Corps uniform; he said that he had just joined up, in the hopes of becoming a pilot after earning his degree.

"Well, I'm with the Black Panthers now," Kerkow blurted out in response, greatly exaggerating her involvement in order to maximize the shock factor. "I know they have some different ideas, but I've come to agree with them." Krummel was every bit as floored as she had hoped.

In the late summer of 1971, Kerkow received a phone call from Beth Newhouse, her close friend from the Marshfield chorus. A rebel in her own right, Newhouse had married a surfer ten years her senior shortly after graduating from high school. But that relationship had quickly disintegrated due to her husband's alcoholism, and Newhouse had fled to San Diego to convalesce with an older sister. Instantly smitten by the city's perfect weather and raucous party scene, she decided to stay and reap the benefits of being a young divorcée in the era of free love. She first moved into an apartment near Ocean Beach, a hippie enclave full of head shops and health food stores, where rock bands often played impromptu shows on the sand. When the rent there became unaffordable, Newhouse found a cheaper place in El Cajon, on the city's eastern edge, and took on a roommate.

When that roommate left without warning, Newhouse became desperate to find a replacement before the next month's rent was due. She offered the bedroom to Kerkow, who seized the chance to escape her dead-end life in Coos Bay. She dropped out of SWOCC, packed up her Volkswagen Beetle, and struck out for southern California.

San Diego was a revelation for Kerkow, a wonderland of sunny days and easy sex. She dated a galaxy of men who seemed fantastically exotic to a cloistered Coos Bay girl: Mexican bikers, greasy rockers, the bronzed and preppy scions of La Jolla's yachting elite. As she sampled San Diego's menu of bachelors, she discovered that she was especially drawn to black men; she confessed to Newhouse that, for reasons she couldn't fathom, she found such men "unusually attractive." Though Kerkow loved to press her mother's buttons, she never dared tell her about this romantic predilection during their occasional phone chats; she worried that Patricia would be appalled.

Kerkow also concealed the seedy means by which she earned her keep in San Diego: she worked at the International Massage Parlor on 4th Avenue, in the run-down Hillcrest neighborhood. Though she had fancied herself too worldly for Coos Bay, she was hopelessly naïve by San Diego standards; when she started at the parlor, she genuinely believed the job would entail nothing more than kneading kinks out of muscles. Kerkow was horrified when the first naked client flipped onto his back and insinuated that he would like a sexual favor; when other similarly smutty requests soon followed, it dawned on her why the manager hadn't cared about her total lack of experience. Against her better judgment, she satisfied her customers' urges in exchange for tips, letting her mind wander to more pleasant thoughts as she rubbed and tugged.

Kerkow told her mother that she worked as a receptionist at a doctor's office.

Right after Christmas 1971, a sleazy gangster who owned adult businesses throughout San Diego convinced Kerkow to come work for him. He offered her a job at a downtown strip club, where customers were barred from touching the topless dancers. But she opted to remain a masseuse, moving to one of the man's upscale parlors in suburban Spring Valley. She and Newhouse also ran a sideline business in marijuana, peddling ounces purchased from a small-time hoodlum they knew only as Fast Eddie.

Kerkow was adrift in this sordid world when Roger Holder came knocking in January 1972. He, too, had gone astray since their fleeting encounter at Empire Lakes some thirteen years earlier. But his troubles ran much deeper than Cathy's, inflamed by experiences far more brutal than she could imagine.

THE ROGER HOLDER who returned to Alameda with his family in the fall of 1959 was not the same boy who had left for Oregon that August. The expulsion from Coos Bay had scarred him; once a devout Christian like his father, Holder now questioned what sort of God would see fit to crush his family's modest dreams. He channeled his melancholy into a solitary pursuit: building intricate models of trains, planes, and helicopters. The geeky hobby reminded him of the happy moments he had spent with his dad in Virginia, watching naval shipbuilders weld together the beams of aircraft carriers.

On the rare occasions he ventured outside, Holder faced relentless teasing by his peers. While waiting for the Navy to complete a new housing complex in Alameda, his family lived in a predominantly black section of neighboring Oakland. The boys there ridiculed Roger for a cruelly ironic reason: they considered his behavior too white.

They mocked him for his models, his elocution, his skateboard—anything that smacked of habits favored by residents of the Bay Area's paler precincts. Confused and stung by this rejection, Holder retreated even deeper into a world of his own.

But when he entered Encinal High School in 1964, Holder discovered that girls of all races were actually charmed by his quirks. Adept at exuding a pensive cool, the long-limbed teenager attracted the sorts of female admirers who were just beginning to hang Beatles posters on their bedroom walls. Holder capitalized on their curiosity by mastering the art of the pickup. He started riding his skateboard to the coffeehouses frequented by students from Mills College, an all-girls school in Oakland's foothills. He convinced more than a few pretty English majors to accompany him to Leona Heights Park, where he would pretend to dig their sappy poetry before moving on to lewder diversions.

Holder was a careless lover, a foible that led to predictable results: in the summer of 1966 he learned that one of his girlfriends, a sixteen-year-old Encinal sophomore named Betty Bullock, was pregnant by him—with twins, no less. That November, to earn money for his children's care, he dropped out of the eleventh grade and joined the family business by enlisting in the U.S. Army; he had to lie to the recruiter about his age, since he was still just seventeen. Holder was at basic training the following February when Bullock gave birth to his daughters, Teresa and Torrita.

Though he lacked a high school diploma, Holder was extremely intelligent and scored well on his Armed Forces Qualification Test, the exam the Army used to determine its recruits' assignments. In March 1967 Holder was sent to Bad Hersfeld, West Germany, home of the 11th Armored Cavalry Regiment, to take a course in tank warfare. That October he received the inevitable order to join the 11th ACR's contingent in Vietnam. On his way to Southeast Asia, Holder made a quick stop in California to marry Bullock and bid farewell to his infant daughters.

When Holder arrived in Vietnam, the 11th ACR was in the midst of an extended operation to pacify Long Khanh, a province northwest of Saigon that teemed with Vietcong fighters. The guerrillas launched daily ambushes on vehicles traveling the region's muddy roads, battering their prey with rockets before melting back into the jungle. The primary mission of the 11th ACR, better known as the Blackhorse Regiment, was to plow its armored vehicles through Long Khanh's dense wilderness in search of the elusive enemy.

The Blackhorse Regiment's mainstay was the M113 armored personnel carrier, a trapezoidal twelve-ton beast with the power to obliterate all foliage in its path. Holder manned one such vehicle's M60 machine gun, shielded by a steel plate stenciled with the regiment's unofficial motto: FIND THE BASTARDS THEN PILE ON. In the thick of the jungle, Holder and his crewmates would try to detect signs of Vietcong activity—the camouflaged hatches of underground lairs, the suspiciously neat piles of leaves that concealed grenades. But with visibility often limited to ten feet or less, their first inkling of the enemy's presence was typically a hail of AK-47 fire.

Holder grew enamored of this perilous search-and-destroy work. He relished the adrenaline of combat, the glee of blindly pumping hundreds of .308-caliber rounds into the jungle after surviving yet another Vietcong onslaught. And he loved tinkering with the M113's mechanical systems, much as he had once loved building model trains in the dim light of his bedroom. While his comrades counted down their days to freedom on homemade calendars shaped like *Playboy* models, Holder intended to stay in Vietnam for as long as possible.

But Holder's passion for combat did not make him immune to the war's psychological toll. The Vietcong were masters at fomenting paranoia, littering the jungle with clever booby traps that made the Americans question their every footstep. Ordinary objects like soda cans and rice bowls were rigged with explosives powerful enough to kill; 11 percent of American deaths in Vietnam were due to such improvised devices. And nightly Vietcong mortar attacks deprived the troops of much-needed sleep, jangling their frayed nerves even further. So as the Blackhorse Regiment pushed toward the Cambodian border in the waning days of 1967, Holder began to suffer from spells of overwhelming anxiety. He self-medicated with copious amounts of marijuana, purchased from peasants for ten cents a joint. The drug numbed him to the fear that his next foray into the bush could be his last.

On January 14, 1968, Holder awoke at dawn with a scorching fever—he had contracted a bad case of malaria. There was no time for medical treatment, though: the Vietcong's Tet Offensive was in full swing, and Holder's unit had orders to root out enemy fighters in the rubber groves by Loc Ninh. Holder chain-smoked a few joints, a ritual he referred to as "the breakfast of champions," then hopped aboard his M113.

Holder and his crew ventured down a dirt trail that dead-ended at a crumbling Buddhist tomb. Worried that the bushes around the gravesite might conceal booby traps, the M113's driver reversed into a patch of tall grass. The stoned and malarial Holder turned his head to check for incoming fire as the vehicle backed up.

Then Holder's eardrums shattered, and his world went white. The next thing he knew, he was lying in the middle of the road, his shirt and helmet gone. He instinctively stumbled back to the M113, which a land mine had turned into a heap of twisted steel. One of his crewmates had been torn clean in half by the blast; another had clumps of brain leaking out from behind his right ear.

Holder heard the whirr of a helicopter and looked up at the sky. As he did so, he collapsed onto his back and fell unconscious; his spine had nearly been severed. He would spend the next six weeks recuperating at a hospital near Saigon, where his back healed but his mind did not: Holder could not stop envisioning the explosion's aftermath, nor shake his survivor's guilt.

There was more tragedy to come for Holder once he returned to action. On May 19 he lost his closest friend in the Blackhorse Regiment, a private from Los Angeles named Stanley Schroeder who shared Holder's love of model trains. The eighteen-year-old Schroeder was killed by a booby trap that sheared off both his arms, leaving him to bleed to death in a thicket of bomb-scorched trees. The death weighed heavily on Holder, who felt that Schroeder was the Blackhorse soldier who best understood his idiosyncrasies. But he dared not mourn, for fear that open tears would be regarded as a sign of weakness. He instead hid his emotions behind a warrior's countenance: decked out in black Ray-Ban sunglasses and a radio-equipped crash helmet, his worn khaki shirt unbuttoned to reveal his sinewy torso, Holder cut an imposing figure atop his M113 perch.

When his yearlong tour was finished in October 1968, Holder did not hesitate to sign up for another six months in Vietnam. The Army rewarded him with a trip back to California to visit his wife and their twin daughters. On his second night in Alameda, a drunken Holder stumbled into Bullock's apartment, expecting to find her waiting for him. Instead, he surprised her in bed with one of his high school classmates, whom he stomped into a pulp. Holder soon learned that Bullock had been sleeping with numerous men, allegedly for pay. Heartbroken by this revelation, he cut short his leave and returned to war, though only after his parents promised to take charge of raising his daughters. Holder knew his marriage was over, yet he continued to wear his gold wedding band; he didn't want his Army comrades to have any inkling of Bullock's betrayal.

Back in Vietnam, Holder was promoted to the rank of Specialist Fourth Class and allowed to choose his next assignment. He decided to ditch the Blackhorse Regiment in favor of one of the Army's most glamorous and demanding gigs: flying with the 68th Assault Helicopter Company, stationed at Bien Hoa Air Base just east of Saigon.

Nicknamed the Top Tigers, the 68th AHC was charged with airlifting South Vietnamese troops into the war's hairiest combat zones. The unit's single-engine Huey helicopters would alight in clearings to disgorge a dozen soldiers each, then dodge Vietcong rockets as they whooshed away with guns blazing. In his role as a crew chief, Holder was responsible for maintaining the Hueys in flight as well as firing the mounted M60s that hung from their doors. Unlike his experience in the jungles of Long Khanh, Holder could now see his targets clearly—men who scattered through the elephant grass upon hearing the hum of the Top Tigers' blades. Holder dutifully mowed these fleeing figures down, their skulls distorting into scarlet blobs as his bullets found their marks.

But the transition from ground to air did not alleviate Holder's mounting sense of dread, which he tried to suppress with ever-vaster amounts of marijuana. His behavior grew more eccentric, to the puzzlement of his fellow Top Tigers. They thought it odd, for instance, that he liked to address everyone as "nigger," regardless of their race. And they took note of the fact that he never ventured down to the Paradise Bar to purchase the affections of slinky hostesses and guzzle cans of Carling Black Label. He preferred to spend his off-duty hours at the Bien Hoa barracks, listening to jazz and reading the works of James Baldwin and Frantz Fanon.

Roger Holder relaxing at Bien Hoa Air Base, 1969.
PRIVATE COLLECTION OF JOY HOLDER

The Top Tigers tolerated Holder's peculiarities, however, because he was an excellent crew chief—up at five a.m. each morning to prep the Hueys for battle, then cool under fire in the field. When Holder re-upped for another six-month tour in April 1969, his stellar performance earned him a transfer to the 120th Assault Helicopter Company's gunship platoon, the so-called Razorbacks. The Razorbacks were responsible for securing Saigon's forested perimeter; they often operated in the dead of night, ferreting out enemy infiltrators with high-intensity searchlights. Given the high volume of Vietcong fighters that its Hueys dispatched, the unit's motto was fitting: "Death is our business; business is good."

Joining the Razorbacks was an excellent career opportunity for

Holder, a chance to prove his mettle with one of the Army's showpiece units. But as he began his stint with the 120th AHC, the nineteen-year-old was swiftly losing the ability to hold his demons at bay. The fracture of his marriage to Bullock, the separation from his daughters, the memories of his brush with death near Loc Ninh, his feelings of isolation from his comrades—all these hardships combined to chip away at his fragile psyche.

Holder was also developing an intense dislike for the Army brass. In August 1969 eight Green Berets were arrested for murdering a South Vietnamese intelligence officer whom they suspected of spying for the North. Holder was incensed that the Army would turn on its most dedicated soldiers; were the generals really so oblivious to the nasty work of war? He likewise seethed at the military bigwigs who rarely ventured out of Saigon, yet loudly boasted that the Vietcong were running scared. He began to wonder why he was killing Vietnamese teenagers in the name of such vain and callous men.

Holder's fury peaked after he made a fateful error. In late September, just weeks away from wrapping up his third tour, Holder drove into Saigon to buy some marijuana. Once he secured a pack of prerolled joints, he foolishly decided to smoke one on the roadside before heading back to base. He didn't realize he had entered a neighborhood that had recently been declared off-limits to American troops; the streets were teeming with military policemen looking for violators.

A moment after Holder lit the joint, an MP pulled up alongside his vehicle and placed him under arrest. Holder was escorted back to Tan Son Nhut Air Base, where he was stunned to learn of the punishment he now faced: six months in the stockade and a demotion to private.

Unfortunately for him, Holder had been nabbed in the midst of a marijuana panic. Politicians on the home front had become alarmed by new research alleging that the drug was crippling the war effort. One study, published in the *Journal of the American Medical Association,* had warned that marijuana was causing American soldiers to experience psychotic episodes in which they could easily murder comrades or wander into minefields. Senator Thomas J. Dodd of Connecticut cited such research in claiming that the My Lai Massacre of March 1968, in which American soldiers had slaughtered hundreds of Vietnamese villagers, had been caused by marijuana abuse. He informed the Department of Defense that he planned to conduct congressional hearings "to let our people know if our soldiers in Vietnam have suddenly become brutal storm troopers or whether, as I consider more likely, some of them have become the victims of a drug problem that has already torn asunder the fabric of American society."

The Army responded to this political pressure by declaring war on pot—"the first popular war we've had in a long time," quipped one Pentagon official. Drug-sniffing dogs were called in from Okinawa to search soldiers' footlockers; suspected farms were doused with herbicides; and those arrested were shown little legal mercy, regardless of how faithfully they had served. Despite having earned six service stars during his twenty-three months in Vietnam, Holder was court-martialed for marijuana possession and handed the maximum sentence.

Holder was sent to the Long Binh Jail, or LBJ, a military prison notorious both for its overcrowding and for its tense racial climate. Originally built to house 350 inmates, LBJ's population had soared to more than a thousand by late 1969. Over 90 percent of those inmates were black, and many complained that they had been singled out for incarceration because of their skin. ("A white guy goes out and kills 13 gook babies and gets away with it," a former LBJ denizen carped to a United Press International reporter. "A brother doesn't shine his boots one day and he gets nine months.") The guards, by contrast, were uniformly white, a situation that exacerbated the inmates' feelings of injustice. The year before Holder began his term at LBJ, the prison had been roiled by a two-day riot in which the facility was nearly destroyed; sixty-three guards were wounded, and an inmate was beaten to death with a shovel.

Holder did not experience such violence while at LBJ, but the prison's skewed demographics reminded him of the harsh lesson that he had learned in Coos Bay: achievement could never trump race.

Still, Holder was not quite ready to give up on the Army: as soon as he was granted early release from LBJ after serving twenty-nine days, he signed up for a fourth tour in Vietnam. No longer welcome in the Razorbacks, he was transferred four hundred miles north to Phu Bai, where he was assigned to the 101st Aviation Battalion's assault helicopter unit, the Comancheros.

But Holder lasted just three months at Phu Bai. He had mistakenly assumed that accepting another tour would exempt him from the demotion that had been part of his sentence for marijuana possession. Upon learning that he had been knocked down to the lowly E-2 pay grade, he angrily confronted a colonel whom he held responsible for giving him the shaft. The colonel took exception to Holder's profane tirade, which he considered a sign that the twenty-year-old crew chief had become too psychologically unwound to remain in Vietnam. He ordered that Holder be shipped home immediately to finish his six-month commitment at Fort Hood, Texas.

Holder's long journey back to the United States began on January 30, 1970. He caught a flight to Yokota Air Base outside Tokyo, where he was supposed to switch to a plane bound for Hawaii. But instead of making the connection, he took a taxi into the heart of the city and checked into a luxury hotel that he could scarcely afford. He spent the night knocking back a bottle of whiskey and surveying Tokyo's neon glow, deep in thought about his years at war. Self-pity, rage, and regret all boiled inside his liquor-addled mind.

When he finally reached Fort Hood a few days later, Holder knew his Army days were over. Having become accustomed to the frantic pace of Vietnam, he couldn't handle the drudgery of fixing engines in Texas. Nor did he feel like dedicating any more of his life to an organization that he felt had treated him with blatant disrespect. So after three weeks at Fort Hood, he walked off the base one morning, never to return. He pawned his wedding band in San Antonio and bought a one-way Greyhound ticket to San Diego, where his parents had recently relocated with his twin daughters in tow. He told his mother and father that he had received an honorable discharge; the Army, meanwhile, listed him as AWOL, though it couldn't spare the resources to track him down.

Holder had a difficult time readjusting to civilian life. His father got him a job working in the kitchen at the Port Hueneme Naval Base north of Los Angeles, but he didn't last long; after flying Hueys in Vietnam, chopping onions for minimum wage struck him as demeaning. He quit and moved back to San Diego, where he used a fake Social Security number to obtain a driver's license in the name of Linton Charles White—an alias to help him avoid detection by the Army. He used the license to open up a checking account at Southern California First National Bank; the bank also loaned him the money to buy his yellow Pontiac Firebird. When Holder started a job at Spin Physics, a manufacturer of magnetic tape recorder heads, he did so masquerading as White.

When he wasn't soldering wires on the assembly line, Holder devoted the bulk of his energy to making up for lost time with the ladies. Having been cuckolded while at war, he exacted a strange measure of revenge by seducing the wives of men still serving in Vietnam. He would find them at lounges near Point Loma, nursing daiquiris and looking forlorn. He became skilled at convincing them that he understood their loneliness, and at sweet-talking them into giving him loans that he never repaid. The racket made him feel dirty, though not enough to stop.

Holder also had to deal with a more searing form of guilt. He was haunted by visions of the carnage that he had witnessed in Vietnam: his M113 crewmate's brains seeping into the grass, the bullet-riddled corpses of Vietcong contorted into unnatural shapes. Seeking to liberate his mind from these memories, Holder experimented with LSD; he spent long hours driving up and down Interstate 5 while enraptured by hallucinations of dancing Hueys.

In August 1971 Spin Physics laid Holder off. Rather than look for new work, he decided to make ends meet by writing bad checks in the name of Linton Charles White. In a four-month span, he bounced eighty-eight checks worth $1,801 as he whiled away the days at Ocean Beach, working his pickup artistry on sweet young things.

Three days before the dawn of 1972, police pulled Holder over while he was driving to his parents' house to see his daughters. There was a warrant out for the arrest of Linton Charles White on eight counts of fraud. Holder was taken into custody, fingerprinted, and released on his own recognizance, though he was instructed to show up for a March court date. He knew that that hearing could only end in disaster—he would either be jailed under his alias or handed over to the Army if he admitted his true identity.

Desperate for guidance on how to right his troubled life, Holder immersed himself in the literature of astrology. As he tore through stacks of books and scrolls, he came to believe that the adversities he faced were actually signs that an extraordinary destiny was at hand: the universe had selected him to be a figure of far greater importance than his current circumstances suggested.

Holder looked everywhere for omens that would instruct him how to fulfill this cosmic calling. He was convinced that the counsel he sought would be encoded in a subtle clue—an image from a vivid dream, or sage words proffered by a stranger. But by bringing Cathy Kerkow back into his life, the universe had tricked him—instead of being sly with its wisdom, it had given him a sign that no man could miss. By Holder's occult logic, there was only one possible reason that fate had arranged for him to reunite with the salamander catcher from Coos Bay: the two of them were meant to do something special together—something spectacular.

3

"I DON'T WANT TO BE AN AMERICAN ANYMORE"

PRIOR TO THE spring of 1961, there had never been a hijacking in American airspace. A handful of incidents had occurred in other parts of the world, typically involving defectors from the Communist bloc. In 1949 a dozen Poles strong-armed a LOT Airlines crew into flying them to Copenhagen, where they were granted political asylum. A year later Czech soldiers from an elite aviation unit seized three planes bound for Prague simultaneously; the men had heard rumors that they were about to be swept up in a purge. At West Berlin's Tempelhof Airport, American officials greeted the Czechs and carefully referred to them as "escapees" rather than the pejorative "hijackers," a word that Prohibition-era tabloids had coined to describe truck thieves.*

The American government later applied this same euphemism to the numerous Cubans who hijacked planes to Florida throughout 1960, the year after Fidel Castro overthrew the pro-American dictator Fulgencio Batista. Whenever one of these purloined aircraft arrived in Miami or Key West, a square-jawed advertising executive named Erwin Harris would instantly lay claim to it, arguing that Cuba still

*Etymological lore holds that the verb *to hijack* derives from the slangy directive issued by gangsters who commandeered freight trucks: "Hold your hands high, Jack!"

owed him $429,000 for a tourism campaign that Batista had commissioned. Eager to irritate Castro in any way possible, the United States let Harris auction off eleven of these Cuban planes.*

The notion that American planes could be hijacked, too, was considered too far-fetched to be worthy of contemplation. The Cold War's flow of refugees was assumed to point in only one direction, from the repressive Soviet sphere to the open and prosperous West. Even when travel between the United States and Cuba became largely forbidden in January 1961, no one imagined that Americans eager to join Castro's revolutionary experiment might resort to desperate measures.

That Americans might hijack a plane to a destination other than Cuba seemed an even more absurd proposition. American citizens were free to travel to every other country within easy flying distance of the United States, so there appeared to be no good reason for someone to hijack a flight when they could simply buy a ticket. A few distant nations might be willing to harbor an American hijacker—North Korea, for example—but getting there would require a herculean, multistop effort; the range of the Boeing 707, then the world's mightiest passenger jet, topped out at 5,400 miles.† And no American criminal could possibly be foolish enough to try and hijack a plane to a domestic airport—police would have the aircraft surrounded before it even rolled to a stop.

There had been one bizarre incident in 1954, when an emotionally disturbed fifteen-year-old boy named Raymond Kuchenmeister had attempted to hijack a plane at Cleveland Hopkins Airport. A social outcast due to his gargantuan size—he stood six foot seven and weighed well over three hundred pounds—Kuchenmeister sneaked onto an American Airlines DC-6 and aimed a revolver at the pilot while issuing a stark demand: "Fly to Mexico or be shot." The pilot

*Harris also made a habit of impounding freight shipments bound for Cuba. His biggest haul, taken from the Palm Beach, Florida, docks, consisted of 3.5 million pounds of lard.

†A later version of the Boeing 707, the 707-320B, could travel an additional 1,200 miles without refueling.

responded to this ultimatum by reaching into his flight bag, pulling out his Colt .38, and shooting the giant teenager to death.* But this violent episode was so little noticed that Congress didn't even bother to make hijacking a crime when it passed the Federal Aviation Act of 1958, which empowered the federal government to regulate the airline industry. Seizing control of an American aircraft was thus perfectly legal, at least according to the letter of the law.

That legislative omission would prove deeply embarrassing in light of what occurred over a three-month span beginning on May 1, 1961. On that day a Miami electrician named Antulio Ramirez Ortiz boarded a National Airlines Convair 440 bound for Key West. The plane had just taken off when Ramirez entered the cockpit, held a steak knife to the pilot's throat, and demanded immediate passage to Cuba's capital. "If I don't see Havana in thirty minutes," he said, "we all die." Ramirez claimed that Rafael Trujillo, the Dominican Republic's dictator since 1931, had offered him $100,000 to assassinate Castro. He wanted to warn the Cuban leader of his Caribbean rival's treachery.

With a serrated blade pressed to his windpipe, the National pilot had no choice but to make a beeline for Havana. After initially threatening to have the plane blasted with antiaircraft fire, perplexed Cuban air traffic controllers let it land at a military base south of the capital. Once soldiers dragged away Ramirez and his eighty-five pounds of checked luggage, the flight's passengers and crew were treated to a chicken lunch and then allowed to depart for Key West, ninety miles to the north. America's first hijacking ended up delaying the flight's scheduled arrival by a mere three hours.†

---

*The pilot, William Bonnell, was traumatized by the shooting. He tried to pay for Kuchenmeister's funeral, but the Cleveland police talked him out of doing so. Bonnell never carried a gun again, and he eventually burned the hundreds of congratulatory letters and telegrams he received from admirers around the nation.

†Ramirez, who returned to the United States in 1975, was interviewed by the House Select Committee on Assassinations in 1978, while serving time in prison. He stated that while working for Cuba's intelligence service, he had seen a file that identified Lee Harvey Oswald as "Kennedy's future assassin." The committee ultimately

The FBI dismissed Ramirez as delusional, noting that he had flown under the pseudonym "Elpirata Cofresi"—a clue that he might have considered himself an incarnation of Roberto Cofresí, a nineteenth-century Puerto Rican pirate. The hijacking, explained an FBI spokesman, was nothing more than the deed of "a wild eccentric with no purpose in mind" and thus was highly unlikely to be repeated.

But a similar incident occurred on July 24, involving a former Cuban policeman who had emigrated to the United States in the late 1940s and become a Miami waiter. He hijacked a Tampa-bound Eastern Air Lines flight to Havana, leaving behind a distraught wife and two young children. This time Castro elected to keep the $3.5 million plane, vowing to return it only if Erwin Harris gave back a Cuban naval vessel that had been hijacked to Key West. This extortionate ploy convinced many American politicians that Castro himself was behind the hijacking and that a dramatic military response was in order. "If we allow a little pipsqueak like Castro, with lice in his beard, to defy the United States of America, nobody is going to have any respect for us," thundered Representative Wayne Hays of Ohio, in a speech arguing for the bombing of Havana. (The plane-for-boat swap did eventually take place.)

Eight days after the Eastern flight's diversion to Cuba, an inebriated oil worker named Bruce Britt tried to hijack a Pacific Air Lines DC-3 from Chico, California, to Smackover, Arkansas, where he hoped to reconcile with his estranged wife. He was subdued by several passengers before the flight could leave the Chico airport, but not before he shot both a Pacific ticket agent and the plane's captain, the latter of whom was blinded for life. Britt's attack confirmed that hijackers were not afraid to follow through on their threats of violence.

Less than forty-eight hours later a forty-one-year-old parolee named Leon Bearden and his sixteen-year-old son, Cody, boarded Continental Airlines Flight 54 in Phoenix. The Boeing 707 was supposed to

---

rejected Ramirez's claim, concluding that "the essential aspects of his allegation were incredible."

reach Houston near dawn, after making stops in El Paso and San Antonio. But the Beardens, who had two loaded handguns tucked into their carry-on bags, had no intention of finishing their trip in Texas.

A WOMAN'S PANICKED scream roused Leonard Gilman from his slumber. In all his years of air travel, the lanky forty-three-year-old Border Patrol agent had never heard such a piercing cry of distress. He was about to leave his seat to investigate when the plane's intercom switched on.

"We have some men up here, they're asking me to ask for . . . volunteers," announced a clearly shaken stewardess. "They're telling me they need four men to come up here to the front of the plane—no soldiers. They say they'll let everyone else go. But . . . they need four volunteers."

Gilman and three other male passengers responded to this cryptic plea for hostages, walking through the darkened cabin of Continental Airlines Flight 54 to the first-class bar beside the cockpit. When they got there, they were surprised to discover who their captors would be: a jittery, gaunt-faced man with a receding hairline and a dour teenage boy. Leon and Cody Bearden both held guns to the heads of stewardesses; the hammer on the boy's .45-caliber pistol was cocked, his finger disconcertingly tight on the trigger.

The elder Bearden told the volunteers that he had ordered the pilot to keep flying to El Paso, Flight 54's next scheduled stop. After the plane refueled, he and Cody would release all the passengers, save for the four hostages. The plane would then veer southeast to Havana, where the Beardens hoped to earn Cuban citizenship by giving Prime Minister Fidel Castro the $5.4 million jet as a gift.

As the plane began its descent to El Paso in the wee hours of August 3, 1961, Gilman gently asked Leon Bearden why he wished to go to Cuba with his son—was he a card-carrying Communist, or a great admirer of Castro's fortitude? "I'm just fed up," replied the convicted bank robber and unemployed father of four. "I don't want to be an

American anymore." Cody said nothing, just snarled and posed with his gun like some B-movie cowboy. Gilman sensed that the youth was itching to kill someone.

By the time Flight 54 touched down in El Paso at two a.m., President John F. Kennedy had been briefed on the developing crisis. The year's two previous hijackings to Cuba had been embarrassing enough, but the Flight 54 situation was an order of magnitude worse. This was no mere commuter flight in Florida—it involved transcontinental travel and the jewel of Boeing's fleet. And the perpetrators appeared to be white Everymen, whose arrival in Havana would give Castro a golden opportunity to declare that the American people were losing faith in their government. Loath to hand his Cuban nemesis yet another public relations victory, President Kennedy authorized the FBI to do everything in its power to prevent the hijacked plane from leaving Texas.

At the FBI's behest, Continental's ground crew stalled for time after the passengers were released, pretending that the jet required hours of maintenance to prepare for the fifteen-hundred-mile journey ahead. As the sun began to rise that morning, Leon Bearden became highly agitated by the endless delays. He commanded Flight 54's captain to take off at once, punctuating his directive by firing a bullet between the co-pilot's feet.

But the trip to Havana lasted less than fifty yards. As the Boeing 707 pivoted toward the runway, a dozen federal agents opened fire with submachine guns, shredding the jet's landing gear and destroying one of its engines. Now stripped of their only means of escape, the Beardens agreed to let an FBI negotiator come aboard to discuss a possible resolution to their predicament.

But Leon Bearden had become too unhinged to strike a deal. "Do you see those policemen out there?" he screamed at the negotiator while gesturing wildly with his revolver. "They would as soon kill as not! They'd rather kill me. I would rather be killed myself than go to prison. I'd rather kill myself!"

An instant after making this suicidal threat, Bearden heard a commotion in the main cabin. He glanced back to see the stewardesses sneaking out the plane's rear exit.

Before Bearden could do anything drastic, Gilman punched him in the ear with all his might, shattering a bone in his right hand in the process. As the hijacker crumpled to the floor, the FBI negotiator spun and tackled Cody, who had let down his guard while listening to his father's rant. Within minutes the two Beardens were lying prone on the tarmac, hands and feet chained behind them as if they were hogs. The dozens of newspaper photographers and camera crews who had gathered around the plane documented their humiliation; the media instinctively grasped the appeal of a lurid hijacking yarn.

On the afternoon of August 4, the Senate Aviation Subcommittee convened an emergency hearing to address the rash of hijackings. A weary Leonard Gilman, his broken right hand heavily bandaged, testified about his heroism aboard Flight 54. The head of the Federal Aviation Administration (FAA), Najeeb Halaby, presented a six-point antihijacking plan that called for cockpit doors to be locked and for pilots to receive firearms training. A Justice Department official announced that his boss, Attorney General Robert Kennedy, had authorized a $10,000 reward for information leading to the arrest and conviction of anyone involved in "the actual, attempted, or planned hijacking of aircraft."

The senators, meanwhile, decried their colleagues' failure to make hijacking a crime back in 1958, a blunder that meant the Beardens could be prosecuted only for run-of-the-mill kidnapping. Senator A. S. Mike Monroney of Oklahoma vowed to rush through legislation that would make air piracy punishable by life imprisonment. But Senator Ralph Yarborough of Texas pronounced that penalty too light. "When civilized nations begin hanging air pirates," he said, "piracy will disappear from the air lanes."

In the midst of all this aggressive posturing, a senator asked the FAA's Halaby if he and President Kennedy had discussed the possibility of requiring airlines to screen passengers—perhaps by searching carry-on bags, a tactic that likely would have prevented the Beardens from boarding Flight 54. But Halaby scoffed at the idea as wholly impractical: "Can you imagine the line that would form from the ticket counter in Miami if everyone had to submit to police inspections?"

Satisfied by Halaby's curt dismissal, the committee did not raise the issue again.

Four days after the Senate hearing, a frustrated artist named Albert Cadon left his Manhattan apartment without saying goodbye to his wife. He surfaced a day later aboard a Pan Am jet bound for Guatemala City, holding a gun and demanding to be taken to Havana. Cadon told the crew that the hijacking was a protest against America's failure to support Algeria's National Liberation Front in its long and vicious war of independence against France.*

One of his hometown tabloids, the *New York Daily Mirror*, splashed Cadon's story on its front page. The bolded headline invoked a neologism that would soon become a much-used part of the American lexicon: PAN AM JET SKYJACKED TO HAVANA.

ALL OPPOSITION TO Senator Yarborough's get-tough approach vanished within hours of Albert Cadon's arrival in Cuba. On August 10 the Senate unanimously passed an air piracy bill that made the crime a capital offense. President Kennedy signed the bill into law on September 5, 1961; twelve days later American newspapers reported that Cuba had executed two of its own failed skyjackers by firing squad. The rest of the year passed without a single hijacking attempt aboard an American or Cuban airliner.

The following year was free of American skyjackings, too, as were 1963 and 1964. The spate of incidents in the spring and summer of 1961 quickly faded from memory; once again skyjacking came to be viewed as a phenomenon unique to the Communist realm, an option

---

*A year prior to the hijacking, Cadon had been arrested for vandalizing the New York City headquarters of the Chemstrand Corporation. He told police that he was upset that Chemstrand was marketing a synthetic fiber called "Cadon" without his permission.

of last resort for those who could no longer tolerate the dictatorship of the proletariat. There were at least two such hijackings in the Soviet Union in 1964 and 1965: one involved a pair of ex-convicts whom the Kremlin's official press agency dubbed "Fatso" and "Crewcut," the other a young Armenian couple who yearned to reach Istanbul. All four of these hijackers were arrested and presumably executed; their grim fates elicited brief nods of sympathy from Americans who skimmed the "World Roundup" sections of their newspapers.

The domestic lull in skyjackings lasted until the summer of 1965, when a fresh outbreak originated in one of the nation's most far-flung locales. On August 31 of that year, a fourteen-year-old boy named Harry Fergerstrom boarded a Hawaiian Airlines DC-3 in Honolulu and announced that he was taking over to protest the newly minted state's lack of political sovereignty. Six weeks later, in nearby Molokai, two disgruntled Navy sailors whipped out hunting knives on an Aloha Airlines flight and demanded transportation to their respective hometowns of White Earth, Minnesota, and Watonga, Oklahoma; unlike Fergerstrom, who surrendered peacefully, the sailors had to be forcibly subdued with shotguns and flares. It was no coincidence that both hijackings took place in Hawaii: as would soon become evident, each skyjacking tended to influence the next, in terms of both location and modus operandi.

A wave of hijackings to Havana then ensued, inspired by a small thaw in U.S.-Cuba relations. In October 1965 Fidel Castro allowed a few thousand refugees to leave the island by boat. Buoyed by the hope that his family might finally be able to join him in Miami, a twenty-year-old exile named Luis Perez tried to hijack a National Airlines flight bound for Key West. His asinine plan was to arrange a personal audience with Castro, whom he planned to beg for his parents' and siblings' freedom. One of the pilots ended the hijacking by knocking away Perez's gun with a fire ax, thereby sparing the young man certain disappointment in Havana.

Three weeks later a sixteen-year-old runaway from Brownsville, Texas, named Thomas Robinson hijacked a National plane out of

New Orleans. The boy fired several shots into the fuselage before he was tackled by three passengers, all officials with NASA's Gemini space program. When questioned by police, Robinson claimed to have a patriotic motive: he wanted to organize a jailbreak for Cuba's political prisoners, to show the world that Castro's regime remained wicked despite its relaxed emigration policy.

When he arrived for his son's arraignment at New Orleans's federal courthouse, Robinson's father was besieged by reporters. The man, a junior college mathematics professor, pronounced himself baffled by the whole affair; his son, he emphasized, was an honor roll student who had never been in trouble with the law. But when pressed by the throng of journalists who surrounded him on the courthouse steps, the elder Robinson decided to speculate on his son's rationale: "I presume he just thought and thought and thought, and then decided within his own mind he must express himself in some way or he wouldn't hold his self-respect."

That observation, made by a bewildered man under duress, would prove to be one of the era's wisest assessments of the skyjacker psyche. Though the men and women who hijacked planes would claim dozens of different motives over the years, they all shared a keen sense of desperation—a belief, however deluded, that they were so cornered by circumstance that only the most extreme of measures could redeem them. And in a nation smitten with the ingenious machines that plied its furthest frontier, no measure was more extreme than skyjacking.

"Oh, yeah, something had to be done—and I did something, for better or worse," one captured skyjacker would later state when questioned about the prudence of his crime. "It [was] better than eighteen years of therapy, or whatever. It just seemed like the answer."

MOST SKYJACKERS EARNESTLY believed that upon reaching Havana, their sole destination during the mid to late 1960s, they would be hailed as heroes. Cuba had, after all, proven itself quite hospitable to notable American exiles such as Robert F. Williams, a North Carolina civil rights activist who had fled the United States after being falsely accused of kidnapping.* Though they were all far less distinguished than Williams, skyjackers expected that they, too, would be free to enjoy the supposed fruits of Castro's revolution. "In a few hours it would be dawn in a new world—I was about to enter Paradise," one skyjacker recalled thinking as the runway lights at José Martí International Airport came into view. "Cuba was creating a true democracy, a place where everyone was equal, where violence against blacks, injustice, and racism were things of the past. . . . I had come to Cuba to feel freedom at least once."

But though Castro welcomed the wayward flights in order to humiliate the United States and earn hard currency—the airlines had to pay the Cuban government an average of $7,500 to retrieve each plane—he had little but disdain for the hijackers themselves, whom he considered undesirable malcontents. After landing at José Martí, hijackers were whisked away to an imposing Spanish citadel that served as the headquarters of G2, Cuba's secret police. There they were interrogated for weeks on end, accused of working for the CIA despite all evidence to the contrary. The lucky ones were then sent to live at the Casa de Transitos (Hijackers House), a decrepit dormitory in southern Havana, where each American was allocated sixteen square feet of living space; the two-story building eventually held as many as sixty hijackers, who were forced to subsist on monthly stipends of forty pesos each. Skyjackers who rubbed their G2 interrogators the wrong way, meanwhile, were dispatched to squalid sugar-harvesting camps, where conditions were rarely better than nightmarish. At these tropical gulags, inmates were punished with machete blows, political agitators were publicly executed, and captured escapees were dragged across razor-sharp stalks of sugarcane until their flesh was stripped away. One

*While in Cuba, Williams established Radio Free Dixie, an hour-long AM radio show that could be heard in several American states. He used the platform to broadcast subversive messages, including calls for black soldiers to desert the Army and stage an organized coup d'état.

American hijacker was beaten so badly by prison guards that he lost an eye; another hanged himself in his cell.

Yet as word of this brutal treatment filtered back to the United States via newspaper reports, the epidemic only grew worse; every skyjacker was an optimist at heart, supremely confident that his story would be the one to touch Castro's heart. A twenty-eight-year-old who claimed to be the heir to a New Mexico real estate fortune hijacked a Delta Airlines jet while inexplicably dressed as a cowboy; a sociology student from Kalamazoo, Michigan, forced a Piper PA-24 pilot to take him to Havana because he wanted to study Communism firsthand; a thirty-four-year-old Cuban exile diverted a Northwest Orient Airlines flight back home because he could no longer bear to live without his mother's delicately seasoned *frijoles*. By July 1968 the situation had become dire enough to warrant another Senate hearing.

The FAA was represented at the hearing by a functionary named Irving Ripp, whose testimony was devoid of even the slightest hint of hope. "It's an impossible problem short of searching every passenger," Ripp testified. "If you've got a man aboard that wants to go to Havana, and he has got a gun, that's all he needs."

Senator George Smathers of Florida countered Ripp's gloom by raising the possibility of using metal detectors or X-ray machines to screen passengers. He noted that these relatively new technologies were already in place at several maximum-security prisons and sensitive military facilities, where they were performing admirably. "I see no reason why similar devices couldn't be installed at airport check-in gates to determine whether passengers are carrying guns or other weapons just prior to emplaning," Smathers said.

This modest proposal was something the airlines feared far more than hijackers. For the industry was convinced that enduring periodic skyjackings to Cuba was financially preferable to implementing invasive security at all of America's airports.

In the grand calculus of business, an airline's bottom line barely suffered when one of its vessels was diverted to Havana. The price to bring a hijacked aircraft and its passengers back to the United States was around $20,000, a sum that included the costs of having to cancel flights and reward abducted crew members with extra vacation days. That figure struck the airlines as chump change compared to the fortunes they imagined losing should electronic screening be made compulsory. Would passengers swear off flying if asked to empty their pockets by uniformed guards, or if forced to reveal the contents of their suitcases? With business booming as never before—the number of miles traveled by American commercial aircraft had risen over 600 percent since 1961—the airlines were not willing to find out.

Having turned a profit of more than $360 million in 1967, the airline industry had ample resources to hire Washington, D.C.'s, top lobbyists, who made the FAA well aware of their employers' strident opposition to electronic screening. Among these highly paid persuaders was Najeeb Halaby, the former head of the FAA, who had become Pan Am's chief lobbyist right after leaving his government post.*

With such influential voices railing against metal detectors and X-ray machines, the FAA's views on the matter had come to mirror those of the airlines. And so Irving Ripp parried Senator Smathers's suggestion as certain to have "a bad psychological effect on passengers. . . . It would scare the pants off people. Plus people would complain about invasion of privacy."

Exactly as had occurred seven years earlier, the Senate committee was swayed by the forcefulness of the FAA's stance. It quietly dropped the matter of electronic screening.

Two weeks after the Senate hearing, a deranged forklift operator named Oran Richards hijacked a Delta Airlines flight. Somewhere over West Virginia, Richards jumped from his seat and pulled a pistol on the first passenger he encountered in the aisle—a man who just happened to be Senator James Eastland of Mississippi. Though the Delta crew eventually talked Richards into surrendering in Miami, the skyjacking of a national political figure represented a dangerous

---

*Halaby would later serve as Pan Am's CEO from 1969 to 1972. His eldest daughter, Lisa, grew up to become the last wife of King Hussein of Jordan.

new twist to the epidemic. Almost immediately the State Department proposed a novel antiskyjacking solution: free one-way flights to Cuba for anyone who wished to go, provided they vowed never to return to the United States. But Castro refused to accept these "good riddance flights"; he had no incentive to help America curtail its skyjackings, which gave him excellent fodder for his marathon sermons against capitalist decadence.

Unwilling to spend the money necessary to weed out passengers with dark intentions, the airlines instead focused on mitigating the financial impact of skyjacking. They decided that their top priority was to avoid violence, since passenger or crew fatalities would surely generate an avalanche of bad publicity. As a result, every airline adopted policies that called for absolute compliance with all hijacker demands, no matter how peculiar or extravagant. A November 1968 memo that Eastern Air Lines circulated among its employees made clear that even minor attempts at heroism were now strictly forbidden:

> The most important consideration under the act of aircraft piracy is the safety of the lives of passengers and crew. Any other factor is secondary. . . . In the face of an armed threat to any crew member, comply with the demands presented. Do not make an attempt to disarm, shoot out, or otherwise jeopardize the safety of the flight. Remember, more than one gunman may be on board. . . . To sum up, going on past experience, it is much more prudent to submit to a gunman's demands than attempt action which may well jeopardize the lives of all on board.

To facilitate impromptu journeys to Cuba, all cockpits were equipped with charts of the Caribbean Sea, regardless of a flight's intended destination. Pilots were briefed on landing procedures for José Martí International Airport and issued phrase cards to help them communicate with Spanish-speaking hijackers. (The phrases to which a pilot could point included translations for "I must open my flight bag for maps" and "Aircraft has mechanical problems—can't make Cuba.") Air traffic controllers in Miami were given a dedicated phone line for reaching their Cuban counterparts, so they could pass along word of incoming flights. Switzerland's embassy in Havana, which handled America's diplomatic interests in Cuba, created a form letter that airlines could use to request the expedited return of stolen planes.

As the airlines labored to make each hijacking as quick and painless as possible, the American public grew to accept unscheduled diversions to Havana as a routine risk of air travel. Comedians mined the phenomenon for corny jokes, none more mimicked than Jerry Collins's quip that stewardesses were being trained to ask hijacked passengers, "Coffee, tea, or rum daiquiris, sir?" Pundits shrugged their shoulders at the epidemic, convinced that nothing could be done to halt its spread. "It seems the best we can do is add airplane hijacking to the list of things we don't like, along with sin and high taxes," wrote the editorial board of *The Pittsburgh Press* in December 1968, "and pray there are no tragedies."

That same month, in response to the twenty-second American skyjacking of the year, *Time* ran a tongue-in-cheek travel guide titled "What to Do When the Hijacker Comes." "Don't panic," began one of the feature's recommendations. "Hijackers, although unwelcome, can be congenial. One of the three men who took over Pan American's San Juan–bound Flight 281 in November, identified only as Jose, passed out .32-cal. bullets as souvenirs and chatted amicably with passengers." The writer also advised against pushing the stewardess call button, since "the sudden ping in the cockpit might startle the felon and provoke him to fire his pistol."

Once the plane was safely on the ground in Havana, however, there was no point in being glum. *Time* noted that hijacked passengers were typically put up at the Hotel Habana Libre while awaiting transport back to the United States. "You will probably be treated to a nightclub, complete with daiquiris, a chorus line and an audience of gaping Eastern Europeans," the guide cheerfully predicted. "The shopping downtown is better: in addition to cigars and rum, bargains include East German cameras and beautifully embroidered Czech peasant blouses."

BUT IT WAS a mistake to treat skyjacking as a managed risk. The airlines' harm-reduction strategy was contingent on the assumption that the epidemic's basic features would never change—that the perpetrators would always be either sad sacks or Cuban exiles whose sole intent was to reach Havana with a minimum of fuss. But as the hijackings piled up with little apparent resistance from the airlines or the authorities, the crime's appeal broadened to new demographics of the disenchanted.

The epidemic first revealed its metamorphosis on the second day of 1969, when a young African-American couple, Tyrone and Linda Austin, took over an Eastern Air Lines flight en route from New York to Miami. Tyrone was the aggressor, announcing the hijacking by holding a gun to the head of a two-year-old boy and shouting, "Black power, Havana! Black power, Havana!" Though the Austins' revolutionary credentials were sketchy—Tyrone's real objective was to flee a felony arrest warrant in New Jersey*—their success in drawing media attention would soon inspire more sincere black militants to embrace skyjacking as a key tactic in their struggle.

Later that month a nineteen-year-old Navy deserter hijacked a National flight from Key West to Havana, telling a stewardess at knifepoint that he refused to shed blood in Vietnam. It was the first American hijacking in which a member of the military cited his opposition to the war as a motive. It would by no means be the last.

By the second week of February 1969, eleven flights had been

*The Austins' stay in Cuba was brief. In April 1971 Tyrone was killed by police while attempting to rob a Manhattan bank. Linda remained at large until 1988, when she was located in Albany living under the name Haziine Eytina; she had married a lawyer, raised five children, and become a preschool teacher since her skyjacking days.

commandeered in the United States—a record pace. In addition to the Austins and the Navy deserter, the hijackers included a former mental patient accompanied by his three-year-old son; a community college student armed with a can of bug spray; a Purdue University dropout with a taste for Marxist economics; and a retired Green Beret who claimed that he intended to assassinate Castro with his bare hands.

At the behest of the House Committee on Interstate and Foreign Commerce, the FAA formed a special antihijacking task force to develop possible solutions to the crisis. The group was immediately inundated with thousands of letters from concerned citizens, who recommended inventive ways to frustrate skyjackers: installing trapdoors outside cockpits, arming stewardesses with tranquilizer darts, making passengers wear boxing gloves so they couldn't grip guns, playing the Cuban national anthem before takeoff and then arresting anyone who knew the lyrics. The most popular suggestion was for the FAA to build a mock version of José Martí International Airport in a South Florida field, so that skyjackers could be duped into thinking they had reached Havana. That idea sparked serious interest at the agency but was ultimately discarded as too expensive.

As the FAA's task force sifted through the mountain of proposals, the hijackings continued apace, each more outlandish than the last. A seventy-four-year-old World War I veteran pulled a knife on an Eastern stewardess in the skies above South Carolina; a Black Panther, wanted for his role in a San Francisco shoot-out, hijacked a TWA Boeing 707 over Nevada; an alcoholic used-car dealer from Baltimore took over an Eastern flight while wearing Bermuda shorts and sandals, so that he could hit the beach upon landing in Havana.

The United States was not suffering through this chaos alone. Skyjackings were occurring at an alarming rate in every corner of the world, as insurgents discovered the ease with which airplanes could be seized and flown to friendly countries; in the terminology of public health, the epidemic had morphed into a pandemic, no longer confined to a discrete geographic area. Leftist guerrillas in Colombia seemingly hijacked Avianca Airlines flights every few weeks, often murdering crew members who dared resist; Eritrean separatists diverted Ethiopian airliners to Sudan, where the ruling junta was sympathetic to their goals; a Greek dissident escaped to Albania by hijacking an Olympic Airlines DC-3, bringing his wife and two sons along for the ride.

Leila Khaled smiles for the camera in Jordan, October 1969.
BETTMANN/CORBIS/AP IMAGES

But it was supporters of the Palestinian cause who became the world's best-known practitioners of skyjacking, thanks to the hauntingly beautiful face of Leila Khaled. On August 29, 1969, the twenty-five-year-old Khaled, a veteran commando for the Popular Front for the Liberation of Palestine (PFLP), helped hijack a TWA flight to the Syrian capital of Damascus. (The date was picked to coincide with the opening of the seventy-second annual meeting of the Zionist Organization of America.) After freeing all 120 passengers, she and her accomplice destroyed the plane's cockpit with dynamite. By the time the Syrians released her that October, Khaled had become an international celebrity, idolized as much for her fashion sense as for her terrorist exploits: she let her jet-black hair pour jauntily from her loose-fitting kaffiyeh, and she wore a shell-casing ring that symbolized that she was "engaged to the revolution." Khaled's fame garnered the PFLP countless new supporters; it also forced her to undergo extensive plastic surgery, since her natural face became too recognizable for covert operations.

The international response to these skyjackings was tepid at best. The United Nations agency responsible for global aviation policy drafted a multilateral treaty that would make "the unlawful seizure of aircraft" an international crime, thereby obligating all parties to either extradite or prosecute hijackers. But that treaty, eventually known as the Hague Hijacking Convention, was initially signed by fewer than four dozen nations, many of which then dragged their feet on formal ratification. The world would remain full of potential "hijacker havens."

Cuba was among the many countries that refused to sign the convention. Fidel Castro's government instead tried to negotiate a bilateral "extradite or prosecute" agreement with the United States, working through Swiss intermediaries in Havana. But these secret talks stalled over Castro's stubborn insistence that the United States also send him Cubans who had fled the island on stolen boats—an unthinkable concession for President Richard Nixon, who had close political ties to South Florida's 300,000-strong Cuban community.

As American and Cuban diplomats bickered through the Swiss, the FAA trumpeted a slight slowdown in skyjackings in the early fall of 1969. The agency credited the improvement to an advertising campaign that reminded travelers that air piracy was punishable by death. The head of the FAA's Miami office waxed optimistic when asked about the decelerating pace of skyjackings, which had dropped to just two or three per month. "It's possible," he said, "that the fad has just died out."

AFTER SIXTEEN MONTHS of charging up booby-trapped hills in South Vietnam, where he earned a Purple Heart, Lance Corporal Raffaele Minichiello returned home a bitter man. A native of Melito Irpino, Italy, who had immigrated to Seattle as a teenager and enlisted in the Marines at the age of seventeen, Minichiello had come to despise his commanders for their casual racism. "The leaders of my platoon just think of me as cannon fodder," he would later recall in his thick Neapolitan accent. "I really get mad. Always, they send me first up the road with the minesweeper so they can walk safe and not get blown up. 'Send the wop,' they say."

Upon arriving at California's Camp Pendleton in April 1969, Minichiello decided that he no longer trusted the Marines with his money. He demanded the $800 that he had asked to be set aside from his military salary while he was in Vietnam. But his unit's paymaster said that Minichiello had miscalculated—he had managed to save only $600, not $800. Minichiello's anguished pleas to the contrary fell on deaf ears. Despite the relative pettiness of the disputed sum, the nineteen-year-old Marine considered himself the victim of a great betrayal.

One night in May 1969, Minichiello decided to exact his own form of justice. He guzzled eight cans of beer and broke into the Camp Pendleton post exchange, where he took precisely $200 worth of radios and wristwatches. When he was court-martialed for the burglary three months later, Minichiello became enraged: had he not simply taken back the $200 that the Marines stole from him?

Rather than face a possible six-month prison term, Minichiello opted for a radical solution to his problem. He took a bus to Los Angeles International Airport and bought a $15.50 ticket for a TWA flight to San Francisco. His carry-on bag contained a disassembled M1 rifle and 250 rounds of ammunition.

Minichiello made his move after downing two quick shots of Canadian Club. He put together the gun in the lavatory, then pointed it at a stewardess and asked to be taken to New York. The stewardess had never heard of such a thing—every skyjacker wanted to go to Havana. But Minichiello kept insisting—New York, New York, he wanted to go to New York.

They stopped in Denver first, where Minichiello released all the passengers. As the Boeing 707 refueled for the next leg of its trip, he informed the captive crew that New York was not his ultimate destination: he was actually trying to get back to his native Italy, a country that would understand why he considered the Marines' $200 slight such a grave affront to his honor.

Confusion reigned at John F. Kennedy International Airport when the flight arrived. The FBI was desperate to stop Minichiello; letting a skyjacker go anywhere other than Havana would set a terrible precedent. The agents were aghast to learn that TWA had every intention of cooperating with Minichiello, in accordance with the airline's official hijacking policy; as long as no blood was spilled and the jet was returned undamaged, TWA was happy to fly the Marine wherever he wished to go.

The FBI had other plans. Agents in bulletproof vests surrounded the jet and crept forward, hoping either to frighten Minichiello into surrendering or to mount a decisive assault. They were yards away from the plane when they heard a single gunshot—Minichiello had fired a round from his M1 into the roof of the fuselage. The startled agents backed off and allowed the plane to depart on its long journey to Rome, via Bangor, Maine, and Shannon, Ireland.

Minichiello avoided capture at Rome's airport by taking a carabiniere officer hostage and stealing the policeman's car. He found brief sanctuary in a rural church, where police tracked him down on the morning of November 2—his twentieth birthday. "*Paisà, perché m'arresti?*" he asked as he was hustled off to Rome's Queen of Heaven prison—"Countryman, why are you arresting me?"

The Italian public shared Minichiello's belief that he didn't deserve punishment. He was lauded as a folk hero, a man courageous enough to stand up to America, a country increasingly despised in Western Europe for its muscular foreign policy. Girls swooned over the wiry, brooding Marine, whom they considered akin to a matinee idol. "He's even better than Giuliano Gemma," one seventeen-year-old admirer squealed to an Italian reporter, referring to a handsome star of spaghetti Westerns. Minichiello "played a real-life role while Gemma does only films. I would like to marry him!" Movie producer Carlo Ponti, the man behind such hits as *Doctor Zhivago* and *Blow-Up*, vowed to make a hagiographic film about Minichiello's life titled *Paisà, perché m'arresti?*

Bowing to public pressure, the Italian government refused to extradite Minichiello to the United States, deciding instead to try him in

Rome—though only for relatively minor offenses such as weapons possession, since air piracy was not technically a crime in Italy. Minichiello's defense lawyer gave a virtuoso performance at the eventual trial, comparing his client to one of literature's most beloved figures: "I am sure that Italian judges will understand and forgive an act born from a civilization of aircraft and war violence. A civilization which overwhelmed this uncultured peasant, this Don Quixote without Dulcinea, without Sancho Panza, who instead of mounting his Rocinante flew across the skies."

Given Minichiello's stratospheric popularity, the trial's outcome was a foregone conclusion: he was convicted of a single charge and ended up serving just eighteen months in jail. After his release, he signed a contract to star in a spaghetti Western.*

The Nixon administration was dismayed by Minichiello's escape from American justice. Italy was supposed to be a close ally, a founding member of NATO that had sent millions of its sons and daughters to the United States over the decades. Yet now it was not only providing sanctuary to a fugitive hijacker; it was lionizing him for his courage and hailing him as a sex symbol. Once American viewers saw footage of Minichiello and his moon-eyed teenage fans, how long would it take for others to try and follow his lead?

The answer was roughly a week. In Norwood, Ohio, a troubled fourteen-year-old boy named David Booth watched Minichiello's saga unfold on the evening news. On November 10, he ditched school and caught a bus to Greater Cincinnati Airport, where he pulled a knife on an eighteen-year-old ballerina as she bade farewell to her grandmother. "You're going with me, you're going to Sweden," Booth told his hostage as he prodded her through the terminal and onto a Delta DC-9. Once on board, he told the pilots to head for Stockholm, evidently unaware that a DC-9 cannot cross the Atlantic.

---

*Years later Minichiello would briefly own a Roman pizzeria called Hijacking. He now lives in Afragola, Naples, where he kindly receives visitors who still regard him as a folk hero.

Booth was persuaded to surrender as the jet idled on the Cincinnati tarmac. But though that incident ended peacefully, it signified that the skyjacking epidemic had entered an erratic new phase: even the most tranquil and law-abiding countries were being sucked into the madness. The United Nations, declaring itself "deeply concerned over acts of unlawful interference with international civil aviation," soon passed a resolution calling for all of its members to criminalize air piracy and punish hijackers as harshly as possible. The final vote was 77–2, with only Cuba and Sudan voicing opposition.

Raffaele Minichiello speaks to the adoring press in Rome. AP PHOTO

In the eighteen days between the UN resolution's passage and the dawn of the next decade, another six planes were hijacked around the world.

4

SWEET BLACK ANGEL

CONVINCED THAT FATE had brought Cathy Kerkow back into his life as part of some grand design, Roger Holder quickly became a fixture at her shared apartment in El Cajon. He would often drive her to and from her job at the Spring Valley massage parlor, then spend the nights regaling her with gory tales from Vietnam and lessons on astrology. Sometimes they would head to Ocean Beach to stroll amid the head shops plastered with antiwar graffiti, or catch dollar matinees at the Strand movie house on Newport Avenue. No matter where they went in San Diego, the young couple always attracted stares: even in the city's most open-minded precincts, interracial romance still carried a whiff of the taboo.

As they strolled through a Point Loma park one evening, Holder and Kerkow were accosted by a group of white men who vulgarly advised Cathy to date someone paler. Holder responded with a challenge to fight, which caused the men to slink away. When Holder turned to check on Kerkow, he saw that she was digging in her purse for something. A moment later she pulled out a black-handled switchblade.

"I wanted them to see it," she sighed, clearly disappointed that she had missed her chance to scare the punks. She had been carrying around the weapon for weeks, hoping to have the chance to show Holder that she was more than just some fun-loving girl from Coos Bay.

Kerkow's obvious infatuation with Holder baffled her friend and roommate Beth Newhouse, who had always disliked the reedy Vietnam vet. She confronted him regarding his occasional use of the name Linton Charles White, which was how he had introduced himself to her when they were neighbors the year before. Holder explained that he had adopted the alias because he was an Army deserter trying to avoid a court-martial. He further claimed that he had fled from Vietnam to swinging London, where he had mingled with artists, musicians, and aristocrats who appreciated his nuanced opposition to the war. Newhouse correctly dismissed this tale as pure fantasy meant to impress girls with hippie leanings. She suspected that Holder was a con man at heart.

Newhouse's boyfriend, a moody rocker name Lee Davis, had an even lower opinion of Holder. He was unsettled by the way Holder's eyes flitted around the room during routine conversation, as if he were scanning for eavesdroppers. And Davis was struck by the fact that Holder didn't seem to have a single black friend, nor any apparent desire to socialize with members of his own race. Like the Oakland youths who had teased Holder a decade earlier, Davis slagged Holder as an Oreo.

In early March 1972, Holder decided to skip his court date for the bad checks that he had written as Linton Charles White. He planned to evade the resulting arrest warrant by shedding his alias once and for all, a maneuver that would require a final reckoning with the Army. Once that situation was resolved, he would be free to forge a remarkable new life with Kerkow, just as fate intended.

To scrap his false identity, Holder destroyed his fraudulent driver's license, abandoned his rented apartment, and sold the yellow Pontiac Firebird that he had purchased under White's name. Then he went to his father, Seavenes, and confessed that he had been AWOL for nearly two years. His boast about having received an honorable discharge had been an utter lie.

This revelation was upsetting for Seavenes, a career Navy man who prided himself on devotion to country. But part of him also understood that Vietnam had changed his son in ways that even Roger was struggling to comprehend. Seavenes dutifully drove his second-born child to Naval Base San Diego, where he arranged for the military police to notify Fort Hood of his son's surrender.

By this late stage in the Vietnam War, the Army was accustomed to dealing with soldiers who had fled from service; between 1968 and 1971, five percent of its enlistees deserted.* Rather than fill its stockades with men who lacked the will to fight, the Army typically offered a deal to fugitive soldiers who turned themselves in: instead of facing a general court-martial, which carried the risk of a lengthy prison term, they could accept an undesirable discharge. This type of discharge, also commonly handed to drug abusers and psychiatric casualties, was not without severe consequences: recipients were barred from receiving virtually all future military benefits, and they often became pariahs to potential employers. But in order to dodge the threat of incarceration, most defendants opted to accept "bad papers."

Holder was galled to learn of the Army's deal, which also included demotion to the lowest possible rank. He thought it terribly unjust that he would receive the exact same discharge as some basic-training washout who had never spent a day in Vietnam, let alone twenty-eight months. The way he saw it, all his problems traced back to that lone marijuana charge in September 1969. If the Army had given him a break in Saigon, he never would have butted heads with that colonel in Phu Bai, nor been shipped back to Fort Hood against his will. Now the Army wanted to sever all ties, as if he had never existed. He could not believe that one ill-advised joint had led to such bitterness.

But twenty-nine miserable days in the Long Binh Jail had taught Holder to avoid the stockade at all costs. As much as it infuriated him to do so, he accepted the undesirable discharge.

Before he was given his separation papers, Holder saw an Army doctor, to whom he described the images of combat that still haunted

*The Army's annual desertion rate today typically ranges between 0.3 and 0.8 percent.

him—the mangled bodies in the elephant grass, the blood of the wounded congealing on the floor of his Huey. The doctor prescribed him tranquilizers and sent him on his way. Due to the nature of his discharge, Holder would not be entitled to any further medical care.

Embarrassed by their son's deceit, Holder's parents made clear that he was no longer welcome in their home, except to visit his twin daughters. Right around this time, Holder also had a quarrel with Lee Davis that nearly turned violent. Afterward Davis and Newhouse decided they could no longer tolerate the constant presence of Holder, who had essentially moved into the El Cajon apartment; rather than risk a serious altercation, they began to look for a place of their own.

But Kerkow's love for Holder only deepened by the day. She found it exhilarating to be dating a genuine soldier who had been on the lam for two years; he seemed like such a man of action compared to the many poseurs she had encountered at San Diego's bars and beaches. Most of those boys considered themselves brave for attending a peace rally in Collier Park, or for spray-painting PIG STY on the wall of a police station. But Holder had spent his nineteenth birthday mowing down Vietcong from atop an M113, then risked his freedom to flee the Army. Kerkow had never shared her bed with anyone so gutsy, so far-out, so *real*. And though she didn't quite buy Holder's contention that celestial forces had reunited them after thirteen years, she took pleasure in the fact that he had once been reviled in Coos Bay—even though she still lacked the courage to tell her mother whom she was dating.

Holder grew more possessive of Kerkow as their relationship wore on. One evening when she returned home from work at the massage parlor, she found him perched on the edge of her waterbed, tensely sucking down a Pall Mall. "You're never going back to that place, not ever again," he said. "That's no job for a lady like you."

Kerkow was touched by Holder's concern—she hadn't realized how much he was disturbed by the thought of her pleasuring customers. But she asked how they would pay the bills if she left the massage racket. She made a little extra cash by selling dime bags of Fast

Eddie's marijuana, but her drug-dealing skills were shoddy at best; she let Holder and other acquaintances smoke away too much of her supply.

Holder motioned for her to sit beside him. He stroked her hair as he calmly assured her that the universe would provide; they would never want for anything.

Though Kerkow had the utmost faith in Holder, she couldn't help but worry about their finances. Every few days she checked the dwindling balance in her Security Pacific National Bank checking account, an exercise that only elevated her anxiety. But Holder refused to look for work, telling Kerkow that his undesirable discharge barred him from any job worth having. He instead spent his days trying to divine the cosmos's intentions. He consulted astrological charts and studied books on dream interpretation, carefully underlining passages on how to determine when dreams presage events in the waking world. A well-worn copy of Madame Blavatsky's *The Secret Doctrine* became his constant companion, a source he consulted again and again to solidify his understanding of the Zodiac. He was confident his careful scholarship would reveal the path he was meant to choose.

For a time, Holder thought he and Kerkow were supposed to move to Costa Rica and conduct groundbreaking zoological research in the jungle; later he toyed with the notion of defecting to China, where President Nixon had recently completed a historic visit. But he ultimately rejected these ideas as too trivial: the more he contemplated his shadowy destiny, the more he felt it must somehow involve Vietnam.

Holder thought he had uncovered the perfect explanation for his acrimonious break with the Army: fate had ordained his undesirable discharge so that he could express his inmost feelings about the war. He—and not some coddled hippie who wouldn't last a second in the rubber groves near Loc Ninh—would be the one to finally open the nation's eyes to the moral inequities of Vietnam.

Though he now had a hazy purpose in mind, Holder struggled to come up with a specific course of action, one that would be theatrical enough to alter history. Then, one day in April, while looking for inspiration in a copy of *The San Diego Union*, he came across a story about the murder trial of Angela Davis.

DURING HER BRIEF tenure at the University of California at Los Angeles, Angela Davis had managed to gain far more notoriety than the typical entry-level philosophy professor. An avowed Communist fluent in the lingo of revolution, she had been hired by UCLA in the spring of 1969, to little fanfare. But by the time the fall semester rolled around, word had spread about her radical politics and her penchant for calling police officers "pigs." California governor Ronald Reagan openly lobbied to have her fired for breaching the university system's long-standing rule against granting faculty positions to Communist Party members. Nearly two thousand UCLA students voiced their opposition to Reagan's meddling by flocking to Davis's class "Recurring Philosophical Themes in Black Literature," where the twenty-five-year-old professor expounded on the works of Karl Marx and Frederick Douglass.

After a ten-month legal struggle, Governor Reagan finally got his way. "As head of the Board of Regents, I, nor the board, will not tolerate any Communist activities at any state institution," the triumphant governor wrote in a June 1970 memo informing the UCLA faculty of Davis's ouster. "Communists are an endangerment to this wonderful system of government that we all share and are proud of." Davis was out of a job, but the ruckus over her drawn-out dismissal had turned her into a countercultural celebrity.

Shortly after her firing, Davis gave several guns to seventeen-year-old Jonathan Jackson, a bodyguard she had enlisted after receiving numerous death threats. On August 7, 1970, Jackson used those guns to mount an assault on the Marin County Hall of Justice in northern California, where a black inmate named James McClain was on trial for stabbing a prison guard. That stabbing had occurred as part of a tit-for-tat feud between the guards and the Black Guerrilla Family prison gang—a gang that been co-founded by Jackson's brother, George. In addition to being a radical author of some repute, George Jackson was also one of the so-called Soledad Brothers, a group of prisoners charged with murdering a guard in retaliation for the January 1970 killing of three inmates.

The goal of the courthouse attack was ambitious, to say the least: Jonathan aimed to seize hostages, take over a nearby radio station, broadcast a message about the squalid conditions endured by California's black inmates, and then demand the Soledad Brothers' immediate release from prison.

Using the guns registered to Davis, Jackson managed to free both McClain and two other prisoners who were waiting to testify at his trial, including a convicted kidnapper named Ruchell Magee. The liberated men took five hostages, including Judge Harold Haley, to whose neck they tied a sawed-off shotgun. They marched their captives into the courthouse corridor, where they urged members of the press corps to document their escape attempt. "You take all the pictures you want," one of the men told a *San Rafael Independent-Journal* photographer while aiming a revolver at Judge Haley's head. "We are the revolutionaries."

But the trip to the radio station was not to be. As the kidnappers tried to drive their hostages out of the courthouse parking lot, several police officers opened fire on Jonathan Jackson's van. Jackson and two of the escapees were killed in the ensuing shoot-out, as was Judge Haley, whose face was blown off when someone fired the shotgun attached to his neck. Magee was the only kidnapper to survive, though he suffered multiple gunshot wounds.

Once the provenance of Jackson's guns was established, Davis became the focus of a nationwide manhunt. In October 1970, two months after being placed on the FBI's Ten Most Wanted list, she was arrested at a Howard Johnson's Motor Lodge on Manhattan's West Side. She had disguised herself by concealing her trademark Afro beneath a tight-fitting wig.

The ensuing murder trial was a circus from the start. "I stand before the court as the target of a political frame-up which, far from pointing to my culpability, implicates the state of California as an agent of political repression," she declared at her arraignment in January 1971. Her codefendant Magee was just as defiant in court, though far less eloquent; he engaged in frequent outbursts, at one point kicking his attorney in the face while calling him an operative for the Ku Klux Klan. Bailiffs began shackling Magee to his chair for his court appearances; his case was later separated from that of Davis, in the hopes of toning down the courtroom theatrics.

As Davis languished in her cell, working on her doctoral dissertation about Immanuel Kant's concept of force, her cause was taken up by defense committees in nearly six dozen countries. Day-Glo posters and sympathetic pamphlets featuring her beautiful visage became ubiquitous on campuses from Paris to Bombay. The Rolling Stones pleaded for her freedom with the song "Sweet Black Angel," contending that she was "Not a gun-toting teacher / Not a Red-lovin' schoolmarm" but rather a "sweet black slave." And a coalition of Soviet artists, headed by the composer Dmitry Shostakovich, wrote an open letter to President Nixon, begging him to "use his influence to release Miss Davis." When she was finally granted bail in February 1972, her $102,500 bond was posted by a total stranger who put up his family's dairy farm as collateral; he did so because he believed that Communist ideals were consistent with the teachings of Jesus Christ.

Like virtually everyone else in America, Roger Holder had been aware of the Davis case for months. But as he read an account of the trial that April day, an inexplicable anger overwhelmed him. The story described how prosecutors were trying to introduce a series of fawning letters that Davis had sent to George Jackson, the Black Guerrilla Family leader whose liberation had been the courthouse assault's ultimate goal; apparently unaware that she was a lesbian, the state theorized that Davis had participated in the plot in order to elope with Jackson. (Jackson had subsequently been killed by guards at San Quentin Prison, during an alleged escape attempt in August 1971.) "That so much love could exist anywhere, in any two people, even between us, I never realized," she had written in one of her intellectual mash notes. "It makes me feel all fluttery and weak, not though in the sense of succumbing to weakness, for it makes me feel so much stronger, with you my strength without end, my life-long husband."

Holder was incensed by the prosecution's efforts to use Davis's private letters against her, a tactic he deemed disrespectful. Now drawn to the ex-professor's cause, he went to the library to read up on her legal travails. As he thumbed through back issues of newspapers, one courtroom photograph from 1971 caught his eye: that of a cheerful Davis giving a black power salute while a glum Ruchell Magee sat at the defense table, arms bound behind his back.

Holder meditated on that image and the juxtaposition of hope and despair contained within it. His blood boiled at the humiliation of Magee, a man who bore a passing resemblance to Holder himself. And he fixated on the wry purse of Davis's lips, which belied the intense focus apparent in her eyes. Holder didn't think she was beautiful, exactly—he much preferred fresh-faced white girls—but he still felt some magnetic tug at his heart, as if her clenched fist were a signal directed only at him.

In that moment, everything clicked for Willie Roger Holder. He finally knew how he and Cathy Kerkow were meant to leave their mark.

5

"I'M HERE AND I EXIST"

When the FAA's antihijacking task force first convened in February 1969, its ten members knew they faced a daunting challenge—not only because of the severity of the crisis, but also due to the airlines' intransigence. Having spent vast sums on Beltway lobbyists, the airlines had the political clout to nix any security measure that might inconvenience their customers. So whatever solutions the FAA proposed would have to be imperceptible to the vast majority of travelers.

John Dailey, a task force member who also served as the FAA's chief psychologist, began to attack the problem by analyzing the methods of past skyjackers. He pored through accounts of every single American hijacking since 1961—more than seventy cases in all—and compiled a database of the perpetrators' basic characteristics: how they dressed, where they lived, when they traveled, and how they acted around airline personnel. His research convinced him that all skyjackers involuntarily betrayed their criminal intentions while checking in for their flights. "There isn't any common denominator except in [the hijackers'] behavior," he told one airline executive. "Some will be tall, some short, some will have long hair, some not, some a long nose, et cetera, et cetera. There is no way to tell a hijacker by looking at him. But there are ways to differentiate between the behavior of a potential hijacker and that of the usual air traveler."

Dailey, who had spent the bulk of his career designing aptitude tests for the Air Force and Navy, created a brief checklist that could be used to determine whether a traveler might have malice in his heart.* Paying for one's ticket by unconventional means, for example, was considered an important tip-off. So, too, were failing to maintain eye contact and expressing an inadequate level of knowledge or concern about one's luggage.† Dailey fine-tuned his criteria so they would apply to only a tiny fraction of travelers—ideally no more than three out of every thousand. He proposed that these few "selectees" could then be checked with handheld metal detectors, away from the prying eyes of fellow passengers. Most selectees would prove guilty of nothing graver than simple eccentricity, but a small number would surely be found to be in possession of guns, knives, or incendiary devices.

In the late summer of 1969, the FAA began to test Dailey's antihijacking system on Eastern Air Lines passengers at nine airports. When a man obtaining his boarding pass was judged to fit the behavioral profile, he was discreetly asked to proceed to a private area, where a federal marshal could sweep his body with a U-shaped metal detector. One of Dailey's assistants secretly videotaped this process, so the FAA could ascertain whether travelers took offense at the intrusion.

Dailey pronounced the experiment a roaring success, noting that his profile selected only 1,268 out of 226,000 passengers; of those beckoned aside for a brief date with the metal detector, 24 were arrested on weapons or narcotics charges. More important, selectees rarely seemed to mind the extra scrutiny; when interviewed afterward, most said they were just happy to know that something was finally being done to prevent hijackings.

---

*Dailey rejected the notion that skyjackers could be female. "Women almost never get involved in situations where they need a knowledge of guns or explosives, such as might be used by a hijacker," he told Congress in February 1969.

†The exact details of Dailey's profile remain a closely guarded secret. The 1972 case *United States v. Bell*, for example, established that both defendants and the public must be cleared from courtrooms before the profile can be discussed by lawyers or witnesses.

Satisfied with the subtlety of Dailey's system, the airlines began to voluntarily implement the program in November 1969, right after Raffaele Minichiello's highly publicized escape to Rome. Almost immediately, hijackings in American airspace dwindled to a handful—just one in January 1970, and one more the following month. Janitorial crews started to find guns and knives stashed in the potted plants outside airport terminals, possibly left there by aspiring skyjackers who lost heart after seeing posted notices that electronic screening was in force.*

But there were two fatal flaws in how the FAA's system was implemented. The first was that pilots and stewardesses were not told which of their passengers were selectees. If a hijacker claimed to have a bomb, the crew had no way of knowing whether he had been searched prior to boarding—and thus no way of determining whether his threat was a bluff. All they could do was err on the side of caution and obey the hijacker's every command.

The system's more fundamental weakness, though, was the fact that it depended entirely on the vigilance of airline ticket agents. They, rather than professional security personnel, were responsible for applying Dailey's checklist to every passenger they encountered. Over time the agents' attention to detail was bound to flag as they processed thousands upon thousands of harried customers each day. It is simply human nature to grow complacent.

ARTHUR GATES BARKLEY finally snapped after the Supreme Court gave him the cold shoulder. He had been embroiled in near-constant litigation since 1963, when he lost his job as a truck driver for a Phoenix bakery. (He was fired for harassing a sales manager, who claimed that Barkley kept calling him to critique his job performance.) Barkley had initially sued his former employer for shorting him on nineteen

*One Eastern Air Lines employee complained to the FAA that the system adversely affected his company's New York–to-Miami route, which catered to Mafia figures. Because these criminals refused to fly unarmed, he said, they began to drive to Florida instead of fly.

days' worth of sick-leave pay. He later turned his ire toward the IRS over a $471.78 tax bill, arguing that his wages had been miscalculated. After his federal lawsuit against the IRS was dismissed for lack of substance, he asked the Supreme Court to hear his appeal. He opened his petition with a memorable line: "I am being held a slave by the United States."

Barkley was certain the nine wise men of Washington, D.C., would recognize the depth of his persecution and deliver the vindication he had been seeking for seven years. But as they do with 99 percent of the petitions they receive, the justices denied his request without comment. Barkley resolved to make them pay for their insolence.

Over breakfast on June 4, 1970, Barkley informed his wife, Sue, that he would be flying to Washington, D.C., later that morning. The forty-nine-year-old World War II veteran had made the trip a few times before, to plead his case to indifferent bureaucrats at the IRS and the National Labor Relations Board. He promised Sue that this would be his very last visit to the nation's capital. "I'm going to settle the tax case today," he said as he kissed her goodbye.

When Barkley arrived at Phoenix Sky Harbor International Airport, the ticket counter at his TWA gate was mobbed. The airline's lone metal detector was on the fritz, and the two overwhelmed ticket agents were unsure what to do if anyone fit the FAA's skyjacker profile. They decided to avoid that dilemma by giving each passenger the most cursory of glances as they speedily issued boarding passes. Barkley, a ruggedly handsome man with slick blond hair and a pressed plaid blazer, did nothing to arouse suspicion as he checked in for Flight 486 to Washington, D.C.'s, National Airport.

As the Boeing 727 passed over Albuquerque, Barkley casually walked into the cockpit holding a .22-caliber pistol, a straight razor, and a steel can full of gasoline. In accordance with TWA policy, the pilots assured Barkley that they were willing to take him wherever he wished to go; they just hoped he was intent on Havana rather than some more exotic location.

But escape to another country was not Barkley's plan. He confounded the pilots by instructing them to head to Dulles International Airport in northern Virginia, about thirty miles from their intended destination. Aside from requesting this minor adjustment to Flight 486's itinerary, Barkley had but one other demand: $100 million in small-denomination, nonsequential bills, to be taken directly from the coffers of the Supreme Court. If the money wasn't waiting for him at Dulles, he vowed to splash gasoline all over the passengers and light a match.

TWA officials were blindsided by Barkley's demand for ransom. They, like everyone else in the airline industry, had always assumed that skyjackers were interested solely in obtaining passage to a foreign land. It had never occurred to them that a skyjacker might try swapping passengers for money, like some garden-variety kidnapper. The airline had no procedure in place for dealing with this type of extortion.

TWA knew the Supreme Court didn't have $100 million in cash, nor the capacity to pay even a fraction of that ridiculous sum. But the airline was scared to break that bad news to Barkley. TWA had to take his threat quite seriously in light of a violent episode that was still fresh in everyone's mind: three months earlier one of that year's relatively rare skyjackings had ended tragically when a man named John DiVivo had killed an Eastern Air Lines co-pilot near Boston, before himself being shot by the flight's captain. Like DiVivo, who had ordered the Eastern pilots to fly toward Europe until the plane ran out of fuel and crashed into the Atlantic, Barkley appeared disturbed enough to kill: he kept transmitting radio messages in which he demanded that President Nixon, Secretary of Labor George Shultz, and the nine Supreme Court justices be informed that they were all "unfit to rule."

With scant time to debate the pros and cons of giving in to Barkley, TWA made the fateful decision to try to mollify him with money. Airline employees were dispatched to two Washington-area banks to round up as much cash as they could on short notice. They returned to Dulles with a total of $100,750.

The airline assumed that Barkley would be reasonable and settle for this lesser sum. But the litigious former truck driver was in no mood for compromise. As soon as the canvas sack containing the money was delivered to the idling Boeing 727, Barkley pawed through its contents and realized that he had been shorted by a factor of a thousand. He made his extreme displeasure known by pouring the cash onto the cockpit floor. Up to his shins in hundred-dollar bills and his face purple with rage, Barkley ordered the plane to take off without delay.

As the jet ascended over the Virginia countryside beyond Dulles, Barkley radioed back an icy message that he addressed directly to President Nixon: "You don't know how to count money, and you don't even know the rules of law."

The plane circled Washington, D.C., as Barkley pondered his next move. The pilots tried to sell him on the idea of Cuba, but Barkley wouldn't bite. He seemed suicidal at times and eager to take his fifty-eight hostages with him to the grave. "When you go, you shouldn't go alone," he told the pilots at one point. "You should take as many people and as much money as possible. Never go alone." The North American Air Defense Command ordered four F-106 fighter jets to shadow the hijacked flight, in case Barkley tried to crash the plane into a populated area.

But after two hours Barkley decided to give TWA one last chance to deliver his $100 million. This time the chastened airline let the FBI take charge of the situation. At Barkley's behest, FBI agents lined the runway with a hundred mail sacks, each allegedly stuffed with $1 million. (They were actually full of newspaper scraps.) As soon as the Boeing 727 landed and rolled to a stop, police marksmen shot out its landing gear. A panicked passenger reacted to the gunfire by kicking open one of the jet's emergency exits and scrambling out over a wing. The other passengers followed his lead, collapsing into the grass beside the marooned plane—some out of sheer exhaustion, others because they had been drinking whiskey nonstop since the hijacking began.

Barkley peeked his head out of the cockpit to see that only a single passenger remained, a photojournalist who instinctively trained his

Nikon on the startled hijacker. The man snapped five quick pictures before leaping onto the wing, just as Barkley aimed his gun to fire.

Moments later FBI agents swarmed up the aft stairs that dropped from the Boeing 727's rear like a collapsible attic ladder; the pilot had stealthily lowered them while Barkley was preoccupied with the photographer. When he saw the agents running up the aisle, Barkley ducked back into the cockpit and shot the co-pilot in the stomach. The FBI responded with a hail of bullets, one of which perforated Barkley's right hand. He was handcuffed as he flopped around in a pile of cash, blood gushing from his busted nose.

Late that night reporters descended on Barkley's shabby Phoenix home to get comment from his wife. Unlike most skyjacker spouses, who typically professed bewilderment regarding their husband's exploits, Sue Barkley struck a defiant tone. "He believes in this country and the Constitution, he believes in what he was fighting for in World War II, but [the government] wouldn't even listen to him," she said while showing off her husband's cartons of legal papers. "He did it to get someone to pay attention to him. He was trying to help us! But he made it worse."

THOUGH HIS COMICALLY ambitious revenge had ended in failure, Arthur Gates Barkley was not without his fans. His novel demand for ransom had turned the skyjacking of TWA Flight 486 into one of the year's most compelling media spectacles: dozens of cameras had captured the dramatic transfer of money from tarmac to plane, and *Life* soon ran a major spread on Barkley, featuring the blurry photographs snapped by his final hostage. The story was so enthralling because Barkley had lived out a common, if ignoble, fantasy: by briefly ruling the skies above the nation's capital, an unemployed truck driver had forced the government to finally treat him with respect. Anyone who felt like an abject nobody could grasp the appeal of commanding such a powerful platform.

All too predictably, then, Barkley's escapade touched off a new wave of skyjackings, one that laid bare the limitations of the FAA's unobtrusive screening process. A man armed with a bottle of nitroglycerin took a Pan Am Boeing 747 from New York to Havana, where Castro personally inspected the brand-new airplane and asked in-depth questions about its design; an Army private hijacked a Philadelphia-bound TWA flight to the Cuban capital by duping the pilot into thinking that he had a bomb-toting accomplice on board; a black AWOL Marine seized a Delta flight en route to Savannah, Georgia, claiming that he could no longer endure his commanders' penchant for calling him "nigger."

President Nixon at first paid little attention to the epidemic's resurgence. He was too busy pressing Congress for anticrime legislation that would stiffen penalties for domestic bombings—an effort to end a spate of attacks on university campuses, where antiwar radicals were targeting laboratories with Pentagon ties. With the congressional midterm elections approaching that November, Nixon's decision was smart politics: Republican voters were convinced that shaggy-haired students represented the Vietcong's fifth column. Skyjackers did not yet elicit the same emotional response from the conservative "silent majority."

But a coordinated series of hijackings in the Middle East forced the president to alter his priorities. On September 6, 1970, four teams of operatives from the Popular Front for the Liberation of Palestine simultaneously hijacked four planes, three of which belonged to American carriers and were en route to New York. Among the hijackers was Leila Khaled, the female commando who had become a global fashion icon the year before. She managed to avoid preflight detection thanks to her new face, the product of multiple surgeries that had clipped her nose and stretched back her cheekbones.*

Khaled and her partner were overpowered by passengers before completing their mission, but the three other PFLP teams succeeded.

---

*Khaled claims to have undergone six surgical procedures to alter her appearance and to have refused anesthesia each time.

One Pan Am plane was flown to Cairo and, after the hostages were released, destroyed with hand grenades. The other two planes were taken to a desert airstrip in Zarqa, Jordan, where masked gunmen paraded the weary passengers and crew past reporters; eighty-six of the hostages were American citizens. Five days after that humiliating display, the PFLP dynamited the planes in front of several Western film crews. Startling footage of the jets' fiery obliteration led the evening newscasts on all three American networks; the nation's major newspapers, meanwhile, ran front-page photos of jubilant guerrillas dancing on the planes' blackened wreckage.

On the night of September 8, as the doomed planes sat on the tarmac in Zarqa, President Nixon called his top advisers to the Oval Office to formulate an emergency antihijacking plan. The PFLP operation had struck a nerve with the president, who recognized the danger of letting foreign militants believe they could take American hostages with impunity. Secretary of State William Rogers, Secretary of Defense Melvin Laird, and FBI director J. Edgar Hoover were all at the meeting, as was Henry Kissinger, then serving as a special presidential assistant. They worked into the wee hours, brainstorming measures that could be implemented by executive order.

On September 11 President Nixon made a somber national address in which he outlined his advisers' seven-point plan. "Most countries, including the United States, found effective means of dealing with piracy on the high seas a century and a half ago," he declared in his gruff baritone. "We can—and we will—deal effectively with piracy in the skies today."

Most of the plan's directives were fairly dull, such as a promise to study the best security practices of foreign carriers and a vague commitment to develop "new methods for detecting weapons and explosive devices." But one of the president's decrees was truly radical:

> To protect United States citizens and others on U.S. flag carriers, we will place specially trained, armed United States government personnel on flights of U.S.

> commercial airliners. A substantial number of such personnel are already available and they will begin their duties immediately. To the extent necessary they will be supplemented by specially trained members of the armed forces who will serve until an adequate force of civilian guards has been assembled and trained.

The details of this sky marshal program did not emerge until five days later, when FAA chief John Shaffer appeared on a one-hour ABC television special devoted to the hijacking epidemic. Shaffer revealed that the United States planned to have four thousand undercover agents in the air by early 1971, at an initial cost of $80 million per year. The marshals, armed with .38-caliber pistols, would be instructed to shoot to kill; no man was supposed to qualify for the job unless he could fire twelve bullets in twenty-five seconds with enough accuracy to kill a hijacker from forty-five feet away. The force would be overseen by Lt. Gen. Benjamin O. Davis, Jr., whom President Nixon had appointed to the newly created post of Director of Civil Aviation Security. Davis, a retired Air Force general who had recently resigned as supervisor of Cleveland's troubled police department, was essentially the nation's first skyjacking czar.

The airlines dreaded the prospect of sky marshals. They worried that planes could lose pressure and crash if their bulkheads were punctured during midair shoot-outs. And they feared the legal fallout should a passenger be slain by a marshal's errant bullet; a civil court might be sympathetic to a lawsuit alleging that an airline's ticket agents should have flagged a skyjacker before boarding.

The airlines' discontent turned to rage when they learned how the Nixon administration planned to pay for the armed guards: by increasing the tax on each domestic ticket by half a percent, and on each international ticket by two dollars. "The airlines see no justification for the imposition of these new taxes," the head of the Air Transport Association of America, the industry's primary trade group, told the Senate Finance Committee at an October hearing. "The taxes are discriminatory in their application because they would be levied on many persons who could not benefit from the purpose for why they are proposed to be imposed." In other words, because only a minuscule percentage of flights would actually have sky marshals aboard, the industry thought it grossly unfair that all travelers should be expected to pay for protection they probably wouldn't enjoy.

Several senators were swayed by this selfish logic, though perhaps more by the airlines' threats to slash service should the tax be imposed. The Senate Finance Committee's deliberations became bogged down in acrimony, with senators touting pet amendments that would exempt Alaska-bound flights from the tax or prioritize the hiring of unemployed pilots as sky marshals. The powerful American Automobile Association, meanwhile, became a major proponent of the tax, hoping the surcharge would convince many travelers to drive instead of fly.

By early December the so-called skyjacking tax was dead in the water, the victim of too much lobbyist meddling. Deprived of critical funding, the sky marshal program had to drastically scale back its ambitions. The manpower goal was slashed to twelve hundred guards, though high turnover meant that as few as eight hundred eventually ended up on duty at any given moment. The training regimen was trimmed to a mere one-week course at Virginia's Fort Belvoir, a move that raised questions about the marshals' marksmanship. "The program is a menace to the people who ride airplanes," one marshal warned the Associated Press. The airlines instructed their ticket agents to bump marshals off full flights in favor of paying customers.

But even if the tax had passed, a full complement of well-trained marshals would have done little to curtail the epidemic. There were 5.1 million airline departures in the United States in 1970; even if four thousand guards were on the job around the clock, the odds of a sky marshal and a skyjacker winding up on the same flight were infinitesimal. The program was akin to placing a single sprinkler in a twenty-story office tower, in the vain hope that any fire would start right beneath it.

It was even more foolish to presume that skyjackers could be deterred by the remote possibility that one of their hostages might be a sky marshal. As Thomas Robinson's father had observed back in 1965, after his son's failed attempt to reach Havana, the rational calculus of risk and reward meant nothing to a skyjacker. These were lost souls bent on salvaging their self-worth, on seeking the transformative high of reigning supreme in America's most distant frontier. As long as they could board aircraft with guns or bombs or jars of acid tucked inside their bags, they would gladly risk death for a chance to right their wayward lives.

And so the hijackings kept right on going as the calendar flipped to 1971. A seventeen-year-old Alabama boy tried to hijack a National flight to Montreal, where he believed the large community of American draft dodgers would understand his adolescent angst; a former New York City police officer threatened to blow up an Eastern Air Lines Boeing 727 unless he was given $500,000, a plan foiled by an airline official who tackled the hijacker during the ransom exchange in the Bahamas; a fifty-eight-year-old West Virginia coal miner, suffering from a terminal case of black lung, demanded that a United Airlines crew fly him to Tel Aviv, where he hoped to curry favor with the Almighty by working on a kibbutz.

Convinced that the epidemic was only destined to get worse, Lloyd's of London began to offer hijacking insurance to travelers in the United States. For a $75 premium per flight, a traveler could earn $500 per day of captivity, plus $2,500 in medical coverage, and $5,000 in the event of death or dismemberment.

NO ONE WAS surprised when the first passenger was killed. With skyjackers striking nearly every week during the summer of 1971, and their demands consistently growing more outrageous, such a tragedy was inevitable. But to those who knew him well, Gregory White seemed an unlikely murderer.

The only remarkable thing about the twenty-three-year-old White was his unusually gangly physique, which he accented with a bushy goatee. He lived in a working-class Chicago suburb with his wife and two children, whom he supported as a six-hundred-dollar-a-month clerk for the Illinois Central Railroad. His sole vice was liquor, which he used to overcome an innate shyness that bordered on the pathological. He sometimes acted foolishly when drunk; his criminal record was marred by several charges for disorderly conduct. But nothing about White's history suggested that he was capable of violence, or that he had any particular interests aside from keeping food on his family's table and his bar bills paid.

Shortly after eleven p.m. on June 11, 1971, White showed up at Chicago's O'Hare International Airport carrying only a folded umbrella. He strolled through the terminal and onto the tarmac, where he queued to board a TWA flight to New York. He made it to the top of the Boeing 727's stairs before a stewardess asked to see his boarding pass. Rather than comply with this polite request, White pulled a pistol out of his umbrella, grabbed the stewardess by the throat, and pressed the gun to her forehead.

"North Vietnam," said White, his slurred speech revealing that his bravado was fueled by whiskey. "We're going to North Vietnam."

A man who had boarded the flight immediately ahead of White, a sixty-five-year-old management consultant named Howard Franks, turned around and moved back toward the stairs. Perhaps he meant to help the imperiled stewardess, or maybe he was oblivious to the drama and just wanted to retrieve an item from his hanging coat. His true intent will never be known, because the spooked White shot him twice—first in the head, then again in the back, as Franks's limp body twisted to the jet's carpet.

The murderous deed done, White whipped his gun back to the stewardess's head; she could feel that the barrel was still hot. "You're next," said White.

Screaming passengers stampeded off the plane, pushing past the hijacker, his captive stewardess, and Franks's corpse. When the chaos settled, White reiterated his demand to the pilots: North Vietnam. And he wanted $75,000, too, as well as a fully loaded machine gun.

After Franks's body was removed from the nearly empty plane, the flight proceeded to John F. Kennedy International Airport, where White was told he could transfer to a larger jet capable of travel to Southeast Asia. While on the ground in New York, White stuck his head out the cockpit window to survey the scene. He saw something move in the darkness beneath the plane's right wing—a man crouched low to the asphalt, creeping forward inch by inch. White fired once at the trespasser and missed; the man, an FBI agent who was working his second hijacking in as many weeks, fired back and pegged White in the left biceps. The bleeding skyjacker meekly surrendered at once.

Two days later, as White was wheeled out of the hospital by federal marshals, a reporter shouted out, "Why were you going to Vietnam?"

"I wanted to bring arms to help the people there fight," yelled back White, who had never before expressed the slightest hint that he cared about the war.

In the days that followed, TWA was widely criticized over the security loophole that had led to Howard Franks's murder: White had been permitted to walk onto the tarmac and ascend all the way to the plane's entrance despite the fact he didn't have a boarding pass. Because White was not a ticketed passenger, no TWA agent had compared him to the FAA's skyjacker profile.

But TWA rejected the notion of altering its security policies even one iota. "How far can the airlines go?" replied a clearly irritated TWA spokesman when asked whether his employer planned to make any changes to its boarding procedures. "Restrict everyone from the terminal except those who have a ticket? Stop everyone from entering the airport area except those who have a ticket?"

The Gregory White hijacking did, however, increase the airlines' faith in the FBI. The agent who wounded White did so in the dark, firing upward from fifty feet away. His pinpoint accuracy under pressure convinced the airlines that the FBI could be trusted to use lethal force, though only if no passengers were present.

That was precisely what happened six weeks after White's capture, when a former Navy aviation mechanic named Richard Obergfell hijacked a TWA flight as it departed New York's LaGuardia Airport. Obergfell demanded passage to Milan, where he intended to propose marriage to a female pen pal. The Boeing 727 he had commandeered lacked the ability to cross the Atlantic, but Obergfell was promised a long-range jet if he released his hostages. He did so back at LaGuardia, keeping only a twenty-one-year-old stewardess as he boarded a maintenance van bound for nearby Kennedy Airport, where a Boeing 707 was waiting to take him to Italy.

As he walked toward the new jet with his gun pressed against the stewardess's back, Obergfell had no idea he was being marked for death. An FBI sniper had climbed halfway up the ten-foot metal wall that stood behind the 707's tail. Clad in tight white trousers that hiked up to his calves, the sniper balanced his high-powered rifle atop the wall and peered through his telescopic sight. But Obergfell was too close to his hostage for the sniper to fire safely.

A few feet away from the Boeing 707's stairs, the stewardess accidentally stepped on Obergfell's toes. The hijacker momentarily lost his balance and staggered back a foot. The sniper took advantage of the split-second opportunity.

The stewardess heard two shots and thought, *I'm dead—he killed me.* But then she heard the thump of a body hitting the tarmac and realized there was no longer a gun barrel lodged against her spine.

"I looked around, and [Obergfell] started to get up on his elbow," she would later recall. "He looked a little dazed. When I saw he was still on the ground, I thought he was going to shoot me, and I started to run, run, run."

But Obergfell never managed to pull his trigger. One of the sniper's bullets had shredded his vital organs; he was pronounced dead at Jamaica Hospital thirty minutes later.

TWA did not hide its elation over Obergfell's demise. "TWA is grateful to the FBI for forestalling the further hijacking of a TWA aircraft to Europe, with all the potential tragedy that might result from an armed man in charge of a crew," the airline wrote in an official statement. "The assurance of prompt and swift justice is the most certain method of discouraging acts of armed aggression against the passengers and crews of aircraft."

For the first time since early 1970, when the debut of the FAA's behavioral profile had coincided with a sudden downturn in skyjackings, there was genuine hope that the epidemic had entered its sunset phase. The publicity surrounding Obergfell's death seemed certain to dissuade potential hijackers, since they now knew that the FBI had the means and the authority to kill at will. Perhaps the occasional hijacker could still get away with flying direct to nearby Cuba, where he would likely end up in a tropical gulag. But those with grander ambitions would always need to stop on American soil to obtain fuel or ransom. And the more time a skyjacker spent idling at an airport, the greater the odds that he would be felled by a sniper's bullet.

But though the skyjackers may have been a delusional bunch, psychological illness does not necessarily interfere with raw intelligence. Those who aspired to commit the crime studied their predecessors' failings and took away a vital lesson: the best way to avoid law enforcement was to avoid the ground.

PAUL JOSEPH CINI might have become a celebrated figure in criminal folklore if he hadn't been so assiduous with his wrapping.

When the twenty-six-year-old Cini hijacked a Calgary-to-Toronto Air Canada flight on November 13, 1971, he did so carrying a brown-paper package bound tightly with twine. No one paid much attention to the parcel, for they were more concerned with the weapons that Cini was brandishing: a sawed-off shotgun and ten sticks of dynamite, one of which he rudely stuck into the mouth of an unfortunate flight attendant. Falsely claiming to be a member of the Irish Republican Army,* Cini demanded $1.5 million and passage to Ireland. Air Canada scrounged up $50,000, which it delivered to Cini at the small air-

*The day after the hijacking the IRA took the unusual step of publicly declaring that it had nothing to do with Cini. "Our job is to organize the working-class people of Northern Ireland in their struggle," a Vancouver-based spokesman for the

port in Great Falls, Montana. Unlike Arthur Barkley, who had freaked out when TWA shorted him by $99,899,250, Cini didn't mind the lesser ransom.

The DC-8 was en route back to Calgary to refuel when Cini decided to spring his surprise: he told the crew to open one of the plane's emergency exits so he could parachute to freedom. In preparation for his jump, he started to unwrap his brown-paper package, which contained a parachute he had purchased from a Chicago skydiving shop.

Cini had been planning this stunt for over a year. In September 1970, while downing shots of vodka in his Victoria, British Columbia, apartment, Cini had seen a television news segment about a failed hijacking in California. His alcohol-fuzzed mind somehow managed to produce a eureka moment: a hijacker could escape with his ransom only if he jumped from the plane.

Cini initially had no designs on attempting this himself, for he was deathly afraid of heights. But the more he contemplated the risky caper, the more he became convinced that it represented his one shot at improving his lackluster life. "I wanted recognition," he would later explain. "I wanted to stand up and say, 'Hey, I'm Paul Cini and I'm here and I exist and I want to be noticed.'"

Cini spent months preparing for the crime. He cased airports, studied aircraft design, and asked copious questions at a Calgary skydiving school. Worried that his red-and-yellow parachute would be too conspicuous in the sky, Cini dyed it dark blue and then paid a Canadian paratrooper to repack it properly. On the morning of the hijacking, he filled a suitcase with candy bars and survival gear, just in case he had to spend days wandering through the Albertan wilderness.

But one minor error was Cini's undoing: he wrapped the parcel containing his parachute too tightly.

Unable to loosen the package's twine, Cini asked one of the pilots to lend him a sharp instrument to cut free his parachute. When the

---

organization said. "Terrorizing innocent people aboard airplanes has no part in that mission."

pilot offered him the DC-8's fire ax, Cini absentmindedly laid down his shotgun to accept it. Seeing that the hijacker was now unarmed, the pilot kicked away the shotgun and grabbed Cini by the throat. Another crew member took the ax and smashed it into Cini's head, fracturing his skull. Paul Joseph Cini would be remembered not as the world's first "parajacker" but as a fool.

The fame that Cini had so desperately craved would instead go to a man who called himself Dan Cooper. Just eleven days after Cini's misadventure, Cooper boarded a Northwest Orient Airlines flight in Portland, Oregon. Shortly after takeoff, he informed a stewardess that he had a bomb in his briefcase. He requested $200,000 in cash and four parachutes, all of which he received after the plane landed in Seattle. After releasing the hostages, Cooper asked to be flown to Mexico City, with an agreed-upon refueling stop in Reno, Nevada.

But shortly before the Boeing 727 reached the Oregon border, Cooper jumped from the aft stairs into a wicked hailstorm. He was never seen again, though tattered bills from his ransom were later discovered along the banks of the Columbia River.

Experienced skydivers scoffed at the notion that Cooper could have survived his jump. The man seemed to know virtually nothing about skydiving, as evidenced by the fact that he jumped without a reserve chute and didn't ask for any protective gear. The plane was traveling at roughly 195 miles per hour when Cooper exited, a speed that even experienced parachutists consider unsafe; it is possible that Cooper was knocked unconscious immediately after jumping.* Even if he did survive the initial plunge through subzero air temperatures and pounding hail, the terrain below was lethal—nothing but hundred-foot-tall fir trees and frigid lakes and rivers. Like so many

*No professional skydivers attempted to jump from a Boeing 727 until the 1992 World Freefall Convention in Quincy, Illinois. One participant, who jumped at an airspeed of "only" 155 miles per hour, was amazed by the violence of the experience. "The first thing you noticed after exit was the heat from the jet engines and the smell of jet fuel," he said. "There was a dead void, then the blast from jet steam. It felt like I was being tackled from behind."

skyjackers before him, Cooper was probably too psychologically askew to have thought his plan all the way through.

But a massive search through the forests of southern Washington and northern Oregon turned up no trace of Cooper, dead or alive. The case's lack of resolution gave the public free rein to mold the skyjacker into a folk hero, a quasi–Robin Hood figure who stole from the rich to prove the machismo of the average American male. "His was an awesome feat in the battle of man against the machine," declared a University of Washington sociologist who pronounced himself a Cooper expert. "One individual overcoming, for the time being anyway, technology, the corporation, the Establishment, the System."

Known to the public as D. B. Cooper due to a reporter's transcription error, the mysterious skyjacker was celebrated in both art and commerce. A twenty-nine-year-old Seattle waiter made a small fortune selling T-shirts depicting a suitcase full of money attached to a parachute; a Portland lounge singer scored a minor hit with "D. B. Cooper, Where Are You?," which featured the admiring couplet "D. B. Cooper never hurt no one / But he sure did blow some minds."

By now well versed in the contagious nature of skyjacking, the airlines and the FBI both braced for the inevitable post-Cooper outbreak. But they were still woefully unprepared for the utter mayhem of 1972.

6

OPERATION SISYPHUS

PLANNING HIS MISSION to liberate Angela Davis became Roger Holder's full-time occupation in late April 1972. He started off with a broad concept: he would hijack a plane and swap the passengers for Davis, who was on trial in San Jose, California. Then he would fly the Communist philosophy professor to North Vietnam, where the nation's grateful prime minister would grant her political asylum. The resulting media circus would somehow force America to confront the blunt realities that had turned Holder against the war: the senseless deaths from booby traps, the generals' baseless optimism, the Army's lack of sympathy for its most loyal soldiers.

But how would Holder gain control of the aircraft? How would he avoid FBI snipers while on the ground? And most important, what would he and Cathy Kerkow do after they safely delivered Davis to Hanoi?

Holder spent hours pondering these vital details, filling page after page of a spiral-bound notebook with his fastidiously neat handwriting. The ideas poured out of him at such a furious clip that he had trouble keeping them all straight. The more intently he focused on the project, the more his thoughts sprawled into a jumble. He increased his intake of marijuana to cope with his mania, much as he had once relied on the drug to tune out the bedlam of Vietnam.

Holder carefully concealed his planning from Kerkow, who was busy trying to peddle enough of Fast Eddie's marijuana for the couple to stay afloat. Sometimes Holder would disappear for an entire day, later telling her that he had taken his twin daughters to the beach or the zoo. But he had actually spent the time flying between San Diego and San Francisco, scoping out the airlines' security procedures and the layouts of their jets. He was able to make these trips thanks to the kindness of a Pacific Southwest Airlines stewardess with whom he'd had a fling the year before: whenever space was available, airline employees were allowed to give complimentary tickets to friends.

As Holder shaped his plot to free Angela Davis, his living situation with Kerkow hit a snag. Beth Newhouse and her boyfriend, Lee Davis, finally moved out of the El Cajon apartment on May 1, having decided they could no longer tolerate Holder's kooky vibes. The place was too pricey for Holder and Kerkow to keep on their own, so they stiffed the landlord on the May rent and began to look for cheaper accommodations.

Around that same time, Holder decided that he needed to go to his parents' house to retrieve one of the few possessions he had kept from his Army days: a May 1966 manual titled *Guide to Selected Viet Cong Equipment and Explosive Devices*. The booklet contained diagrams of numerous improvised bombs, including a briefcase-size model of particular interest to Holder. The device's detonation was controlled by an ordinary wristwatch connected to an alkaline battery.

Kerkow drove Holder to his parents' place in her beat-up Volkswagen Beetle—the first time she had ever done so. While he searched for the explosives manual, she introduced herself to his mother and father, Marie and Seavenes. They were not pleased with their son's choice of girlfriend: Kerkow's Coos Bay connection reminded them of a demeaning chapter in their family's history, one they had spent the past thirteen years trying to forget.

But Holder was oblivious to his parents' scorn. Every scrap of his mental energy was dedicated to planning the perfect hijacking. He knew in his heart that he would be the one to succeed after so many others that year had failed.

"WHEN I GET up, you have to watch the other one. Otherwise we're all gonna crash."

Ida Robinson was puzzled by this cryptic instruction, whispered into her ear by her boyfriend, Allen Sims. The couple's Pacific Southwest Airlines flight was just minutes away from landing in Los Angeles, and Robinson was focused on her five-month-old son, Atiba, who was asleep in a cradle next to her. She figured that a combination of exhaustion and the engines' roar had caused her to mishear Sims.

But when Sims reached into Atiba's cradle, Robinson suddenly understood what was about to happen and what would be expected of her.

Sims whipped out a sawed-off shotgun that he had stashed beneath Atiba's blankets and jammed it into a passing stewardess's nose. Robinson then pulled a pistol from the cradle and aimed it at the flight's other stewardess. She had no clue why her boyfriend had decided to hijack the plane, but the bookish college student trusted him a thousand percent. She was crazy in love with the charismatic Sims, a disciple of the radical Third World Liberation Front, and totally unaware that he had been hospitalized for paranoid delusions just four months earlier.

Sims demanded passage to Africa, though he didn't specify a country. But even if he had, he would have been out of luck: Pacific Southwest's operations were confined to California, so the airline didn't own a single jet capable of traversing the Atlantic Ocean. Sims was enraged to learn of his error and took out his frustrations on a long-haired male youth, whom he clubbed with his shotgun while yelling, "Fuck you, hippie!"

Robinson, meanwhile, started to loosen up and enjoy her dalliance with absolute power. She ordered one stewardess to feed Atiba his formula, and the other to crochet the baby a hat.

With Africa out of the question, the hijackers settled for a trip to Havana, reaching the Cuban capital on the afternoon of January 8, 1972, after a refueling stop in Tampa. It was America's first hijacking of the year; compared to the multitude that would follow, it was a relatively mundane affair.*

By month's end, another five planes had been hijacked in American airspace—the most in a single month since January 1969. The boldest caper involved a former Army paratrooper named Richard LaPoint, who commandeered a Hughes Airwest Airlines DC-9 by showing the crew what appeared to be ten sticks of dynamite taped together. (They were actually road flares.) After obtaining $50,000 in ransom and two parachutes at the Reno, Nevada, airport, LaPoint jumped from the plane over northeastern Colorado. Unlike the mysterious D. B. Cooper, he knew a fair bit about skydiving—he requested a crash helmet, for example, as well as a steerable parachute that allowed him to alight in a wheat field. But he made a poor choice of footwear, electing to jump in zip-up cowboy boots that provided little support. As a result, he sprained his left ankle upon landing on the frozen earth. Totally immobilized by his injury, LaPoint was quickly tracked down by the FBI, which had arranged for him to receive parachutes bugged with radio transmitters.

At his arraignment two days later, the judge informed LaPoint that he was entitled to adequate medical care for his busted ankle. The Vietnam War veteran grumbled a reply that resonated with untold thousands of ex-soldiers struggling to cope with life after combat: "How 'bout some mental assistance instead?"

Considering what happened to two of his fellow skyjackers that month, LaPoint was lucky to have suffered a mere sprained ankle. A former mental patient named Garrett Brock Trapnell was shot in

---

*Robinson sneaked back into the United States in 1975, leaving Sims in Jamaica. She was arrested in 1987 after Atiba tipped off the authorities; he alleged that Robinson and her boyfriend had tried to kill him after he ran away from home. Robinson, who served nearly half of a twenty-year prison sentence, now heads a San Francisco organization that helps female inmates reconnect with their children.

the hand and shoulder after a nine-hour standoff at New York's Kennedy Airport; the shooter was an FBI agent who managed to board the TWA flight by disguising himself as a relief pilot. Another skyjacker, a forty-five-year-old father of seven named Heinrich von George, was decapitated by an FBI agent's shotgun blast while trying to flee the Albany, New York, airport with a $200,000 ransom. His family later claimed that von George had hijacked Mohawk Airlines Flight 452 because he needed money to pay for his eldest son's open-heart surgery.

In response to this latest rash of hijackings, Lt. Gen. Benjamin O. Davis, Jr., the nation's skyjacking czar since September 1970, ordered all American airlines to submit reports detailing their security protocols. Davis was stunned to learn that several airlines had stopped using the FAA's behavioral profile, deeming it too much of a hassle. "You know, we get an awful lot of funny people coming aboard our aircraft every day," an Eastern Air Lines ticket agent explained to *The Washington Post*. "If I tried to stop everybody who fits the skyjacker syndrome, I don't think very many planes would take off from my gate." Of the nine most recent hijackings, seven had occurred on flights whose passengers hadn't been screened at all.

The airlines' reports to Davis revealed a second major problem with the FAA's antihijacking system: metal detectors were in short supply, and the airlines refused to purchase more. America's airports handled roughly 15,000 commercial flights per day, yet they had just 350 functioning detectors among them. These handheld devices had to be shuffled from gate to gate as planes prepared to board, a virtually impossible task at the busiest airports. Rather than delay a flight's departure until a detector arrived, ticket agents usually skipped screening altogether.

Since the security status quo was clearly untenable, the FAA issued an emergency order making its screening system mandatory rather than voluntary, at least for flights longer than a couple hundred miles. That meant airlines could no longer instruct their ticket agents to ditch the behavioral profile for reasons of expediency. But the FAA stopped short of requiring the airlines to search all passengers whom the profile red-flagged, bowing to the industry's argument that such an obligation was not feasible due to the dearth of metal detectors. Airlines were instead given the option to decline to search selectees who could present valid photo identification.

A few weeks after the FAA issued its order, an entirely new threat emerged, one that could not be stopped by screening passengers: extortion by phone.

Shortly before noon on March 8, a man called TWA's corporate headquarters in Manhattan and said there was a bomb aboard a flight that had just departed New York for Los Angeles. The caller instructed the airline to check a rented locker at its Kennedy Airport terminal. The specified locker contained two empty duffel bags and a note stating that there were bombs stashed aboard four TWA planes. Unless the bags were filled with $2 million and delivered to a location yet to be determined, the bombs would explode at six-hour intervals.

The flight to Los Angeles was rushed back to New York and its forty-five passengers evacuated. An explosives-sniffing German shepherd named Brandy was brought aboard to hunt for the alleged bomb. At 12:48 p.m. she began to paw furiously at a black briefcase in the cockpit. It was the sort of briefcase that pilots used to carry flight plans and technical guides; it was even labeled CREW in white block letters. An armored member of the New York City Police Department's bomb squad carefully opened the briefcase and peered at its contents through the slit in his steel-and-nylon helmet. He saw a five-pound lump of C-4 plastic explosive attached to an alarm clock. The alarm was set to go off in twelve minutes.

The officer dashed off the plane, clutching the briefcase to his flak jacket. He knelt down on a remote section of the tarmac and clipped the wires that connected the C-4 to the detonator. He waved his arms as the signal for "all clear" at 12:55 p.m.

TWA grounded more than two hundred flights to search for additional bombs, all the while keeping up negotiations with the anonymous caller. The airline dispatched a private jet containing $2 million to Atlanta, where the extortionist said he would arrange a meeting to obtain the money. But after the jet landed, TWA never heard from the man again.

Around one a.m. that night, a bomb exploded in the cockpit of an empty TWA jet at the Las Vegas airport; the massive blast would have caused the death of everyone aboard had the plane been aloft. The airline's inspectors had somehow missed the device despite having searched the plane twice.

Over the next two days, a dozen more bomb threats were phoned into various airlines throughout the United States, with extortion demands ranging from $25,000 to several million. Though no more bombs were discovered, tens of thousands of frightened Americans canceled their air-travel plans. Empty seats suddenly outnumbered passengers on flights that had routinely been overbooked.

For the second time in eighteen months, President Richard Nixon felt compelled to address the nation about the crisis in aviation security:

> Our transportation system faces a new threat in the form of vicious extortion plots like the ones which have been directed at air traffic across the country this week. We must not be intimidated by such lawlessness. Rather we must and will meet this blackmail on the ground as vigorously as we have met piracy in the air.

The president ordered the airlines to restrict access to their baggage facilities, so that nonpassengers couldn't sneak luggage onto flights. He also toyed with the idea of forbidding the airlines to pay money to extortionists or skyjackers. But his legal advisers concluded that only Congress could enact such a ban, and even then it would have to include exceptions for extreme circumstances—a private company could not be forced to let its customers die.

The five largest airlines in the United States, meanwhile, banded together to create a special $250,000 reward fund, hoping to tease out information about bomb plots and skyjackings. And they gave their crew members new preflight duties to help ensure that planes were free of explosives before takeoff. TWA, for example, instructed its stewardesses to check all first-aid kits for bombs and to throw any grenades they found into an unoccupied lavatory.

A THOUSAND THEORIES bloomed regarding the skyjackers' psychological motives. John Dailey, the psychologist who had developed the FAA's behavioral profile, believed the typical skyjacker was an egomaniac who yearned for instant fame. The only reward that such a man truly cared about was not money or political gain, but press coverage. "He is like the Indian scalp hunter," Dailey testified before Congress. "If the other Indians didn't know when he scalped someone, he wouldn't do it."

William Davidson, president of a Beltway think tank called the Institute for Psychiatry and Foreign Affairs, took a more sympathetic view of skyjackers, whom he considered protesters against an increasingly heartless society. "They are the dispossessed," he wrote of the skyjackers in a *Washington Post* op-ed. "They do not care about their own lives or the lives of others. They feel utterly powerless, and the airplane is an enormous symbol of power and of the technology that overwhelms. So they seize it and make it their own with little or no thought that at some point, inevitably, the adventure will be over." Davidson argued that the only way to curtail the epidemic was to provide members of the "psychological rock-bottom of society" with meaningful jobs that didn't involve "tightening screws on a metal plate 480 times a day."

But in the spring of 1972 the most celebrated commentator on the skyjacker mind-set was a Dallas psychiatrist named David Hubbard, author of the national best seller *The Skyjacker: His Flights of Fantasy*. As a consultant for a federal prison hospital in Missouri, Hubbard had interviewed more than three dozen skyjackers since January 1969. These conversations had convinced him that all these men were shaped by childhood traumas that caused them to fixate on flight.

The American skyjacker, Hubbard concluded, was the offspring of a violent, alcoholic father and a devoutly religious mother. He'd had a difficult time learning to walk and was subsequently bullied at school for his lack of physical coordination. Later in life his relationships with women were all dismal failures due to his feelings of sexual ineptitude. As a result of these ordeals, the skyjacker developed a keen interest in airplanes, which he subconsciously associated with both graceful movement and liberation from past humiliations. To commandeer such an awesome vessel was tantamount to triumphing over gravity, the force that had once vexed the skyjacker as a wobbly toddler.

"Skyjackers seem intent to stand on their own feet, to be men, to face their God, and to arise from this planet to the other more pleasing place," wrote Hubbard. "Just as when an infant first dares to stand in the 'unknown' of vertical posture, [skyjackers] must assume not only the load of a heavy burden, but the possibility of falling and being destroyed." Hubbard also argued that skyjackers drew an erotic thrill from their crime: pulling a gun on a stewardess, he said, "may be the first sexually aggressive act of their lives."

The Skyjacker was a sensation in 1972 and not just because of its timely topic. Psychoanalysis was one of the year's hot self-improvement fads, touted by Hollywood stars and featured in sitcoms, and Hubbard possessed a certain genius for tapping in to the public's curiosity about the theories of Sigmund Freud. Hubbard's bearded, avuncular visage became a staple of network news segments about the skyjacking epidemic, and magazines often highlighted his research in their weekly skyjacking roundups. *Life* hailed him as "the one man who probably knows more than anyone else about the psychology of the hijacker."

Hubbard was also prized as a pundit because he was unafraid to court controversy. He openly blasted the FAA's behavioral profile as "a fraud" that would lead to "an expensive police state based on fallacious assumptions." He believed it was futile to try and catch skyjackers on the ground, for the truly dedicated would always find a way to outwit security. Hubbard instead recommended measures designed to make skyjacking seem unappealing to the psychologically unwell. These included the public dissemination of medical research linking the crime to sexual inadequacy; an end to FBI sniper attacks, which Hubbard criticized as catering to a universal "death wish" among skyjackers; and the training of female astronauts, so that potential skyjackers would be less prone to associate the concept of flight with machismo.

Hubbard's oddest notion, though, was that skyjackings could be prevented in the womb. He believed that all skyjackers suffered from physiological deformities of the inner ear, which explained their poor equilibrium. Hubbard suspected that these deformities were caused by prenatal diets that lacked sufficient manganese and zinc. To test this hypothesis, he conducted a series of experiments at his Dallas research facility, the Aberrant Behavior Center: Hubbard and his staff injected toxins into the ears of baby monkeys, then compared the animals' locomotion to that of monkeys whose mothers had been deprived of manganese and zinc while pregnant. Hubbard foresaw the day when all expectant mothers would take nutritional supplements containing those two minerals, thereby nipping any future skyjacking epidemics in the bud.

As Hubbard's fame grew, jealous critics and rivals lampooned his more outlandish theories. The FAA's John Dailey mocked Hubbard's focus on the sexual dynamics of skyjacking, half-jokingly accusing him of wanting to place prostitutes on flights in order to distract sexually immature hijackers. James Murphy, the director of the FAA's security office, likewise scoffed at Hubbard's insistence that all screening should be abandoned as pointless. "The public," he said, "wants us to keep the bastards off the planes."

The airlines, on the other hand, were big fans of Hubbard's analysis, since it largely absolved them of responsibility for skyjackings. Virtually every airline hired him as a consultant, to brief their pilots on how best to deal with hijackers. Perhaps not coincidentally, Hubbard became a vocal defender of his employers, placing the lion's share of blame on the same media that adored him. He denounced the press for "communicating skyjacker techniques like Typhoid Mary in a nursery" and proposed that news organizations be sued for publishing communications between hijacked pilots and air traffic controllers.

Seasoned journalists could only laugh at Hubbard's naïveté about their business. The skyjacking surge was one of the biggest stories of 1972, right up there with President Nixon's landmark trip to China. Even the dullest skyjacking made for scintillating copy. And the truly sensational ones were like gifts from the journalism gods—especially those involving men who managed to elicit sympathy from what Hubbard so eloquently termed the "little bit of skyjacker in all of us."

RICARDO CHAVEZ ORTIZ had an ulcer, a really nasty one that made it so he couldn't get through an hour without vomiting. He was in no shape to travel, but he felt an irresistible urge to leave Albuquerque at once. He had been in the city for just thirty-six hours, having come to seek work as a cook—a last-ditch effort to support his wife and eight children back in Los Angeles. But after a sleepless night at a fleabag motel, Chavez Ortiz had changed his mind: after nineteen years of living hand-to-mouth, he was finished with the United States. He would return to his native Mexico, to become a cop in Tijuana. The pay would be dreadful compared to what he could earn flipping eggs in America, but at least his own people wouldn't call him *spic* and try to cheat him at every turn.

Chavez Ortiz spent virtually all his remaining cash on two items: a Frontier Airlines ticket to Phoenix and a .22-caliber pistol. He planned to take the bus from Phoenix to Tijuana, then sell the gun on the black market at a $50 profit—enough to tide him over until his first paycheck. After a few months on the police force in Tijuana, he would send for his eldest son, Jorge, to save the teenager from joining an East Los Angeles gang.

As Frontier Airlines Flight 91 climbed over Albuquerque on the morning of April 13, 1972, Chavez Ortiz meditated on the hardscrabble life he was leaving behind. He had worked so many fifteen-hour days washing dishes and cleaning toilets and spent so many nights sleeping in cockroach-infested flophouses far from his family. One of his children had been born prematurely and died at seven months, a tragedy that Chavez Ortiz blamed on himself; he hadn't been able to afford a special nutritional supplement that might have saved the baby's life. Now the barrio streets were trying to steal Jorge from him, too.

Suddenly, a sense of purpose crystallized in his distraught mind. After a lifetime of being a patsy, he would take a stand:

> So many boys, they begin to live the best part of their lives and they are sent to kill people. I see many millions of children here in this country, mostly the poor people, the black man, and they use drugs and spoil things. Then I see the oceans, the rivers, the lakes polluted. The food—the best thing in life—polluted . . . So I say, "Oh, Christ, somebody must listen to me. They know they are destroying the whole world." So I think, what can I do? We can do something. But somebody have to listen to me.

Chavez Ortiz placed his unloaded .22-caliber pistol on his lap and told the stewardess that he would like to speak with the pilot.

Upon seeing an armed man enter the cockpit, the pilot readied himself for what was sure to follow: the ever-popular demand for money. Just six days earlier a Mormon Sunday school teacher and former Army Green Beret named Richard McCoy had obtained $500,000 after hijacking a United Airlines flight out of Denver. McCoy had parachuted from the plane near his Provo, Utah, home, relying on his extensive skydiving experience to execute a perfect jump; unlike Richard LaPoint, McCoy had made sure to wear combat boots to guard against ankle injuries. Though McCoy had been swiftly captured after his fingerprints were discovered on the hijacked plane, the airlines knew from experience that his sensational plot would inspire copycats.*

But Chavez Ortiz had no interest in ransom. He asked only that the pilot fly past Phoenix and land in Los Angeles, where he would gladly release all the hostages on one condition: that reporters from the city's Spanish-language media be brought on board to hear his statement regarding the indignities he had suffered in the United States.

"I don't want to hurt no one, please," Chavez Ortiz told the pilot in his slightly broken English. "This is for save my sons and your sons, too. I am trying to save America, to save the whole world, because we are all crazy. We are mad."

He was true to his word. He let the passengers disembark at Los Angeles International Airport, keeping only the flight's four crew members. A pack of journalists came on board, including audio engineers from a pair of local radio stations that planned to air the statement live. Once the microphones were switched on, he began his oration: "*Buenas tardes. Esta es su amigo, Ricardo Chavez Ortiz . . .*"

The rambling speech that followed lasted thirty-four minutes. Chavez Ortiz spoke of everything from the various bosses who had stiffed him on wages to the emasculating nature of America's welfare system. Again and again he stressed that he could easily have asked for a million dollars and flown to Mexico, but that spreading his message verbatim was more important. Once he had spoken his piece, he politely handed his unloaded gun to the pilot while apologizing for the day's inconvenience.

This shambolic performance made Chavez Ortiz an instant hero to the nascent Chicano movement, which was trying to stoke political

---

*McCoy was serving as a National Guard helicopter pilot at the time of the hijacking. The day after he parachuted to safety, he was called upon to take part in the aerial search for the hijacker—that is, for himself. He was arrested at his home less than twenty-four hours later; the ransom was found in a cardboard box, minus $30 that McCoy had already spent.

consciousness among young Mexican Americans. A defense committee formed to gather donations to pay for his $35,000 bail; dozens of families volunteered to put up their homes as collateral. Within a week of his capture, Chavez Ortiz emerged from the Los Angeles County Jail to the cheers of supporters gathered outside. As he awaited trial, the erstwhile cook and dishwasher made the rounds at California's top universities, delivering off-kilter lectures about the immigrant experience while standing beneath giant "Free Ricardo Chavez Ortiz" signs emblazoned with his world-weary face.

Like Raffaele Minichiello, the Italian-American hijacker who had been acclaimed in Rome, Chavez Ortiz had inadvertently tapped in to a wellspring of rage. Though his message was essentially incoherent, its raw spirit struck a chord with segments of society that felt entirely divorced from the political process—opponents of the war whose years of marching had come to naught, or denizens of crumbling cities who lived in fear of street crime while the president fretted about campus bombings. They admired Chavez Ortiz for having the moxie to risk everything to gain a voice, if only for thirty-four minutes.

The praise heaped upon Chavez Ortiz did not escape Roger Holder's notice as he prepared for his mission. Rather, it fueled his belief that he, too, would be lionized once his ingenious plan came to fruition.

CATHY KERKOW WAS down to her last few dollars, a situation that complicated her efforts to find a new apartment for herself and Holder. She finally settled on a one-bedroom flat on Lauretta Street, right behind the University of San Diego campus. She lied to the property manager, telling him that she worked as a receptionist for a company that sold mobile homes. She also concealed the fact that Holder would be living with her, since she knew their interracial relationship was widely frowned upon. The manager was charmed and handed over the keys; Kerkow moved in on May 15, showing up in a borrowed van with her waterbed and little else.

When Holder arrived a few days later, the couple had a frank talk about their future. Kerkow had just sold her Volkswagen to raise cash, but the balance in her checking account was still perilously low. She told him that her father wanted her to visit him in Seattle after Memorial Day. Though his dreams of becoming a full-time jazz musician had never quite panned out, Bruce Kerkow now earned a good living selling real estate. He was willing to send Cathy a round-trip Western Airlines ticket to Seattle and perhaps lend her some money, too. But her father's largesse could only be a temporary solution to their financial predicament—upon her return to San Diego, she and Holder would have to look for work.

Don't worry, said Holder. Everything would be okay. The constellations were aligned in their favor.

While Kerkow got ready to fly to Seattle on May 31, Holder redoubled his efforts to finalize the Angela Davis plan. He pored over newspaper accounts of each recent skyjacking, taking note of what worked and what didn't. The month provided no shortage of intriguing case studies, including a pair of hijackings that took place on the same day. The first involved a young North Dakotan, recently drafted into the Army, who hijacked a Western Airlines flight from Salt Lake City to Havana; he did so with a note stating that he was just one of "several heavily armed members of the anti-imperialist movement" who were working to ensure that "the skies of America will not be safe again until the U.S. government ceases its aggression against the people of Indochina." At almost the exact same moment the hijacked Western plane touched down in Cuba, a forty-nine-year-old Pennsylvanian named Frederick Hahneman bailed out of an Eastern Air Lines Boeing 727 as it flew above northern Honduras. He carried with him $303,000 in ransom, obtained from the airline during a stop in Washington, D.C. Hahneman vanished into the jungle, amid rumors that he planned to donate the money to Marxist insurgents.

But the more information Holder compiled, the more muddled his planning became. He concocted at least seven different skyjacking strategies of varying complexity, yet couldn't quite decide which one to pursue. He scribbled the step-by-step instructions for each scenario in his notebook, along with a list of alternate destinations for both himself and Davis should the hijacking go awry. And he drafted the notes he would use in the course of the skyjacking, trying to nail the right language and tone.

As his notebook began to run out of blank pages, Holder gave his mission a name culled from Greek mythology: Operation Sisyphus, a reference to a sadistic king sentenced to spend eternity rolling a boulder up a hill.

On or around May 24, his head swimming from his mental exertions, Holder took a break to check out the latest Charlton Heston movie—a campy thriller titled *Skyjacked.*

The film was controversial due to its subject matter, and numerous TV stations had refused to run ads for it; one station manager in Washington, D.C., said he feared the movie would impel viewers with "impressionable minds" to seize planes. But *Skyjacked* nevertheless opened strongly at the box office, drawing moviegoers curious to experience the terror of life aboard a hijacked jet.

Despite an all-star cast that included Rosey Grier and Yvette Mimieux in addition to Heston, *Skyjacked* was a dreadful movie riddled with plot holes. Based on a pulp novel called *Hijacked,* the movie was a halfhearted whodunit in which the skyjacker initially communicates his threats by anonymously scrawling messages on a lavatory mirror. It is no great shock when the culprit is revealed to be a stereotypically frazzled Vietnam vet, played by the thirty-one-year-old James Brolin. Upset over his treatment by the Army, Brolin's character decides to escape to the Soviet Union, where he is certain that he will be given a hero's welcome. His daft plan unsurprisingly fails, though not until the Boeing 707 is on the ground in Moscow.

Holder was fascinated by the cheesy *Skyjacked,* for he saw himself in Brolin's morally wounded soldier. Both had gone AWOL upon returning from Vietnam, and both felt disrespected by the Army. In one scene, as the pilot played by Heston bends down to help a dying FBI agent out of the plane's luggage hold, Brolin's character kicks him in the ribs. "That's what you get for doing your duty," he sneers as Heston doubles over in pain. "It's standard."

As the movie's climax nears, Brolin changes into his Army dress uniform so he can meet the Soviet elite in style. Holder liked that cheeky touch; shortly after seeing *Skyjacked*, he retrieved his own dress uniform from his parents' house and had it cleaned and pressed. And he purchased a set of silver captain's bars from a military surplus store, to affix to the uniform's collar; he felt the hijacking would go more smoothly if he masqueraded as an officer.

That weekend Holder told Kerkow they should go out for a special dinner, as he had something important to discuss with her. His parents chauffeured the couple to Anthony's Fish Grotto on North Harbor Drive, a San Diego institution known for its seafood cocktails. The meal was quite an extravagance given the sorry state of the couple's finances, but Holder swore there was good reason for the splurge.

Midway through dinner he reached across the table and motioned for Kerkow to take his hand. The moment had come for him to invite her to join Operation Sisyphus.

Holder did not delve into too many operational details—those were his responsibility, and his alone. But he gave Kerkow a rough idea of what he had in mind, beginning with his plan to hijack a Hawaii-bound jet from Los Angeles; he explained that such a plane would be guaranteed to have the range necessary for the mission.

Once he had command of the plane, he would order it flown to San Francisco International Airport, where he would exchange half the passengers for Angela Davis and a sizable amount of money. They would then head for North Vietnam, stopping in Honolulu to refuel and release the remaining passengers. As they approached Hanoi, Holder would request that Prime Minister Pham Van Dong come to the airport to greet Davis and offer her political asylum. Once he knew Davis was in good hands, Holder would make a public show of donating the ransom money to a Vietcong leader, as a way of assuaging the guilt he felt over his role in the war.

But the hijacking would not end in Hanoi. After dropping off

Davis and the ransom, the couple would fly to Australia, where Holder claimed they would be allowed to homestead in the Outback. They would get married and then send for his twin daughters, whom Kerkow would help raise as her own.

And they would live happily ever after.

Kerkow had never heard anything so incredibly far out. She had always known that Holder had a defiant streak, but this plan was the stuff of true rebellion. There was only one way she could possibly respond to such a deliciously extreme proposal.

"So, what do I wear to a hijacking?"

THERE WAS MUCH to do in those final days of preparation. One of the biggest obstacles that Holder and Kerkow faced was poverty—dinner at Anthony's Fish Grotto had all but wiped out their meager cash reserves, and the tickets to Hawaii would cost in excess of five hundred dollars. Kerkow called her ex-roommate Beth Newhouse to beg for a loan but was coldly rebuffed.

Kerkow then came up with a crafty idea: she would purchase the tickets at the San Diego airport on the morning of the flight, using a check that would inevitably bounce. If questioned, she would claim to have dropped a paycheck into a Security National Pacific Bank deposit box that very morning. By the time the airline uncovered the lie, she said, their connecting flight would already be en route from Los Angeles to Hawaii.

Pleased with the viability of this ticket-buying scheme, Holder briefed Kerkow on how else he expected her to aid the hijacking. The couple would sit apart and pretend not to know each other upon boarding the aircraft. After he executed the takeover, she would remain incognito in the main cabin, keeping an eye peeled for trouble. This role would be especially important while the plane was on the ground, for Kerkow would be responsible for alerting Holder if any FBI agents came sneaking through the exits.

Holder, meanwhile, would communicate with her over the

flight's public address system. He would refer to her by the code name "Stan"—a sly tribute to Holder's best friend in Vietnam, Stanley Schroeder, the eighteen-year-old private who had been killed by a booby trap.

On May 31 Kerkow skipped her planned flight to visit her father in Seattle. That afternoon Holder called United Airlines' central ticket office in Chicago and booked two reservations for travel to Honolulu on June 2; payment would be made at the airport ticket counter. But after consulting some astrological charts a few hours later, he had a change of heart. He called back United and moved up the reservation by twenty-four hours, so that he and Kerkow would be departing the very next morning.

But when he awoke before dawn, Holder decided he couldn't leave without bidding farewell to his family. He had his father come pick him up, stating that he wished to see the twins. At his parents' house, Holder announced that he and Kerkow were about to depart for Australia, where they planned to marry and live off the land. Marie and Seavenes thought this sounded absolutely crazy, but they had come to expect such erratic behavior from Roger since his return from Vietnam. Marie agreed to drive the couple to the airport at seven a.m. the following morning.

That night at the apartment on Lauretta Street, Kerkow cheerfully packed a suitcase for her new life as an Australian homesteader. She knew nothing about the country but assumed there would be ample sun and swimming opportunities. Her clothing choices leaned toward the lightweight—two floral tops, leather Italian sandals, a pair of green knit shorts, a blue Beachmates bikini.

Holder did not bother with luggage. He would travel with just two carry-on items, a small black valise and a Samsonite briefcase. The valise would contain his planning materials—his notebook, the explosives manual, his ransom notes, his favorite astrological charts.

The briefcase would contain his bomb.

7

"THERE ARE WEATHERMEN AMONG YOU"

ROGER HOLDER LEANED close to the bathroom mirror, inspecting every crease and decoration on his Class A Army dress uniform. He rubbed spit on the silver aviator wings pinned to his jacket and fine-tuned his necktie's Windsor knot. Then he delicately cleaned the amber lenses on his wire-rimmed eyeglasses so there would be no spots or smudges. He couldn't bear to look anything less than perfect for Operation Sisyphus.

As he bent down to buff his black shoes, Cathy Kerkow banged on the bathroom door. "Hey, hurry up in there," she said. "I have to shit." Holder hated it when Cathy talked like that; he liked to pretend that beautiful ladies were pristine creatures. He bashfully opened the door to find her holding a cup of breakfast tea. She had chosen a slightly hippie-ish ensemble for the momentous day: purple hip-hugging slacks, a chunky brown belt that she had crafted herself, and a light pink blouse. Like Holder, she wore modish eyeglasses, though their temples were obscured by her cascading brown hair.

Kerkow giggled at the sight of Holder in his uniform. "You look like a robot!" she squealed, then kissed him on the cheek. Holder was unsettled by her breeziness; he worried that she might be underestimating the significance of their mission.

It was 6:15 a.m. on June 2, 1972. The couple's first United Airlines flight of the day, from San Diego to Los Angeles, was scheduled to depart in less than three hours.

UPON DISEMBARKING AT Los Angeles International Airport at 9:25 a.m., Kerkow announced that she once again had to use the restroom. Holder, who was traveling under the pseudonym "C. Williams," promised to wait for her by their arrival gate.

As the waiting Holder lit a Pall Mall, a man in a steel-blue blazer approached him and asked if he was Captain Williams. When Holder replied in the affirmative, the man identified himself as a United customer-services representative.

"We have a bit of a situation we need to discuss here, sir," the representative said, doing his best to sound respectful of Holder's apparent military rank. He explained that there was a problem with the check that Catherine Marie Kerkow had written at the San Diego airport. At the behest of a suspicious United ticket agent, Security Pacific National Bank had carefully reviewed its records concerning Kerkow's most recent withdrawals and deposits. The bank had concluded that her account was actually $2.97 overdrawn; as a result, United could not possibly honor her $580.83 check. The representative politely asked Holder to hand over the couple's tickets for their connecting flight to Honolulu.

As Holder pleaded ignorance regarding the state of his girlfriend's finances, Kerkow returned from her trip to the ladies' room. She swore to the United representative that the bank was mistaken, for she had dropped a paycheck into a branch deposit box that very morning; her check would no doubt clear by day's end. But the United representative would not be swayed by her fibs or her feminine charms. Kerkow and Holder had no choice but to relinquish their tickets.

To make matters worse, the representative told Kerkow that her checked luggage was already in the process of being transferred to the Honolulu-bound flight and thus could not be retrieved. She would have to contact the airline's baggage-handling department to arrange for the recovery of her personal effects.

It was not yet ten o'clock in the morning, and Operation Sisyphus was already going awry.

Having grossly misjudged the banking industry's efficiency, Holder and Kerkow ordered Bloody Marys at an airport bar and chewed over what to do next. They worried that the police would be called if Kerkow tried to pass a bad check at another airline. Yet postponing the mission was not an option: the jury in the Angela Davis case was slated to begin its deliberations that very day.

Their situation seemed hopeless until Kerkow remembered something: the Western Airlines ticket that her father had sent her, the one she had neglected to use two days earlier as she prepared for the hijacking. It was still in her purse.

Kerkow went to the Western ticket counter and asked if she could exchange her unused round-trip ticket to Seattle for two one-way tickets. The agent said that would be fine, then advised her that she was entitled to a twelve-dollar refund—the flight from Los Angeles was slightly cheaper than the one from San Diego. He also suggested that the couple could travel for even less if Holder took advantage of a special Western offer: military personnel who flew standby were entitled to half-price fares.

Absolutely not, said Kerkow. They needed guaranteed seats on the next flight to Seattle—Flight 701, scheduled to depart at 12:50 p.m.

The ticket agent gave the couple a cursory once-over as Kerkow filled out her refund application. Nothing about their behavior struck him as odd. Unlike four of their fellow passengers on Flight 701, Holder and Kerkow were not selected for additional screening.

Boarding passes in hand, the couple returned to the bar for one last preflight cocktail. When they were finished, they coolly parted ways: they would henceforth pretend to be strangers to each other, until the last passengers had been freed en route to North Vietnam.

As she stuffed her copy of the latest *Playboy* into her purse, a grinning Kerkow said a few last words to Holder: "Nigger, you'd better not run off on me." The slur was a private joke between them, a way they poked fun at their racial mismatch.

The flight boarded at 12:35 p.m. There were no assigned seats: he took 18D, on the aisle, while she chose 22D. Approximately fifteen minutes after they settled in, the jet's wheels pulled free of the runway. Operation Sisyphus was a go.

HOLDER WAS ACHING for a taste of marijuana, just a few quick tokes to soothe his nerves. He had a cigarette pack full of joints in his breast pocket, but there was no way he could sneak a puff in the lavatory without attracting unwanted attention. He settled instead for a second round of bourbon, brought to him by a shapely blond stewardess who said her name was Gina. A bump of turbulence caused her to splash some liquor on Holder's jacket, an accident for which she profusely apologized.

"Don't worry about it at all," said Holder. "No harm done."

Still, Gina Cutcher promised to bring him a dry cleaning voucher. Holder turned his head to watch her walk back to the aft galley, her comely figure sheathed in Western's flattering peach uniform. He briefly thought of asking this gorgeous lady to join him and Cathy on their journey, to become part of their happy band of homesteaders in the Australian Outback. But he knew that it would be foolish to deviate from the plan.

When Holder ran out of cigarettes, he bummed a smoke off the man sitting in 18E, an auto-sales executive from suburban Seattle. The man used this exchange as an excuse to make small talk. He started the conversation by asking Holder how long he had been in the Army. "Oh, since before I was born," Holder responded with a laugh, before explaining that his father had spent his entire career in the military.

That was the last true thing that Holder told his seatmate. He proceeded to weave a fantastic tale of derring-do, claiming to be a helicopter pilot who had just emerged from the hospital after suffering grievous wounds in Vietnam. He said he had served in Korea, too, where he had been shot down after flying a secret bombing mission over the 38th parallel. He was heading to Seattle as part of his new gig with Army intelligence, a job he had earned by scoring a genius-level 141 on an IQ test. Once his military career was over, he hoped to train police pilots in the art of evasive maneuvering.

Four rows behind Holder, Kerkow was telling less outrageous lies to her seatmate, a middle-aged homemaker from Los Angeles. She said that she was traveling to Seattle for her father's surprise birthday party, and that she worked as a medical receptionist in San Diego. Soon thereafter the man sitting across the aisle from Kerkow roped her into a game of gin rummy, which she played quite shrewdly.

As the plane passed over Oregon's Mount Hood, Holder felt an acute pang of self-doubt. He worried that he had already waited too long to execute the takeover, a concern that sparked misgivings about the thoroughness of his preparations. He began to compose a new note for the captain, scribbling furiously on a sheet of yellow legal paper. But he stopped writing after five garbled paragraphs, unable to string together a coherent message. His thoughts were slipping away from him.

Holder asked his seatmate for another cigarette and tried to read a *Life* feature about Alabama governor and Democratic presidential candidate George Wallace, who had survived an assassin's bullet on May 15. Though he maintained a veneer of cool, he was desperately trying to muster the courage to go through with his plan.

At around 2:25 p.m., the captain's voice blared over the public address system. He directed the passengers' attention to snowcapped Mount Rainier, which was coming up on the left side of the aircraft. All was running smoothly, he added, and they would be on the ground in Seattle in twenty-five minutes.

Holder closed his magazine and stubbed out his cigarette. *Now or never,* he thought. *Now or never.*

He removed his Samsonite briefcase from beneath the seat in

front of him and replaced it with his small black valise. He opened the briefcase a crack and removed a travel-size alarm clock. He wound it up and then placed it back inside the briefcase.

"Could you watch my seat?" Holder asked the auto-sales executive in 18E. With that, he rose and walked down the aisle toward the rear of the plane.

Kerkow watched him pass by. This was it.

Holder pulled back the aft galley's red curtain to find three stewardesses shoveling beef and broccoli into their mouths. The lovely Gina Cutcher stood closest to him.

Oh no, thought Cutcher. *The voucher. I forgot about his voucher.*

"I need to show you something," Holder said to her, placing two sheets of three-by-five notepaper on the galley's countertop. "Read these."

Cutcher did as she was told. The first note began: *Success through Death . . .*

IT WAS SUPPOSED to be a milestone day for Jerome Juergens, the first time he had ever captained a Boeing 727. The former Marine aviator, who had been with Western since 1959, had been flying 737s for a few years. The older and larger 727, with its unique three-engine design and T-shaped tail, was widely beloved by pilots for its agility and responsiveness; if given a choice of any plane to fly through a thunderstorm, many veteran pilots would pick the Boeing 727.

Juergens's co-pilot, Edward Richardson, had logged hundreds of hours on 727s. He was assigned to Flight 701 to observe and grade Juergens's maiden performance. Rounding out the crew was the flight engineer, Thomas Crawford, a former Air Force pilot who had cut his aviation teeth landing C-130 cargo planes on the Alaskan tundra. He sat directly behind Richardson, facing a massive bank of instruments mounted on the cockpit's right side.

Shortly after 2:30 p.m., as Juergens was easing the plane down toward Seattle-Tacoma International Airport, the cockpit's entrance bell rang twice. In stepped Gina Cutcher and Donna Jones, the flight's lead stewardess. Cutcher thrust forward two sheets of paper. "Captain," she said, "before you go on descending, please, you—you need to read these!"

Though rife with poor spelling, the notes' message was crystal clear: four men, three guns, two bombs. And the briefcase diagram proved that, at the very least, the notes' author was familiar with military explosives.

Juergens had always boasted that he would never relinquish control of one of his planes to a skyjacker. As a proud Marine, he thought he could subdue anyone foolish enough to challenge his command—with bare fists, if necessary. But now faced with the very real possibility of losing all ninety passengers on board, Juergens kept his bravado in check. "Go back and tell this man we'll comply with anything he wants to do," he told Cutcher.

Juergens made a mental checklist of Western's hijacking procedures, which were detailed in a ten-page section of the airline's pilot's manual. There was a special transponder code that had to be sent to air traffic control in Seattle—"7500" meant a hijacking was in progress, "7700" that lives were in imminent danger. The code word "TRIP" had to be relayed to Seattle, too, along with pertinent information regarding the passengers: whether there were any infants on board, any children traveling alone, any celebrities or politicians. There were even special instructions for travel to such hostile countries as the Soviet Union, China, and North Vietnam, which included specifications for airspeed (400 knots) and the appropriate frequency on which to broadcast distress signals (121.5 megahertz).

Ed Richardson knew these procedures better than any other Western pilot, for he had firsthand hijacking experience. Less than a month earlier, on May 5, he had been part of the crew that had flown a rogue Army draftee down to Havana. That hijacker had been armed with a revolver that he had stashed inside a hollowed-out book; he had also claimed to be part of a paramilitary movement opposed to American imperialism. Richardson had dismissed the doughy youth as a "momma's boy" who was merely afraid to fight in Vietnam. His most vivid memory of the hijacker was the self-proclaimed revolutionary's first utterance to the Cuban soldiers who boarded the aircraft: "Can you have someone get my luggage?"*

CUTCHER ASKED THE Lord for strength as she returned to the aft galley. She'd had a bad feeling about this stewardess job ever since her initial interview, when Western officials had spent more time measuring her bust and thighs than inquiring about her qualifications. How she now wished that she had followed her dream and gone to nursing school instead.

She found Holder leaning against the galley's countertop, staring at his immaculately shined shoes. She haltingly relayed Juergens's words: "The captain says he'll . . . he'll comply with anything you want to do."

"Good, take me to the cockpit now," Holder replied. "You have two minutes to get me up there." The other two stewardesses in the galley, Marla Smith and Carol Clymer, were relieved to be rid of the hijacker; he had frightened them with his mumbled regrets about having failed to destroy the plane.

Few passengers noticed Holder and Cutcher as they marched up the aisle. One who did, a nineteen-year-old woman traveling with her baby, did a double take because of Holder's unusual height. When Holder caught this young lady staring, he flashed back a smile and said, "Peace."

Holder ducked through the open cockpit door and stood over the three-person flight crew. He took a moment to savor the feeling of accomplishment; for the first time in ages, he felt wholly in tune with the universe's intentions for his life. But after that surge of satisfaction ebbed, he struggled to remember what, exactly, he was supposed to do

---

*The hijacker, Michael Lynn Hansen, was returned to the United States in 1975. He became an ardent neo-Nazi during his subsequent five-year stay in prison, after which he founded the Christian National Socialist White People's Liberation Army.

next. At the very moment of his greatest triumph, all of Roger Holder's convoluted plans began to mash together in his head.

"My name is Richard Bradley Williams," said Holder, a trace of anxiety audible in his wavering voice. "I trained as a helicopter pilot at Fort Rucker. Flew Huey Cobras in Vietnam. Been back thirty-six days now, working with Army intelligence. My home's in Oakland. I'm divorced."

Holder sat down in the jump seat behind Juergens and fell silent. The flight crew was baffled, and not only because Holder seemed more interested in recounting his life's story than in making demands. One of the hijacking notes had clearly instructed the pilots to leave the cockpit, four paces apart, and "take seats to the rear of the aircraft." Juergens had been girding himself to argue against that dangerous idea. But Holder appeared to have forgotten all about what he had written.

Holder held up his Samsonite briefcase and wiggled his left index finger, the one with the metal ring around it. The crew could see that the ring was connected to a piece of copper wire that led into the briefcase. "This controls the detonator," explained Holder. "There is a concussion grenade in here, and eight slabs of C-4. Now, Captain, what is your name?"

"Jerry Juergens."

Holder gave the captain a firm handshake, then did likewise with the other two members of the crew. Tom Crawford noticed that the hijacker's hand was clammy and that sweat was trickling down his brow.

"I'm here to tell you that I was visited at my home by the Weathermen," said Holder. He was referring to a notorious radical group, an offshoot of Students for a Democratic Society, that had orchestrated a series of bombings aimed at ending America's involvement in Vietnam. Two weeks earlier the Weathermen had managed to bomb a women's bathroom at the Pentagon.

"They told me they'd taken my children from my wife—kidnapped them," Holder continued. "That's how they're forcing me to do this—they have my girls. *My family.* Four of them are on this plane right now, back there with a bomb. One's a girl—she's the leader. And one's on LSD. I saw them in Los Angeles, at the airport, waiting. But I don't know where they're sitting at now."

Holder removed his spiral-bound notebook from a jacket pocket and flipped to page one. "San Francisco," he said. "They want us to go to San Francisco."

"Not enough fuel for that," said Richardson. "We need to land in Seattle first." Holder objected, saying there was no time for any stops along the way. But Richardson countered that they didn't have a choice—they could barely make it back to the Washington-Oregon border on the fuel they had left.

Then a spur-of-the-moment idea occurred to Holder—a way to turn Operation Sisyphus into an even more elaborate and personal demonstration.

"I want us to land in Coos Bay," he said.

Richardson rolled his eyes at the hijacker's idiocy. He curtly explained that even if they had enough fuel to reach southwestern Oregon, a Boeing 727 could never land at the minuscule airport that served Coos Bay. Either they landed in Seattle at once, or they all died.

Holder relented, though he stressed that refueling would have to take place far from the terminal on an empty runway—he wanted to make it as difficult as possible for police to reach the plane. Crawford radioed the news to Western's dispatch center in Los Angeles, which was charged with handling all hijacking-related communications:

FLIGHT 701: We are going to land in Seattle for refueling. That's the first problem. Will need gas and also might need some money.

WESTERN: Roger.

The brief Seattle stopover arranged, Holder continued on with the demands he ascribed to his imaginary Weathermen handlers: "Money. You said money. They want three million dollars."

Crawford swiveled his chair to the right so he could look Holder in the eye. "Listen, whether you choose to believe this or not is up to you, but my father is a vice president at the Federal Reserve Bank of Cleveland," he said, speaking the truth. Crawford explained that the only banks with $3 million on hand likely followed the Federal Reserve's policy of locking their vaults promptly at five p.m. on Fridays—just over two hours hence. Those locks were controlled by timers, so that absolutely no one could open them until eight a.m. on Monday.

"You want three million dollars today, at this hour, you're not going to find it," said Crawford. "You'll be lucky to find half a million."

"Okay, half a million, then," said Holder. "And Angela Davis. Have her at the airport in San Francisco, on the runway. Wearing something white—a white dress." Holder had put considerable thought into that last detail; he wanted to make sure he could spot Davis from afar.

Crawford passed along these demands to Western dispatch, emphasizing that they were being made by a bomb-toting man who claimed to have armed, LSD-taking confederates among the passengers. The moment Crawford ended his transmission, Holder suddenly remembered something else he wanted.

"And five parachutes. We want five parachutes."

As Crawford took to the radio once more, Juergens pulled up the nose of the plane and banked left. They would have to enter a holding pattern while a runway was cleared. To prepare the passengers for the unexpected brevity of their stay in Seattle, Juergens decided to level with them. He switched on the public address system and began to speak, choosing his words very carefully.

"Ladies and gentlemen, we, uh, have a party up here in the cockpit who doesn't wish to go to our intended destination. Now, we're cooperating with him completely. We're going to land in Seattle soon to take on some more fuel. I'll pass along more details when I have them."

The passengers had seen enough newscasts to understand precisely what was going on. Some stuffed cash and jewelry into their socks, fearful that the hijacker would try to rob them on the way to Havana; others bowed their heads in prayer or dug through their pockets for rosary beads. A woman in first class began to hyperventilate and sob uncontrollably, until her husband muffled her cries by sticking her head inside his blazer; to the stewardesses' relief, the hysterical woman quickly passed out.

But Holder thought Juergens's announcement had not been sufficiently frightening. He wanted the passengers to feel maximum dread, so that no one would be tempted to act rashly. He grabbed the public address system's microphone from the captain.

"Weathermen, relax—we are encountering absolutely no resistance, they are complying with all our demands," Holder said to his fictional overseers. He then shifted the focus of his address to the passengers. "There are Weathermen among you. They have a bomb. One of them is on LSD. Remain calm. Don't try anything. These men will blow us all up if anyone steps out of line."

Eyes darted about nervously as passengers tried to spot the covert hijackers in their midst. Save for children and the elderly, everyone was a suspect.

In seat 22D, Cathy Kerkow could barely suppress a smile. Her future husband's plan was even more clever than she had imagined.

FLIGHT 701 TOUCHED down in Seattle at 3:14 p.m. Per Holder's instructions, the plane immediately taxied to a runway devoid of traffic. As a fuel truck approached the parked plane, a frantic passenger tried to open an emergency exit over the left wing. His seatmate locked him in a bear hug and reminded him of the hijacker's threat: "Weren't you listening? Don't do anything funny."

Holder, meanwhile, became more and more antsy with each passing minute they were on the ground. His research had taught him that a hijacking's odds of success plummeted in direct proportion to its length of time. He was nearly seven hundred miles north of San Francisco, and thanks to the bounced check snafu that morning, the hour was getting late. The moment the fuel truck moved clear of the jet, Holder uttered a command in Juergens's ear: "Okay, white man, get this thing moving."

"Okay, just let me . . ."

"Now. Get it moving now."

Juergens hit the throttle and zoomed the jet down runway 34L. Passengers who had stood to stretch their legs were tossed about like rag dolls.

Once the plane was airborne and headed south, the gregarious Crawford tried to ply Holder for information. "So, the ones in back—these Weathermen. Their bomb the same as yours, with the grenade and the C-4?"

Holder shook his head. "That one has a timing device. They'll reset it every two hours, long as they keep getting what they want."

Minutes later Donna Jones rang the cockpit bell. A passenger had told her that his wife was dying at a Seattle hospital. He had flown up from Los Angeles because she was undergoing emergency surgery. He was desperate to know if she had survived the ordeal. Was there any way the airline could check on her condition?

Crawford asked Holder for permission to transmit the message. This small act of deference pleased Holder, who gave his approval. *This guy's negotiable*, thought Crawford. *We've got a rapport going. I can work with him.*

After receiving word that the distraught passenger's wife was in recovery, Crawford probed Holder even more: "So, after San Francisco, where is it you want us to take you all?"

Holder was caught off guard by the question. He hadn't planned on revealing his destination until after Angela Davis was safely on board. He fumbled with his reply: "Maybe I want to go to . . . errrrm-mmm, North Vietnam?"

Dead silence in the cockpit. This was going to be a problem.

Crawford pointed to the silver wings affixed to Holder's uniform. "You flew Cobras, yeah?"

When Holder nodded, Crawford tapped a row of three meters on his instrument panel. "Okay, then you'll understand this. See, here's the fuel flow on all three engines. Each one's putting out three thousand pounds per hour, yeah? You take nine thousand pounds per hour, we only have five hours of range. Right?"

Holder stared blankly at the fuel gauge. Crawford figured he should clarify his point. "That means you can't get there. To North Vietnam? Can't do it. Not on a 727. Can't possibly do it."

It took a moment for Holder to comprehend the enormity of his mistake. In his haste to find another flight to hijack after losing the United tickets to Hawaii, he had completely forgotten about the issue of range. Now he had accidentally commandeered an aircraft incapable of making it to Honolulu, to say nothing of Hanoi.

But it was far too late to abort Operation Sisyphus. Angela Davis was in her most desperate hour. Holder would have to improvise.

"Get me an airplane that can, then. You know, that can go over water."

Crawford pleaded with Holder to change his mind, to settle for a destination that the Boeing 727 could reach. He explained that Flight 701's crew wasn't qualified to fly long-range jets, so new pilots would have to be located, too. He proposed zipping down to Havana instead, or alighting in some Central American country. But Holder stood firm in his desire for a plane capable of crossing an ocean.

"How about King Salmon, Alaska?" suggested Crawford, recalling an isolated town from his Air Force days. "I know a little strip up there where we can take you. We'll fly away and leave you alone."

"No. I want another airplane."

Crawford rang Western dispatch with the bad news:

FLIGHT 701: We are negotiating here and want to know if we can get another aircraft, ours or someone else's, and a fresh crew for a trans-Pacific flight. Will try and let passengers off and just take crew and parties involved. Desiring aircraft to take to appropriate destination.

WESTERN: Roger. Contact ramp control at SFO for further instructions and info.

Holder now had to contemplate an entirely unforeseen logistical mess: how would he safely move from one airplane to the other? He thought of the late Richard Obergfell, the hijacker who had been cut down by an FBI sniper mere steps from the Boeing 707 that was supposed to fly him to Milan. Holder worried that he could easily suffer the same fate.

ANGELA DAVIS WAS sitting alone in a San Jose café at 3:45 p.m., trying to enjoy a late vegetarian lunch and a rare moment of peace. The previous twenty-four hours had been a nerve-wracking whirlwind, starting with the trial's emotional closing arguments on June 1: her attorney had blasted the case as "a gigantic hoax not only on the defendant, but also against the name of American justice." Hours later someone had phoned in a death threat to the Santa Clara County district attorney's office, vowing that Davis would be assassinated when she showed up for court the next morning. Security had thus been extraordinarily tight for the day's proceedings, which had consisted of Judge Richard Arnason giving his detailed final instructions to the jury. Deliberations in the thirteen-week trial were now finally under way.

The café's manager interrupted Davis's lunch by telling her that she had a phone call from her lawyer. Davis at first assumed he was calling to inform her that a verdict had been reached. But the jury had only been deliberating since noon—how could they have decided the complex case so quickly?

The attorney had no word yet on a verdict, but he did have an important message to relay from Judge Arnason: a group of militants had hijacked a plane near Seattle, and they were en route to San Francisco in hopes of exchanging their hostages for Davis. Three sheriff's deputies were on their way to the café to escort Davis back to the courthouse; Judge Arnason wanted to see her immediately.

Dazed by the news, Davis returned to her table to wait for the cops. This wasn't the first time some misguided soul had thought of using violence to secure her freedom: in November 1970 a man named Ronald Reed had been arrested for plotting to kidnap the governor of Minnesota, hijack a United Airlines flight, then arrange a swap for Davis.* But up until now, no one had come close to actually whisking her away.

The sheriff's deputies arrived around four p.m. and hurried Davis to Judge Arnason's chambers. Dozens of reporters were still at the courthouse when she arrived, waiting to file their stories about the first day of deliberations. They were stunned to see Davis return amid a phalanx of police, her brightly colored shawl pulled high around her face to help conceal her shaken expression.

Judge Arnason could tell that Davis was genuinely shocked by news of the hijacking, and he believed her protestations that she had nothing to do with it. The judge mentioned that the FBI might want Davis to speak with the hijackers, to try and convince them to surrender. But Davis said she wanted nothing to do with such crazies, not even over the telephone.

As Davis slipped away from the courthouse with her police escort, her closest supporters scrambled to distance themselves from the hijacking. The National United Committee to Free Angela Davis distributed a brief, hastily written statement to reporters covering the trial. "We don't know anything about this," the statement read. "We don't agree with this method of obtaining Angela Y. Davis' freedom."

PARANOIA WAS THICK in the cabin of Flight 701 as it made its way to San Francisco. Everyone wondered who might be in cahoots with the hijacker, holding a bomb while stoned on LSD. Holder gleefully stoked this tension by broadcasting messages to his made-up Weathermen.

*The charges against Reed were eventually dismissed, but he was subsequently imprisoned for thirteen years for having robbed an Omaha, Nebraska, bank in October 1970. In 2006 he was convicted of having ambushed and killed a St. Paul, Minnesota, police officer in May 1970. Reed allegedly committed that murder because he wanted to impress the national leadership of the Black Panther Party.

"Stan, we are still on page six, paragraph twelve," he said on one occasion; a short time later he told this mysterious "Stan" to "turn to page sixteen, paragraph two." Holder was trying to convey the illusion that he was running through a point-by-point plan for a military operation.

In scanning the cabin for "Stan," several passengers focused on a man in his late twenties sitting in 17F—the only other black passenger on the plane. It did not matter that the Weathermen were essentially an all-white organization; the prevailing assumption aboard Flight 701 was that a black hijacker like Holder would have an accomplice of the same race.

Suspicions increased after the stewardesses began to pour free champagne for the hostages: the man in 17F was the only adult to decline a glass. Donna Jones, the lead stewardess, overheard several male passengers discussing what implements they might employ to beat the black man to death.

Jones looked over at 17F and saw the man staring out the window, pretending not to notice that he was being singled out for murder.

One row back, meanwhile, Holder's former seatmate noticed that the hijacker had left his small black valise stashed beneath 17D. He unzipped the bag and carefully pawed through its contents. As he did so, a small crowd gathered around row 18, eager to learn more about their skyjacker.

There was plenty of reading material in the bag, including Holder's copy of *Guide to Selected Viet Cong Equipment and Explosive Devices,* marked up with extensive handwritten notes. This was accompanied by a pair of horoscope booklets; one of them, titled *Aquarius 1972,* ended with a lengthy passage about the nature of death, which Holder had underlined in red pen. There was also a book on dream interpretation and a ratty copy of *Steal This Book,* Abbie Hoffman's infamous guide to using petty crimes to subvert the "Pig Empire" of America.

The bag also contained a bottle of tranquilizers prescribed to Holder by an Army physician; documents detailing Holder's undesirable discharge; a map of Southeast Asia clipped from *The San Diego*

Union; a pair of brown bell-bottom trousers; a loose-fitting white shirt; and a packet of Alka-Seltzer tablets. But the passengers were most intrigued by a collection of handwritten notes—apparently drafts of the notes that Holder had used to hijack the plane. Among them was the letter that Holder had attempted to write on the way to Seattle, then abandoned when his thoughts had become too jumbled:

> *Captain,*
>
> *It is with regret that I am to inform you of my discussion with you was of a highly classified nature, and that your open letter to the press has placed you in a very undesirable position with the command.*
>
> *It is with best feelings of admiration that I am to release you of your command.*
>
> *No request to have you contained at this time have been submitted. You are to consider yourself under house arrest.*
>
> *Your performance concerning your duty will be of some credit to you.*
>
> *(All regulations pertaining to this case are to be review ASAP.)*

The passengers gathered around row 18 could only conclude that they were at the mercy of a very bizarre individual.

In keeping with her duty as Holder's eyes and ears in the main cabin, Kerkow leaned into the aisle to survey the commotion in row 18. She could see the assembled passengers rummaging through her boyfriend's bag and examining his private things. She had to put a stop to it.

Kerkow found Gina Cutcher roaming the aisle with a bottle of champagne. "Those guys shouldn't be allowed to do that," said Kerkow, pointing at the men going through Holder's valise. "That's not right." She was visibly upset, her voice on the verge of cracking into a shriek.

Cutcher couldn't fathom why anyone would care about the morality of sifting through a hijacker's possessions. But something about

Kerkow's demeanor convinced her to intervene. She approached the snoops and warned them that their actions might upset the Weathermen lurking about. She put all of Holder's items back in the bag, which she then restowed beneath 17D. But she whispered to Holder's seatmate that he should write down what he had seen—the FBI might find that information useful.

A CLOUD OF marijuana smoke wafted about the pilots' heads as Holder sucked down the first of his joints. Aware that the straitlaced crew disapproved of his indulgence, Holder tried to assure them that he was acting in everyone's best interest. "Don't worry, it doesn't make me irrational," he told the pilots. "It actually gets me right."

But as Flight 701 passed over the forested wilderness of northern California, Holder became irritable rather than relaxed. It was now almost five o'clock, and there had been no word from Western regarding his numerous demands. He decided to ratchet up the pressure.

"Weathermen, we are one half hour out of phase," he announced over the public address system. He told the pilots that this message had signaled one of his handlers to reset the timing device on the Weathermen's bomb, to thirty minutes hence. If their demands weren't met by then, the plane would be destroyed as it circled the Bay Area.

Crawford got on the horn with dispatch in Los Angeles:

FLIGHT 701: Will have to hold SSW of Oakland until you can derive some info we can use in reference to aircraft, crew, Angela Davis, parachutes, and money.

WESTERN: Roger, stand by.

Crawford was about to tell Holder to stay patient when a devious idea occurred to him: how might the hijacker react to a bluff?

"Sorry, they say they can't get ahold of any parachutes," said Crawford. It was only a minor gambit on his part; Crawford had the sense that Holder was too reasonable to detonate his bomb over such a trivial issue, certainly not before making his displeasure known.

Holder just nodded at Crawford's lie, seemingly unperturbed by the lack of parachutes.

Looking for an excuse to try a riskier ruse, Crawford got back to dispatch:

FLIGHT 701: Like to impress the need to expedite the decision making. If there's any info, please let us have it now.

WESTERN: Roger, stand by. Will check and call back in a couple of minutes.

Crawford made his move: "Hey, Angela Davis—you know, they say she got acquitted today."

His mind burbling with manic energy, Holder did not greet this claim with skepticism. He instead marveled at the role that Operation Sisyphus must have played in securing Davis's acquittal. He wondered at what point the jury had been informed of the hijacking, and whether the liberated Davis was thinking of him fondly at that very moment. How would she express her gratitude for all he had done on her behalf?

Once again Holder just nodded at Crawford—Davis would no longer be a topic of negotiation. But he still wanted that second plane capable of reaching North Vietnam—that, he told Crawford sternly, was something his Weathermen handlers could not forgo.

Shortly after five p.m., the radio crackled with an update from Los Angeles:

WESTERN: Arranging for money. Difficult at this time of day. How long, don't know.

FLIGHT 701: Stress fact that money not primary consideration. Getting aircraft with long-range ability primary.

WESTERN: No aircraft in area and no volunteers of use from others.

FLIGHT 701: If unable to get aircraft, can request from military for use of one of theirs. There can be no compromise on this situation. Want to stress, no way out. Have to get long-range aircraft.

WESTERN: Roger.

Satisfied that his orders were being followed, Holder flipped through his notebook, looking for ideas on how to adjust Operation Sisyphus now that Davis was supposedly free. He still wanted to have his say about Vietnam, to shock the nation into understanding the madness of that distant war. But Davis's acquittal seemed like an unmistakable sign that Holder's ultimate goal was slightly off. And Holder was not one to quibble with cosmic advice.

So as Western Airlines Flight 701 swooped toward San Francisco, Holder pondered the list of alternate destinations in his notebook. Perhaps he wasn't meant to reach Hanoi.

8

"CAN'T YOU GET A CHOPPER?"

VISITORS TO WILLIAM Newell's office couldn't help but notice the black-and-white mug shot that hung above his desk. The photograph's subject, a big-eared kid with a patchy mustache, sported an expression halfway between sour and fatigued. The small chalkboard he held to his chest contained a puzzling jumble of letters, the first three of which were "Kfg"—the German acronym for *Kriegsgefangener,* or "prisoner of war."

Newell had been just nineteen years old when he posed for that photo at Stalag Luft I, the German prison camp where he spent the last fourteen months of World War II after ejecting from a damaged P-51 Mustang. He rarely talked about his time in captivity, except to note that he had been sustained by a memento that the guards had failed to confiscate: a single lock of his young bride's hair. But the mug shot alone was enough to impress his peers and underlings at San Francisco International Airport, where Newell served as Western Airlines' chief pilot. Even in a company full of hardy combat veterans, Newell was regarded with a certain sense of awe.

On the afternoon of June 2, 1972, the balding, pugnacious Newell sat hunched beneath his German mug shot, grumpily plowing through a thick stack of paperwork. He knew he would never finish the job by five p.m. and was thus condemned to get a late start on the summer weekend. At the rate he was going, it would surely be close to dark by the time he reached his home in suburban San Mateo.

At roughly a quarter past four, Newell received a phone call from Norman Rose, the head of Western's dispatch center in Los Angeles. Rose had startling news to share: Seattle-bound Flight 701 had apparently been hijacked by a gang of LSD-addled Weathermen armed with multiple bombs. The Boeing 727 was now headed to San Francisco, where the hijackers expected to be given $500,000, five parachutes, and—most bizarrely—a white-clad Angela Davis. A team of FBI agents was on its way to the airport, to set up a command post on the main terminal's fourth floor. The FBI knew the airport and its buildings well; this would be the fourth hijacking the Bureau had handled in San Francisco since 1969.

By the time Newell found the makeshift command post, located in an isolated room protected by a retractable steel gate, the FBI agents had already arrived. One agent was connecting telephones that provided access both to the outside world and to Western's communications system. Another was taping up diagrams of the airport's layout and a Boeing 727's interior. And a third agent was unpacking a duffel bag containing shotguns and flak jackets, neatly arranging the items on a folding table.

The FBI agents were feeling bold, buoyed by a rare victory in the War on Skyjacking: that morning the fugitive Frederick Hahneman, who had parachuted into the Honduran jungle on May 5, had surrendered at the American embassy in Tegucigalpa—albeit without the $303,000 he had extorted from Eastern Air Lines, the fate of which he declined to reveal. The agents wanted to build on that mild success by putting a rapid end to the hijacking of Flight 701.

A Western vice president was at the command post, too, and he updated Newell on the airline's efforts to comply with the hijackers. Angela Davis had steadfastly refused to get involved in the affair, so that particular demand was a nonstarter. But two Western employees were gathering the ransom at the Bank of America on South Van Ness

Avenue; since the FBI was insisting that the bank record every bill's serial number, the process would take at least two more hours. Most important, the hijackers were now requesting a new plane capable of transoceanic travel. The vice president was aware that Western had no such aircraft in San Francisco at that time. He asked Newell to make some calls.

Newell returned to his office and worked his Rolodex, starting with his local counterparts at United and Pan Am. But both airlines were understandably reluctant to lend a long-range jet to Western, especially after Newell admitted that the hijacking involved explosives. Newell then reached out to Western's other bases of operation, in the hope that one of them could spare an aircraft. After much frustration, Newell finally lucked out: a Minneapolis-based Boeing 720H was scheduled to land in Las Vegas a little after six p.m.* He arranged for the plane to be flown to San Francisco as soon as its passengers had disembarked. With any luck, it would arrive around eight p.m.

But Newell worried that the 720H could only be a stopgap. Based on the Weathermen's antiwar ideology, as well as the limited information he had gleaned from Norm Rose, Newell inferred that the hijackers wanted to go to North Vietnam, the rare nation that might grant them asylum. But the 720H had a maximum range of just 4,370 miles, nowhere near enough to reach mainland Asia from San Francisco. The plane could certainly get to Hawaii, where Western could then arrange for a transfer to a Boeing 707-320C with a range of approximately 6,600 miles—almost exactly the distance between Honolulu and Hanoi. It would be prudent to refuel in either Tokyo or Manila, but coordinating such an overseas stop would be difficult for an airline whose most exotic destinations were Edmonton and Mexico City.

The more pressing matter, though, was who would fly the 720H, since Jerry Juergens and his crew were not qualified to do so. Newell nominated himself to be the new plane's captain—as chief pilot, he

*The Boeing 720H was a model unique to Western, a version of the popular 720B that had been modified by the airline's own engineers. It was tweaked to be slightly lighter than the 720B and thus burn less fuel per mile traveled.

felt obligated to take the job. He perused the duty roster to find two more men he could trust. Newell quickly settled on Donald Thompson, a World War II veteran who had been with Western since 1949, to be his co-pilot. Richard Luker, a lieutenant commander in the Naval Reserve who had flown A7 Corsair attack jets in Vietnam, would be his flight engineer.

Newell had Thompson paged first. When they spoke over the airport's courtesy telephone, his instructions were vague and terse: "I'm going to need you to stand by, Don. Looks like we may be going on a trip."

ROGER HOLDER COULD now make out the specks of cars moving across the Bay Bridge. He knew this meant the plane was making its final approach to San Francisco International Airport, after holding near Oakland for forty minutes while a runway was cleared. He asked Tom Crawford to inquire about the status of his money and the long-range jet. The reply from Western upset him greatly:

WESTERN:	The money is being assembled now in downtown San Francisco and will have to be sent by armored truck to the airport and with traffic this time of day will take about one and a half to two hours to get it to the airport.
FLIGHT 701:	Can't you get a chopper to get it?
WESTERN:	Stand by.
FLIGHT 701:	And what is your problem with getting the aircraft? If you can tell us we can react and work out some game plan. Tell why the aircraft is delayed.
WESTERN:	Roger, stand by.
FLIGHT 701:	Make it fast. Will have to make some moves shortly.
WESTERN:	Roger, be back in a couple of minutes.

Western's dithering had become too much for Holder to stand. He picked up the radio microphone next to the jump seat and screamed, "In less than twenty minutes, they are going to kill us! They are holding my family!" His Samsonite briefcase rocked precariously on his lap as he shrieked.

It wasn't just the flight crew that heard Holder's rant—it was everyone at Western dispatch and at the FBI's command post, too. To prepare for landing, Ed Richardson had been about to respond to an air-traffic control inquiry when Holder made his unnerving broadcast. "Uh, say again?" asked a puzzled dispatcher, who feared that it was the co-pilot who had warned that his family was in peril.

Crawford tried to clarify the situation. "These people, they came to this party's house and are holding his family. He is the middle party, a concerned party whose family is, uh, let's say *controlled*. He is on our side. He is a go-between between us and the others. The others are from the Weathermen group, and you know their desires as regards to this country."

The dispatcher confirmed that he understood Crawford's explanation—the crew was dealing with a hijacker who claimed to be under duress. But the eavesdropping FBI agents were still confused. They couldn't distinguish Holder's voice from Richardson's, and they feared that a hijacker might have a gun to the co-pilot's head, forcing him to recant his plea for help. The agents alerted the FBI's field office in Los Angeles, requesting that Richardson's house in nearby Palos Verdes be checked for evidence of a kidnapping.

Flight 701 landed in San Francisco at 6:15 p.m. and taxied to the north end of runway 19R. Just as in Seattle, Holder did not wish to play into the FBI's hands by idling on the ground. He demanded that the plane be refueled quickly, then take off again once its tanks were full. They would circle the airport until his $500,000 and his long-range jet had been delivered.

Back in the main cabin, Cathy Kerkow sprang into action as soon as the plane came to rest. She walked to the rear exit, where Gina Cutcher was sitting in a jump seat. "Hey, what's going on?" Kerkow asked cheerfully. "Anything I can do to help out?" She kept one eye on the jet's folding stairs, checking for signs that they were about to be deployed to enable an FBI ambush.

Cutcher thanked Kerkow for her concern and asked her to return to her seat. As she settled back into 22D, she peered out the window, hoping to catch a glimpse of Angela Davis. But all she saw was a lone Western fuel truck gliding across the tarmac.

UPON RETURNING TO the FBI's command post after arranging for the Boeing 720H, Newell noticed that one of the agents was no longer wearing his dark blue suit. The man had donned the uniform of a Western maintenance worker, complete with a bright orange safety vest. A pair of shiny wingtips peeked out from beneath the frayed cuffs of his borrowed coveralls.

The agents explained that their disguised colleague was planning to sneak aboard the Boeing 727 while pretending to fix an engine. He would assess the situation and then determine whether an assault would be prudent. If anything went awry, or if he glimpsed an opportunity to end the hijacking himself, he would use the pistol tucked inside his sleeve.

There was little time to execute this plan, since the Boeing 727 would be taking off as soon as it refueled. The FBI asked Newell to lend them a Western maintenance truck, a piece of equipment essential to the ruse. But Newell refused to play along.

"Absolutely not," he fumed. "I don't want anyone on that plane with a gun." He had read too many stories about wild shoot-outs between hijackers and the FBI. Newell wasn't about to permit such violence aboard a full flight.

The agents pleaded with Newell, assuring him that they wouldn't do anything to jeopardize the passengers' lives. They argued that their gambit might prevent a true catastrophe, since the Weathermen were obviously cavalier about setting off bombs. But Newell could not be budged.

As the frustrated agents huddled to discuss their options, Newell used the FBI's communications setup to contact Flight 701. He assured the crew that the money and long-range aircraft would be in San Francisco shortly—an hour and a half, tops.

"Roger, but can't delay any longer," replied Ed Richardson. "These people are deadly serious. They mean business."

FLIGHT 701 WENT back in the air at 6:59 p.m., with enough fuel in its tanks to circle the airport for five hours. "Stan, turn to page nineteen, paragraph two," Holder announced to the imaginary Weathermen as the Boeing 727 soared over the San Francisco Bay. He didn't want the passengers to forget about the supposed bomb in their midst.

Kerkow was soothed by the sound of her boyfriend's voice, which she hadn't heard in over an hour. She had no idea why they had taken off again with neither the money nor Angela Davis aboard. Nor did she understand why the plane wasn't venturing out over the Pacific Ocean toward Hawaii. But she still had faith that all would be well. A man of Holder's brilliance surely knew what he was doing.

Holder, though, was struggling to revamp his busted plan. None of the hijackings he'd studied had involved the transfer of numerous hostages from one plane to another. He would have to concoct a safe method for doing so, and fast: Western dispatch was reporting that the Boeing 720H had left Las Vegas and would land in San Francisco at 8:05 p.m.

The operational details in Holder's notebook were providing him with little solace; he needed his astrology charts for peace of mind. He had a stewardess fetch him the black valise stashed beneath 17D, the bag his seatmate had rifled through on the way down from Seattle. He hoped that *Aquarius 1972* would provide him with the guidance he so desperately craved.

Holder excused himself from the cockpit and took the booklets to the first-class lavatory. He smoked another joint while reacquainting himself with the messages encoded in the stars. The logistics of the plane transfer took shape in his mind.

When he returned to the cockpit, Holder was brimming with meticulous directions for the crew. When they landed again in San Francisco, he wanted the money first, brought to the plane's front door by a commissary truck equipped with a hydraulic lift. He insisted that the truck approach on the plane's left-hand side; based on what he had observed about runway 19R, he felt this would give him the best view of the vehicle and its occupants.

Once the money was delivered, Holder wanted the 720H taxied to within two hundred feet of Flight 701. The new crew would stand at the base of the 720H's stairs, their hands atop their heads like captured soldiers. Half of Flight 701's passengers would march to the second jet in a single-file line, with Holder at the rear. Once those passengers were settled in, everyone who had remained aboard the first plane would be free to go.

"So which half you want?" asked Tom Crawford.

Holder scrunched his brow in puzzlement.

"The passengers. You know, which half of the passengers?"

This was yet another key detail that had somehow slipped Holder's mind as he was planning Operation Sisyphus: though he had always intended to free half the hostages in San Francisco, he hadn't devised a method for divvying them up.

"How 'bout one side of the plane?" suggested Crawford. "I'm thinking that would be easiest, don't you?"

Holder nodded.

"Okay, which one you want, left or the right?"

Holder spun the question in his mind, straining to remember which side Kerkow was sitting on. He had last seen her nearly five hours earlier, while marching up the aisle with Gina Cutcher.

"Right."

FLANKED BY BLUE-AND-WHITE police cars with blaring sirens, the armored truck containing the ransom reached the airport at 7:30 p.m. Bank of America had finally managed to amass the requested sum by scraping together $10,000 worth of fivers. The total amount, consisting of 12,500 bills of varying denominations, was transferred to a large canvas sack marked STEREO HEADSETS: PROPERTY OF WESTERN AIRLINES. The filled bag weighed more than thirty pounds.

Bill Newell, meanwhile, was making final preparations to command the Boeing 720H. Dick Luker and Don Thompson, his handpicked crew members, had been apprised of the situation, and neither one had expressed any qualms about flying to Hanoi. Newell had all the charts he needed to get the 720H as far as Honolulu, a daily Western destination; they would have to figure out how to get from there to North Vietnam once they reached Hawaii.

All was going smoothly until Newell overheard Tom Crawford transmit the hijacker's latest demand: all the passengers on Flight 701's right-hand side would be coming aboard the 720H.

Newell had assumed that his only passengers would be the hijacker and his Weathermen associates. Now he had to plan for the needs of Western customers whose routine trip to Seattle could potentially end in the hostile city of Hanoi. Newell paged the senior stewardess on duty, Glenna MacAlpine, who was just about to depart for the weekend. When informed that the hijacked flight needed stewardesses, MacAlpine did not hesitate to volunteer; like Newell, she felt obligated to place herself in harm's way. She made some calls and found three other "girls" willing to assist: Pat Stark, Chris Hagenow, and Deirdre Bowles. All were eating dinner with their husbands when asked to work a hijacked flight; all immediately rushed to the airport, knowing full well that the trip could lead them into a war zone.

As MacAlpine assembled her crew, Newell was called into a conference with the FBI. The agents again expressed their eagerness to prevent the hijacking from proceeding any further. They said they were sensitive to Newell's concerns about gunplay, and they would no longer pressure him to help sneak a disguised agent aboard a plane. All they wanted now was his permission to inspect the Boeing 720H when it arrived so they could familiarize themselves with its layout.

Newell was leery of the FBI's intentions. "You're putting me in a hell of a position," he snapped, pointing out that the hijackers might not react well if they spotted FBI agents prowling about their long-range jet. Newell suspected that the agents still aimed to use violence.

Shortly before eight p.m., the bickering between the agents and Newell was interrupted by a phone call from FBI headquarters in Washington, D.C. It was the office of acting FBI director L. Patrick Gray, passing along some urgent news: a second hijacked plane was on its way to San Francisco.

9

"IT'S ALL A LIE"

GEYSERS OF FUEL gushed from the tanks beneath Flight 701's wings, evaporating into ribbons of white mist as they slammed into the stratosphere. Many passengers who saw the spectacle feared that something had gone terribly wrong in the cockpit, and that they would soon plummet 20,000 feet to their deaths. But Captain Jerry Juergens was dumping fuel for good reason: the $500,000 ransom was ready for pickup, and the plane had to be several thousand pounds lighter in order to land safely.

Juergens informed the passengers that they would be back on the ground shortly, and he thanked them for their patience. He made no mention of the second plane that was flying in from Las Vegas.

Flight 701 landed at 8:09 p.m. and once again taxied to a stop at the north end of runway 19R. Roger Holder leaned forward in his jump seat and peered out the cockpit's left-hand side. A commissary truck was approaching the plane, just as he had instructed.

"I want a girl in the cockpit," Holder announced over the public address system. He needed someone to reach out and grab the money from the truck; doing so himself would make him vulnerable to snipers.

Donna Jones, the lead stewardess, responded to Holder's call for help. But she was rather petite, just five foot two, and Juergens thought she wouldn't be able to lift the money herself. He suggested that Tom Crawford do the job instead. Holder agreed.

Jones opened the aircraft's front door for Crawford. The stereo headsets bag was sitting on the truck's hydraulic lift, all by itself. Crawford hopped onto the lift, picked up the sack, and heaved it back into the plane. It landed with a loud thud in the aisle, attracting the whole plane's attention.

The passengers' hearts lifted in unison. The money had arrived. Surely their freedom was at hand.

THE FBI AGENTS were scrambling to learn all they could about the second hijacking, but details were scarce. All they could gather was that a disheveled young man had forced his way onto a United Airlines Boeing 727 as it was boarding passengers in Reno. The man, armed with a .357 Magnum, was demanding $200,000 and passage to San Francisco. Since the banks were already closed for the weekend, United was trying to obtain the cash from local casinos; the Harrah's on Virginia Street promised to front the airline three-quarters of the ransom.

The Reno hijacker had made no mention of any political motives, but the FBI couldn't write off his desire to reach San Francisco as mere coincidence. The agents fretted that he might be in cahoots with the hijackers of Flight 701, part of a massive conspiracy to free Angela Davis that was just beginning to take shape. If the United hijacker found out that the Weathermen aboard the Western aircraft had been gunned down, would he retaliate by executing his hostages? Or was storming Flight 701 the only way to save lives? The FBI would have to proceed with great caution in determining its next move.

As the agents struggled to gather intelligence about the situation in Reno, the long-range Boeing 720H landed and taxied to a hangar near runway 19R. Seeing that the FBI was momentarily distracted, Newell quietly beckoned his two crew members, Dick Luker and Don

Thompson, to accompany him to the newly arrived jet. There was no time for the men to change into their uniforms; Newell wanted to get out to the 720H right away so he could prevent any FBI agents from sneaking aboard.

The three men got to the hangar at 8:23 p.m. From the cockpit window, they could see the Western commissary truck heading back to the terminal, its delivery mission complete. It was time to make the switch.

HOLDER DIDN'T BOTHER to unzip the canvas bag that contained the half-million dollars. He was too focused on getting to the next plane. But where was it? Darkness had fallen outside, yet the only lights he could see were those that lined the runway or illuminated the distant terminal. No other aircraft was approaching.

"They're going to kill us all if they don't get the plane," Holder told Crawford. "They reset the timer. Now it's almost run out."

Crawford passed along the message to the airport's air traffic control tower:

> FLIGHT 701: We are dealing in minutes now. Get that 720 refueled fast and back out here. No monkey business. It's getting close now. Absolutely no games. Make sure the ramp people know this, and fast.
>
> SFO: Roger.

When the FBI agents heard this ominous communiqué, they looked around for Newell, only to realize that the chief pilot and his crew had given them the slip. One of the agents sprinted toward the hangar where the 720H was refueling. He got there a little after 8:30 p.m., just as Glenna MacAlpine and her stewardesses were arriving.

The agent begged Newell to keep the plane in the hangar. The

FBI still wanted to inspect the 720H and perhaps get a closer look at the area surrounding runway 19R, too. Things were hectic at the moment, with the agents still trying to gauge events in Reno, but they would be ready to conduct their inspection soon. How long was Newell willing to wait?

"I won't taxi out for fifteen minutes," promised Newell. The agent said that was acceptable, and that he would soon return with two colleagues.

As soon as the agent departed, Newell radioed Juergens and told him to get ready—they were heading out to runway 19R immediately. He wasn't going to give the FBI time to cook up some harebrained scheme that might endanger his passengers' lives.

THE MOOD IN the cabin of Flight 701 was close to jubilant as the passengers awaited their release. The plane's supply of liquor and champagne had run dry nearly an hour before, so tipsy passengers toasted each other with glasses of ice water. Strangers hugged and vowed to keep in touch, perhaps even arrange a reunion so they could all laugh about the ordeal they had just shared. Few paid attention to the flashing lights of the Boeing 720H that was slowly rolling toward them.

Donna Jones was urging passengers to keep the aisle clear when she glimpsed the 720H out of a right-side window. She watched it turn onto runway 19R and head straight for Flight 701, angled slightly to the left of the hijacked plane. A maintenance truck followed close behind, towing a set of boarding stairs.

Jones hurried down the aisle to find Cutcher, who was joking with a couple of boisterous passengers about their mutual sense of relief. Jones grabbed her by the shoulders and whispered in her ear: "It's a lie. It's all a lie. It isn't over."

In the cockpit, Jerry Juergens watched the 720H come to a halt about two hundred feet away, its nose facing that of the 727. It was time for him to make the announcement he'd been dreading ever since the stoned Holder had told him of the transfer plan.

"Ladies and gentlemen, we're going to have a transfer to another aircraft here," Juergens said over the public address system. The passengers assumed this was good news; their Weathermen captors were about to depart.

The front door of the 720H opened. Newell and his crew descended the boarding stairs and lined up along the tarmac with hands atop their heads.

Holder didn't like what he saw. The women were all wearing stewardess uniforms, but the men were in civilian clothes—jackets and ties. If this was an FBI trick, he warned Juergens, the consequences would be dire.

Juergens swore that the pilots were authentic. Then he broadcast Holder's orders to the cabin.

"Will the stewardesses please release the air stairs? Ladies and gentlemen, we're going to need everyone sitting on the right side to file out the rear of the plane and up into the other aircraft. Walk fast."

All laughter and chatter ceased at once. Passengers on the right side anxiously looked left, hoping to find empty seats to move to. But those seats were in short supply.

A few brave right-side passengers rose and moved toward the descending stairs in the rear. Cathy Kerkow was among them. She passed by Cutcher at the exit. "I'll be praying for you," the stewardess whispered. "God bless you." Kerkow expressed her gratitude with an appreciative smile.

The rest of the passengers on the right-hand side followed suit, save for a woman who was traveling with her infant son. She stayed put, praying that the hijacker wouldn't make her join the others.

Up in the cockpit, Holder ordered Crawford to carry the ransom to the new plane. The flight engineer did as he was told; Holder walked a few paces behind, clutching the Samsonite briefcase to his stomach with one hand and carrying the black valise in the other. The two men passed by Donna Jones, who was standing in the first-class galley. She glanced at an empty champagne bottle resting on the countertop. *Smash him in the head,* she thought. *Smash him in the head and this is all over.*

But the bomb—what about the bomb? Jones resisted the urge to be a hero.

Toward the rear of the plane, Holder saw the woman and her infant son still sitting on the right-hand side, surrounded by a sea of empty seats. She looked deathly afraid, her arms wrapped tight around her fidgeting baby. The expressionless Holder didn't break his stride as he followed Crawford down the air stairs onto the tarmac.

Don't look around, thought Holder. *Just go.*

From the safety of their command post, the FBI agents used binoculars to watch the single-file procession from one plane to the other. They had been blindsided by the transfer; neither Juergens nor Newell had told them of their plans. The option of posting a sniper near runway 19R was no longer viable.

The furious agents called the nearest Coast Guard air station and requested that a jet be scrambled to tail the 720H after takeoff. Perhaps Newell would listen to the entreaties of a fellow military pilot.

As the unlucky passengers marched toward the new plane, one woman fell out of line and dropped to her knees, struck by a sudden dizzy spell. "Go back, ma'am," Holder told her as he and Crawford passed. Grateful for her unexpected reprieve, she stumbled back to the 727.

Twenty-seven passengers made it on board the 720H. Dazed by their sudden reversal of fortune, they glumly selected their seats. Kerkow settled on 11A, right over the left wing. She still had no idea why they had changed planes, nor why Angela Davis had failed to show, but she had to trust that Holder had the situation under control. They would be sunbathing in the Outback soon enough.

Holder asked Crawford to drop the money on a first-class seat, then nodded farewell—the flight engineer was free to go. As soon as

Crawford stepped back aboard the first plane, Juergens made a weary announcement to the remaining passengers: "For all of you still here, it's over. It's over."

WHEN NEWELL, LUKER, and Thompson entered the cockpit of the 720H, Holder was waiting for them, standing just inside the door. He wasn't what they had expected at all: the pilots had pictured a wild-eyed, scruffy type, not a clean-cut soldier in wire-rimmed glasses.

"There are no heroes here, are there?" Holder asked the pilots.

"What do you mean by that?" Newell retorted. Though he appreciated the delicacy of the situation, he was not one for verbal games.

"You're not going to do anything drastic, are you?" Holder replied.

"No," said Newell. "Are you?"

Holder grinned, as if energized by the brusque exchange. He shook hands with the three pilots, introducing himself as Richard, then settled into the cockpit's jump seat. He was feeling quite pleased with himself—he had managed to keep Operation Sisyphus going despite numerous complications. He was clearly in harmony with the universe's majestic plan.

"Where do you want to go?" asked Newell as he pushed the 720H back from the rendezvous point on runway 19R.

"I'll let you know," said Holder. He honestly hadn't decided yet. Hanoi was still a possibility, of course—that would be the most obvious stage from which to air his grievances about the war. But Holder could not ignore the Angela Davis omen, which had him wondering whether North Vietnam might be a tragic mistake; he now had visions of enemy MiG-17s spraying the Western Airlines jet with cannon fire. Holder once again flipped through his spiral-bound planning notebook to see if any of his alternate destinations struck him as auspicious.

At 9:21 p.m. the Boeing 720H zoomed down runway 19R and began to climb over San Francisco Bay. From that point forward, the plane would be known to air traffic controllers and company dispatchers as Western Airlines Flight 364.

Newell prepared to bank left toward the Bay Bridge, in preparation for rounding the peninsula and heading west out over the Pacific—the first step in the marathon journey to North Vietnam. But he decided to check one last time with the hijacker regarding his desired itinerary.

"Where do you want to go?"

Holder knew it was time to make a decision. He felt the cosmically appropriate answer well up in his throat.

"Algiers."

10

THE CHOICE

THOUGH BILL NEWELL was a worldly man, his North African geography was rusty. *Algiers?* he thought. *Where in God's name is Algiers?* It took him a moment to realize that he needed to head in the exact opposite direction from the one he had envisioned—not west toward Hanoi, but east toward the capital of Algeria.

Newell was partly relieved by the hijacker's decision: at least the United States wasn't at war with Algeria, so there was little danger of getting blasted from the sky on approach. But he also knew that Algeria's government was openly hostile to the West. The nation had broken off diplomatic relations with the United States in 1967, during the Six-Day War between Israel and its Arab neighbors. Since then Algeria had become a prominent supporter of various revolutionary movements around the globe, including the Vietcong. Newell feared that such a virulently anti-American country would have no qualms about impounding his plane and imprisoning his crew.

But Newell's most immediate concern was simply reaching Algeria, rather than figuring out a way to avoid incarceration once he got there. He suggested to Holder that they first fly to New York City, where the plane could refuel and the crew could take on a qualified navigator: because Western didn't operate east of the Mississippi River, the flight would need a navigator who was familiar with transatlantic travel.

Holder gave his blessing to Newell's plan, with the caveat that he would be extremely upset if the navigator turned out to be an FBI agent in disguise. He said that he would be forced to detonate his bomb if there was any hint of deception.

After Dick Luker notified Western dispatch of Flight 364's destination, Newell picked up the radio to ask a favor: "Can you call the wives of the crew members and reassure them that everything is fine, tell them not to worry?" The three volunteer pilots had neglected to phone home before boarding the Boeing 720H; their families were still expecting them for supper.

A few minutes later Luker heard something unexpected in his headset: a transmission from a Coast Guard jet. The jet's pilot stated that he was shadowing Flight 364 and wished to ask some pertinent questions. Could the Western crew determine whether there were multiple hijackers aboard? Had they seen any firearms? What course would they be taking?

Newell told Luker to ignore the Coast Guard inquisitor. He would not stand for any further FBI meddling.

THE PASSENGERS WERE greatly relieved to hear that their next stop would be New York's John F. Kennedy International Airport. A rumor had been circulating that they were bound for Havana, spurred by a stewardess's ill-advised joke that the meal service would feature "Cu-Ban" coffee instead of the typical Yuban. As they tucked into their lukewarm chicken dinners around 10:45 p.m., the passengers had renewed hope that their ordeal still might end on American soil.

But Cathy Kerkow was bewildered by Flight 364's flight plan. Holder had never mentioned the possibility of an eastbound journey. Now, in addition to failing to free Angela Davis, her boyfriend had them flying away from their agreed-upon destinations of North

Vietnam and Australia. Kerkow's faith in Operation Sisyphus was beginning to waver.

Two seats away from Kerkow, in 11C, was a twenty-three-year-old man who had been traveling to Seattle to attend a hydroplane race. He couldn't stop staring at her, his interest stoked by the fact that she clearly wasn't wearing a bra beneath her pink blouse. As the stewardesses came around to fill champagne flutes, the man decided to make the best of a bad situation and try his romantic luck.

But his attempt to strike up a conversation didn't get far, for Kerkow was in no mood to flirt. Though she had been relatively honest with her seatmate on the way to Seattle, she now thought it best to lie. She told the man her name was Marti and that she was a student at San Diego State University majoring in "recreation." When the man asked what classes she had taken last semester, she merely shrugged. He got the hint.

After the conversation petered out, Kerkow excused herself and moved to the empty row of seats on the opposite side of the plane. She stared out the window, watching the wingtip lights flicker in the darkness, until sleep overcame her.

LIKE TOM CRAWFORD before him, Dick Luker was a gregarious sort who figured it might be wise to befriend the hijacker. Once the plane was safely cruising at 33,000 feet, Luker spun his chair ninety degrees and turned to face Holder, who was counting the money in the canvas bag. The flight engineer advised Holder that he needed to retrieve a chart from beside the jump seat.

"Why are you telling me this?" asked Holder.

"I don't want to do anything that might startle you."

"Do anything you want. I trust that you won't try anything that'll jeopardize those people in the back."

Noting that Holder spoke with a smile, Luker sensed an opening to get more personal: "So, you have any children?"

"Two girls. Twin girls. But their mom and I ain't married anymore. The Weathermen have them. That's why I'm doing this."

The two men then spoke at length, with Holder telling many of the same lies that he had shared with his seatmate en route to Seattle: he claimed to have been a helicopter pilot in Vietnam who possessed an IQ of 141. But he also let slip some truths, such as the fact that he had spent time in a military prison, a demoralizing experience that he did not care to repeat. "I've got nothing to lose," he said at one point, a remark that made Luker strongly suspect that the Weathermen were a fiction and that Holder was acting alone.

Luker was surprised at how much he enjoyed chatting with Holder—he was impressed by the hijacker's obvious intelligence and warmth. But as they bantered, he was also debating whether to violate Western policy and use force to end the hijacking. Midnight was fast approaching after a long and eventful day. If Holder dozed off, would Luker dare pry the Samsonite briefcase from the hijacker's limp hand?

But Holder was in too much of a manic state to feel fatigued. He requested a cup of coffee with sugar, his first sustenance since lunch. He then asked Newell to have the first-class section cleared so he could sit there all alone.

After the first-class passengers had been moved to less luxurious quarters in coach, Holder settled into seat 1B and lit another joint. As a momentary calm washed over his body, he contemplated the welcome that awaited in Algiers.

Dozens of reporters and cameramen swarmed the various airports involved in the day's two skyjackings. In Reno, the media throng watched from behind a chain-link fence as a United Airlines ticket agent drove the $200,000 ransom out to the hijacked Boeing 727. She was met on the tarmac by a strange sight: three individuals standing in a tight huddle with a blanket flung over their heads. The concealed trio consisted of two flight attendants and the hijacker, who had his

.357 Magnum cocked. The blanket trick frustrated an FBI sniper who had hoped to end the hijacking with a single bullet.

The United jet finally took off for San Francisco around 11:30 p.m., heading south toward Washoe Lake. Just twenty miles into the journey, the hijacker parachuted out of the rear exit, taking along the cash that United had borrowed from two Reno casinos. He landed safely on the highway that ran along the lake's west side, then vanished into the scrub.

At the San Francisco airport, meanwhile, the passengers and crew from Flight 701 were sequestered in a hallway cordoned off from the media. They snacked on roast beef sandwiches as they waited for their FBI debriefings. One of those interviews proved extraordinarily useful to investigators: the passenger from seat 18E stated that he had rifled through the hijacker's valise, which had contained Army discharge papers for a private named Willie Roger Holder.

For the most part, though, the FBI debriefings were worthless. To the agents' chagrin, a number of the liberated passengers were too intoxicated to recall any useful details from the hijacking; many others, presumably wary of incurring the Weathermen's wrath, claimed they had never gotten a good look at the black man in the Army dress uniform. The press was stymied in its efforts to make sense of the story, too; the initial wire-service reports had described Flight 701's hijackers as four black radicals.

Though the police prevented reporters from interviewing many passengers in San Francisco, there was no such security at Seattle-Tacoma International Airport, where concerned families had remained after Flight 701's brief stop for fuel. The passengers' loved ones gave voice to the growing popular discontent over the government's inability to halt the skyjacking epidemic. "I hope the FBI has a real welcome waiting for [the hijackers], a real warm welcome," snarled the elderly husband of one hostage. "I think we should give them the same thing they're putting our people in danger of getting. We need fewer lawyers and more executioners."

A *Seattle Times* reporter confronted a five-year-old boy whose great-grandmother was aboard Flight 701. He asked the child if he knew why the plane had been delayed. "They got hijacked," the boy replied. "The men wanted money. I think in the hundreds of dollars."

"A commentary on modern society," the reporter lamented. "'Hijacking' part of a five-year-old's vocabulary."

HOLDER STUBBED OUT his third joint of Flight 364 and returned to the cockpit, where Newell had several matters to discuss. The captain first tried to sell Holder on the idea of flying to Havana instead of Algiers, stressing that the Cuban government was a safer bet to greet him with open arms. When Holder declined, Newell raised the possibility of going somewhere in Canada, where Western had some experience taking hijackers: in February 1971 the airline had deposited a nineteen-year-old Army draftee in Vancouver, after he commandeered a Seattle-bound flight in order to avoid basic training.

But the more Newell tried to negotiate the flight's final destination, the more dead set Holder became on the idea of Algiers. He had picked the city on impulse over the likes of Peking and Moscow, trusting his gut to decipher the esoteric messages conveyed by the stars. The captain's protests now made Holder feel that The System was truly unsettled by how Operation Sisyphus was unfolding—confirmation, he believed, that his instincts were correct.

"Algiers," Holder insisted. "That's what they want me to do."

With his cajoling getting nowhere, Newell shifted gears. "But how do they feel about you maybe letting the passengers go in New York? They can't help you anymore. Maybe even be a threat to you if they find out you want to take them all the way to Algiers."

Holder said he had no problem with that. He had always planned to release the remaining hostages before heading overseas, albeit in Honolulu rather than New York.

Newell woke up half the plane with his ensuing announcement. "Ladies and gentlemen, I think I have some very good news for you. I have been negotiating with our passenger up here, and he has agreed to let you off in New York. If anything further develops, I'll let you know."

Kerkow was among those awakened by Newell's address and the cheers that followed. Her aspiring suitor across the aisle noticed that, unlike the rest of the passengers, she expressed no joy at hearing that her freedom was imminent. She just sat there glumly with a blanket tucked around her neck, staring out at the pitch-black sky.

As the plane passed over southern Illinois, Newell walked back to the main cabin—partly to stretch his legs but also to see if he could identify any of the hijackers' accomplices. He discovered that he knew one of the passengers quite well: Bud Brown, a Seattle-based Western pilot who had been deadheading* on Flight 701. Newell asked Brown if he would come along to Algiers, to serve as a relief pilot in case the crew became too exhausted to fly. Brown readily agreed.

When Flight 364 began its descent toward Kennedy Airport at 4:49 a.m. on June 3, Holder gave specific instructions for how the plane would refuel and how the navigator would join the crew. The demand he stressed most was that the nose of the plane should face away from the fence around runway 22R. Holder hadn't forgotten that this was the airport where an FBI sniper had killed Richard Obergfell.

The Boeing 720H touched down at 5:12 a.m. and refueling went off without a hitch. Newell assumed a truck would soon arrive with a set of stairs, so the navigator could come aboard and the passengers could depart. But fifteen minutes passed with no sign of activity. Newell asked the air traffic control tower for an explanation. The response he received was the last thing he wanted to hear:

JFK:	Captain, this is Special Agent in Charge Baker, of the FBI. I'd like to talk to you about having flown all day, and the crew tired from flying the number of hours you spend in the air.

*Aviation slang for when airline crew members travel as ordinary passengers, typically so they can reach their next assignment.

NEWELL:	Well, there's not going to be any crew change, and the sooner we get out of here, the better. Let's get the steps out here, and the navigator!
JFK:	How many hours, as far as safety and everything, have you flown?
NEWELL:	Well, it's not going to be any of your business. We've got to go, so let's get on with it.
JFK:	Captain, could I talk to the hijacker?

It was the first time the FBI had asked to speak directly with Holder. At this late stage in the hijacking, though, he was in no mood for diplomacy:

HOLDER:	What do you want, man?
JFK:	Hello. Are you in the cockpit?
HOLDER:	Right. Say, if you're trying to make big news, I guess you're going to find out now in a few minutes. So, you know, you got a little while now. Get those steps and ladder out here now.
JFK:	We're going to bring the steps and ladder out there now. I'd like to talk to you about—
HOLDER:	I don't want to talk to you.

Newell looked back and noticed Holder tugging on the copper wire attached to the briefcase—a warning, perhaps, that he had been pushed to the brink. "He doesn't want to talk anymore!" Newell barked at the FBI agent. "He wants action. Let's go!"

But a certain degree of procrastination was integral to the FBI's plan. The Bureau was going to try its maintenance-worker ruse once more, sending a disguised agent to the plane along with the boarding stairs. The agent needed just a few more minutes to don a uniform from American Airlines, which was lending its equipment for the operation.

Minutes passed. Holder started to talk to himself, uttering things of a most disturbing nature. "It doesn't matter to me whether I die right here now, or a little bit later," he mumbled. The increasingly nervous Newell demanded the stairs and navigator again, to no avail.

At 5:48 a.m. Holder decided to take matters into his own hands:

HOLDER:	Would you put that FBI agent back on the phone?
JFK:	FBI Agent in Charge Baker.
HOLDER:	Lookie here, motherfucker. You better get this shit out here now, you honky ass. Now.
JFK:	The steps are moving right now.
HOLDER:	I don't want to hear your shit. Just get everything out here right now.
JFK:	Moving right now.
HOLDER:	'Cause you ain't fucking around with no dumb nigger, you understand?

The stairs came into view thirty seconds later, pulled by a yellow truck containing three men. One was the navigator, Ira McMullen, an FAA official who had worked for TWA prior to entering public service. One was a genuine American Airlines maintenance worker. And one was the disguised FBI agent.

Holder came to the door of the cockpit and peeked out the plane's open hatch, where the stairs were being moved into place. He couldn't see who was inside the truck, since its cab was wedged beneath the fuselage. This made him livid.

"Where the fuck are they? Put them where I can see them!" he yelled. "Why aren't you following my instructions? Get them away, get them away!" Holder turned back toward the cockpit and warned Luker that he would set off his bomb in ten minutes if his orders weren't obeyed.

Holder's commotion was audible throughout the plane. Kerkow went to a left-side window and looked out. She saw a man dressed as a maintenance worker walking alongside the plane. He seemed to be moving carefully, almost sneakily, as he glanced up at the passengers' faces in the windows.

Kerkow suddenly realized: she had forgotten to do her job. "I hope they don't do anything foolish!" she shrieked as she bolted down the aisle. She frantically looked for the rear exit door, praying all the while that the FBI hadn't already launched its raid. A stewardess grabbed her by the arm and told her to pipe down and return to her seat. Kerkow complied, though not before assuring herself that the rear exit was still sealed.

McMullen finally came up the steps. Holder waved him toward a seat in first class, satisfied that the FAA employee looked like a genuine navigator. Then he returned to the cockpit and told Newell it was time for the passengers and the stewardesses to leave. Only the Western flight crew, augmented by McMullen and Bud Brown, would accompany him to Algiers.

On Newell's instructions, everyone in the cabin quietly gathered in the aisle as two buses were parked on the tarmac, about three hundred feet from the plane. Once the buses' doors swung open, the passengers began to file toward the exit.

Doubt overwhelmed Kerkow as the line of soon-to-be-free hostages passed by her seat. No one suspected that she knew Holder; she could walk right off the plane without causing a stir. Maybe the FBI would never figure out her connection to the hijacking. But even if they did, she could always lie and claim that she had been forced to tag along, or that Holder had never told her of his plans. She was confident she could dupe any FBI agent by flashing her coquettish smile.

Kerkow slowly stood and glanced about. Holder was nowhere to be seen. The other passengers were giving her curious looks, wondering when she planned on cutting into the swiftly moving line. She looked down at her purse, which was resting on the adjacent seat; it would only take a moment to sling the bag over her shoulder and join the stream of hostages heading for the exit.

Then, all of a sudden, Holder's voice boomed over the public address system: "Cathy, you stay here."

Kerkow slid back down and pulled her hair over her cheeks and mouth so that the other passengers couldn't see her face.

"Aren't you coming with us?" asked Glenna MacAlpine, the flight's lead stewardess, as she passed by Kerkow's row.

Kerkow shook her head. She had made her choice.

ONCE THE PASSENGERS and stewardesses were safely aboard the buses, the American Airlines maintenance worker and the disguised FBI agent came to the foot of the stairs. They were going to board on the pretext of performing a preflight inspection. It would be the FBI's last chance to stop the plane from leaving the United States.

The two men had barely started their ascent when they heard Newell yelling at them from the cockpit window: "Get back! Get back! Don't come up here!" At the same time Newell motioned for Luker to shut the hatch. The veteran pilot had gotten his flight this far without any bloodshed, simply by working with Holder; he saw no reason to antagonize an armed man who had just released thirty hostages.

Their plan foiled, the maintenance worker and the FBI agent carted away the boarding stairs. Back in the airport's control tower, the agent in charge of the FBI's operation made special note of Newell's intransigence. When his superiors inevitably berated him for failing to stop the hijacking, he intended to place the blame on Flight 364's captain.

The Boeing 720H took off at 6:25 a.m., heading slightly southeast toward Jones Beach. Holder once again moved to a seat in first class, where he lit yet another joint as the brilliant postdawn light filtered through the jet's windows.

Luker noticed that Holder had left two pieces of paper on the ground beneath the jump seat. They were handwritten notes, evidently scribbled in New York. The first was rather heartening: "Assure safety of aircraft at dis *[sic]* of Captain."

But the second note was menacing: "I still have two armed bombs aboard."

As the first-class section filled with marijuana haze, Kerkow came forward and sat next to her boyfriend. Holder draped a blanket over their torsos and passed her the joint. It was the first time they had acknowledged each other since the morning before, when they had split up at the airport bar in Los Angeles. But Holder and Kerkow didn't say a word as they cuddled beneath their blanket. They just kept passing the joint back and forth, until it was nothing but ash.

Suitably stoned, Kerkow asked Holder the question that had been bugging her for hours: "Where are we going?"

"Algiers."

The city's name didn't ring any bells for her. She stood up and jabbed a finger in Holder's chest. "You know, I'll never be able to trust you about anything again," she said.

Kerkow's severe expression then melted into a grin. There was something oddly liberating about having no choice but to lose herself in the adventure; perhaps Holder had done her a favor by coaxing her through that brief moment of doubt as the hostages left.

Kerkow leaned down to kiss Holder on the cheek, then beckoned him to follow her back to coach class. "I want to show you something," she said.

In the rear of the plane, she pulled up the armrests on a row of seats and lay down on her back. She shimmied out of her purple slacks as Holder dropped his Army dress pants to the floor.

Damn, it's chilly in here, thought Holder as he exposed his flesh. But once he leaned into Kerkow's embrace, he stopped caring about the cold.

"HI, COULD YOU please turn up the heat?"

The cockpit crew was startled to hear a female voice make that polite request. They turned to see Cathy Kerkow's head ducking through the cockpit door; up until that moment, the pilots had believed that Holder was traveling to Algiers alone. They were flabbergasted to learn that the hijacker had a beautiful female companion who had escaped their notice.

Luker, who had a reputation as a ladies' man, was struck by a thunderbolt of envy. *Maybe I can make something happen here*, he thought as he took stock of Kerkow's figure. But she had no interest in socializing with the crew.

A short time later Newell went to the first-class section to speak with Holder, who was drinking Coca-Cola from a can. Holder first offered the captain some marijuana, suggesting that the drug might help "turn him on." Newell gruffly declined, then began to try to persuade Holder to pick a less perilous destination than Algiers.

According to Luker's calculation, which took into account a stiff tail wind, the Boeing 720H could make it all the way to North Africa without taking on extra fuel. Newell had thus scrapped plans he had made to stop in Shannon, Ireland, a popular refueling spot for American airlines. But he still dreaded the prospect of landing in hostile Algiers; having already spent fourteen months of his life in a Nazi prison camp, he was loath to risk further captivity.

Newell first proposed landing in Madrid, but Holder wouldn't hear of it; he knew that Spain was run by an aging Fascist dictator who wouldn't take kindly to a subversive of his ilk. "Well, another possibility we could do would be Switzerland—Geneva," said Newell. "Would you like to go to Geneva?"

Holder was intrigued. The word *Switzerland* conjured up images of idyllic chalets and pretty Red Cross nurses. He wondered whether the country had any aerospace industry to speak of, since he would like to someday work as an engineer. "You think they'd give me amnesty?" he asked hopefully.

Newell promised to see what he could do. Since Flight 364 was now well beyond the range of any Western Airlines facilities, Newell reached out to TWA's dispatch center at Kennedy Airport, which promised to pass along the request to Western officials. Newell figured those officials would have to inform the FBI, which could then notify the State Department.

But the chain of communication was actually much shorter than Newell realized, for his transmissions were being intercepted by the military. Flight 364 was being shadowed by a KC-135 Stratotanker, which had been scrambled out of Loring Air Force Base in Maine. The jet was ordinarily used to refuel fighters in midair, but its mission this time was to keep the Pentagon apprised of Flight 364's every move. This was highly unusual, but so, too, was the hijacking: no American skyjacker had ever taken a plane to Africa, and there were high-level concerns about how the drama might unfold.

Within minutes of Newell's inquiry about Switzerland, word had filtered back to State Department headquarters in Washington, D.C. The proposal put the Nixon administration in a tough diplomatic spot: though it was obviously reluctant to argue on behalf of any hijacker, it preferred to have the plane land in Europe rather than Algeria. In Switzerland, at least, the recovery of the plane, its crew, and the ransom would be guaranteed. And the Swiss might even be willing to play a trick on the hijacker by withdrawing their offer of asylum once the public's interest had waned.

A call was placed to the Swiss ambassador to the United States, a balding patrician named Felix Schnyder. He felt no need to run the State Department's daft proposal by his bosses in Bern; he flatly rejected the notion of letting the hijacked plane land in Geneva. Switzerland did not wish to become known as the Cuba of the Alps.

It was now clear that Flight 364 had no choice but to continue on to Algeria. The State Department contacted its lone representative in the country, William Eagleton, who headed the U.S. Interests Section at the Swiss embassy in Algiers. He was instructed to alert the proper Algerian authorities, then head to Maison Blanche Airport at once.

HOLDER AND KERKOW took turns sleeping as the plane crossed the Atlantic. As the flight neared the Iberian coast, Holder ducked into a lavatory to change into the white shirt and brown bell-bottom trousers that he had brought in his valise. Having burned through as many as a dozen joints since leaving Seattle, his mental faculties were not at their sharpest; he accidentally left the Samsonite briefcase on the seat next to the dozing Kerkow.

When he heard the lavatory door slam shut, Luker leaned back in his chair and peered into the cabin. He noticed the unguarded briefcase right away. If there was ever a moment to do something about the hijacking, this was it.

A whispered debate began in the cockpit. Ira McMullen, the FAA navigator, was gung-ho to lead the assault. He wanted to crouch behind the lavatory door with some sort of blunt instrument and club Holder over the head as he exited. Someone else could then grab the briefcase, thereby neutralizing Kerkow as a threat.

But Newell vetoed that idea. There were just too many things that could go wrong. What if McMullen failed to knock out Holder on the first try? Or if Kerkow awoke and decided to detonate the bomb beside her, or one of the other ones that Holder claimed to have stashed elsewhere on the plane? Though Newell had serious doubts that the hijackers were gutsy enough to kill, he wasn't willing to risk his aircraft on a hunch.

And so the Western crew did nothing. Holder returned to his seat in civilian clothes, oblivious to how close he had come to botching Operation Sisyphus.

At 5:20 p.m. local time, as Flight 364 flew through Spanish airspace, an Algerian official contacted the plane. In passable English, he asked to speak to the hijacker.

"Do you have affiliation with any political group?" the official asked Holder.

"No . . . ah, well, uh, let's talk about that on the ground. Now I got some questions for you."

"Yes, please."

"Can you guarantee my safety?"

"Safety? Yes, safety. This is not a problem."

"All right, now I'm going to want asylum. You going to give me asylum?"

"Asylum? Yes, okay, I understand. Asylum."

Holder was getting excited about the new life that lay ahead. He thought the Algerians sounded thrilled about his impending arrival. He was sure that such hospitable folks would have no problem granting his final, most important request.

"And listen, I want you to get Eldridge Cleaver to come meet me at the airport."

"Again, please?"

"Eldridge Cleaver. I want Eldridge Cleaver."

11

"WE ARE GOING TO BE FRIENDS"

In 1968, the year Roger Holder spent riding a tank through the jungles of South Vietnam, Leroy Eldridge Cleaver ran for president of the United States. He was only thirty-three years old at the time and thus constitutionally ineligible for the office. But when the 218 delegates of the leftist Peace and Freedom Party gathered for their convention in Ann Arbor, Michigan, Cleaver won the nomination on the first ballot. In humbly accepting the honor, he vowed to burn down the White House and replace it with a "museum or monument to the decadence of the past" should he miraculously win the presidency.

Just two years prior to entering the presidential fray, Cleaver had been an inmate at California's maximum-security Soledad State Prison, serving a fourteen-year sentence for attempted murder. The high school dropout had become an accomplished autodidact while behind bars, devouring the works of Thomas Paine, Voltaire, and Malcolm X. He was eventually inspired to try his own hand at writing, crafting a series of provocative essays on race, sex, and violence. When those essays began to appear in the quarterly political magazine *Ramparts*, Cleaver became a literary sensation, hailed by critics as a man blessed with an "innate gift of language" and a "formidably analytic mind." Cleaver's soaring intellectual reputation helped him win parole in December 1966, after having served just over half his term; upon his release from prison, he joined the *Ramparts* staff.

But Cleaver was far too energetic and ambitious to settle for a mere writing gig. He joined the nascent Black Panther Party in February 1967, after watching one of its co-founders, Huey P. Newton, stare down a pack of heavily armed cops outside *Ramparts*' San Francisco office. Cleaver rapidly ascended to the post of Minister of Information, becoming the party's public face after Newton was arrested for shooting an Oakland police officer in October 1967. His skill at turning the Black Panthers' antiestablishment ideology into a sort of muscular poetry was a wonder to behold—no one else could make the phrase "racist Gestapo pigs" sound like something from *King Lear.*

But Cleaver's zest for verbal combat was also his greatest weakness. "I'm a fat mouth and a fool, you know?" he confessed to one interviewer. "I talk too much."

In March 1968 *Ramparts*' publishing arm released *Soul on Ice*, a collection of Cleaver's prison essays. Just two weeks after the instant best seller received a glowing *New York Times* review, Cleaver and several comrades were involved in a ninety-minute shoot-out with Oakland police. The incident resulted in the death of a seventeen-year-old Black Panther named Bobby James Hutton, as well as Cleaver's arrest for attempted murder.* Though he managed to make bail, Cleaver knew his parole was certain to be revoked. As he hit the campaign trail that summer, he vowed to his wife, Kathleen, that he would never spend another day in prison.

Three weeks after garnering 0.05 percent of the presidential vote, Cleaver fled to Montreal. There he caught a freighter to Havana, where the government stashed him in a luxurious apartment with two minders from the Ministry of Interior. But Cleaver quickly wore out his welcome in Cuba, first by providing sanctuary to two American skyjackers who had escaped from one of Fidel Castro's sugar-harvesting gulags. Then in May 1969 a Reuters reporter tracked down Cleaver

*Though much about this shoot-out remains murky, it appears that the Black Panthers instigated the gun battle in retaliation for the assassination of Martin Luther King, Jr. Hutton was killed by the police after the Panthers had surrendered, reportedly after being disarmed and pushed to the ground.

and published his location in the American press. The resulting uproar, which included loud calls for Cleaver's extradition to California, convinced the Cubans to eject their troublesome guest: they placed Cleaver on a plane to Algeria, telling him he would spend only a week there "to deflect the publicity" caused by the Reuters story.

But just as the Cubans had intended, Cleaver ended up staying in Algeria at the invitation of the nation's dictatorial president, Houari Boumédiène.* An organizational genius known for his asceticism and ruthlessness, Boumédiène had been a top commander for the military wing of the National Liberation Front, the party that had led the independence fight against France. His wartime experiences had turned him into a fierce anticolonialist, committed to supporting revolutions the world over. Algerian oil money flowed to rebel groups in Rhodesia, Eritrea, Portugal, and Palestine, among many other countries. Boumédiène was naturally intrigued by the Black Panther Party, which he viewed as the closest thing America had to a socialist insurgency.

Cleaver proved adept at reading Boumédiène's expectations, adapting his lingo to give it an even more belligerent edge. Shortly after his arrival in Algiers, he told an American photojournalist that he planned to form an organization called the North American Liberation Front, dedicated to the overthrow of the U.S. government and the nationalization of Standard Oil. "I plan to shed my blood and to put my life on the line and to seek to take the lives of the pigs of the power structure in Babylon," he declared, using his favorite nickname for America.

Boumédiène was impressed enough to let Cleaver operate freely in Algiers, as well as give him a five-hundred-dollar monthly stipend. Joined by his pregnant wife Kathleen and a few admirers from the United States, Cleaver established an official branch of the Black Panther Party, which he christened the International Section. At first confined to a bungalow by the Mediterranean Sea, the International

*This was actually the president's nom de guerre. His real name, a closely guarded secret at the time, was Mohammed Ben Brahim Boukharouba.

Section soon upgraded to a gated villa in the tony El Biar neighborhood. The villa was a gift from its former residents, the official delegation of the Vietcong, who were great fans of Cleaver's work. Cleaver repaid their kindness by broadcasting a message on Radio Hanoi, urging African-American soldiers to mutiny: "If you can get up the courage to do it, you should start ripping off those Uncle Toms and those pigs who're giving you orders to kill the Vietnamese people. You should start blowing them away. Throw those hand grenades at them. And put that dynamite up under their houses, up under their jeeps."

As Cleaver became more established in Algiers, more than a dozen Black Panthers came to join him—many of them, like Cleaver, on the run from American law enforcement, which was trying to destroy the party. There was Pete O'Neal, the founder of the party's Kansas City chapter, who fled from a charge of transporting a gun across state lines; Donald Cox, who held the title of Field Marshal and was suspected of participating in the murder of a police informant; and Sekou Odinga, one of the so-called Panther 21, a group of party members facing conspiracy charges in New York.

The International Section also briefly played host to Timothy Leary, the Harvard psychiatrist turned LSD guru. After receiving a twenty-year sentence for marijuana possession in January 1970, Leary promptly broke out of prison with the assistance of the Weathermen. He wound up in Algiers, where Cleaver let him crash in El Biar; he hoped that embracing Leary would help create an alliance between the Black Panthers and white hippies. But then a friend of Leary's showed up with a stereo packed full of LSD, a dangerous substance in a deeply traditional country like Algeria. "Leary would go out to the desert with his wife, they would drop acid and lie naked in the sun, and some goat herder would come along and tell the first cop he saw," Cleaver later grumbled, adding that Leary also distributed the drug to numerous female university students. After a few months of such hijinks, Cleaver declared the professor persona non grata, forcing Leary to seek refuge in Switzerland.

Looking to broaden the Panthers' support, Cleaver traveled extensively throughout Asia as an honored guest of the continent's Communist regimes. He toured North Vietnam, where Prime Minister Pham Van Dong toasted him with the words "In the West you are a black in the shadows, here you are a black in the sun." He spent time in Pyongyang with Kim Il-sung, North Korea's "Great Leader," whom he lauded for his "genius command"; Cleaver would later write the foreword to *Juche*, an English-language collection of Kim's speeches.

Yet by the summer of 1972, the International Section was in sharp decline. With Cleaver's *Soul on Ice* royalties frozen by the U.S. government,* the organization was badly strapped for cash. "We are debt-ridden," Kathleen Cleaver told an American journalist. "Our telephone bill from February to April was $5,000 . . . We rent four houses and the rent is overdue. All the funds are eaten up for seven kids, eight families, clothing, hospital, doctor bills and food. You can imagine what it costs." To make ends meet, the International Section trafficked in fraudulent visas and stolen cars ferried down from Marseilles.

Eldridge was also growing increasingly paranoid, a mood stoked by letters he was receiving that claimed that Huey P. Newton was trying to destroy the International Section. Cleaver did not realize that the letters, which alleged that Newton had called him "a murderer and a punk without genitals," were clever FBI forgeries, designed to cause a rift in the party's leadership.

With his future in Algeria looking grim, Cleaver was greatly intrigued by the surprise phone call he received on the afternoon of June 3, 1972. It was from the office of President Boumédiène, who was out of the country at the time, attending a meeting in Senegal. A presidential aide requested that Cleaver rush to Boumédiène's palace at once.

When Cleaver arrived with Donald Cox in tow, the aide revealed

---

*The U.S. government contended that Cleaver had become a citizen of North Vietnam and North Korea during his Asian travels. As a result, Cleaver's American-based assets were frozen in accordance with the Trading with the Enemy Act.

the reason for his alarm: for the first time ever, a hijacked American airliner was on its way to Algiers. All the government knew was that there was at least one bomb on board, though perhaps several more. And the hijackers were carrying $500,000 in a canvas sack.

Cleaver's eyes lit up at that last detail. The revolution could certainly make excellent use of a half-million dollars.

FLIGHT 364 WAS now so close to Maison Blanche Airport that Holder could make out the beaches along the Mediterranean, still full of bathers soaking up the day's last rays of sunshine. He became ecstatic at the prospect of stretching out in the sand and splashing in the surf. He knew the stars had steered him right by guiding him to Algiers.

"See, this is a place where a man like me can be free," he told the crew, a huge smile stretched across his face. "The only place I can be free."

Newell asked Holder if he might consider leaving the money on the plane so it could be returned to Western Airlines. If he did so, Newell said, the American authorities might let him live in peace. But Holder chuckled at the notion of relinquishing $500,000 without a fight.

"Sorry," he told Newell. "Money's not for me. It's for the poor and needy people all around the world. And maybe if I live that long, I'll buy myself my own airline someday."

The plane landed at Maison Blanche at 6:57 p.m. local time. As it rolled to a stop on runway 22, it was surrounded by at least a dozen military vehicles, each crammed with soldiers. A black sedan pulled up to the boarding stairs that were positioned by the plane's front door. Out stepped a trim man with beady eyes, wearing an extravagantly expensive suit. He walked to the foot of the stairs and waited, his interpreter by his side.

In the plane's cockpit, Holder was too excited to bid a proper farewell. "I left you something in the oven," he told Luker. Then he flung the canvas bag full of money over his right shoulder and walked back into the cabin.

Holder found Cathy Kerkow in row 19, gazing out the window at the soldiers who had surrounded the plane. "You go out first, alone," he said. "They won't shoot at no woman."

Kerkow turned away from the window and stared deep into Holder's eyes. "Roger," she said, "we walk out there together." It was clear from her emphatic tone that she would settle for nothing less.

As the couple approached the front door, Holder paused to remove his shoes and socks. He wanted the world to see him in bare feet, a flourish meant to make his emergence from the plane that much more dramatic.

Just like a runaway slave, he thought.

Halfway down the boarding stairs, Holder was met by the man in the finely tailored suit. The man's interpreter translated his rapid-fire French: "Welcome to Algeria. My name is Salah. You are home now, brother. We are going to be friends. Very good friends."

What choice do I have? thought Holder as he followed Salah Hidjeb down the stairs toward the waiting black sedan. Before he and Kerkow entered the car, a soldier motioned for Holder to hand over the Samsonite briefcase that was still in his left hand. Holder did so gingerly, and the soldier made sure to avoid putting undue pressure on the copper wire.

From the cockpit window, the Western crew watched the sedan drive off across the tarmac. They next heard the sound of two dozen feet clanging up the boarding stairs—Algerian soldiers coming to search for additional bombs.

With Holder's parting words in mind, Luker went back to the galley and looked inside the oven. He found fifty hundred-dollar bills—a tip for the crew's excellent service.

THROUGH HIS INTERPRETER, Hidjeb continued to talk to Holder and Kerkow as the sedan glided toward the Maison Blanche terminal. He expressed his regrets over the fact that President Boumédiène was not there to greet the hijackers in person, but he promised that such a meeting would be arranged upon His Excellency's return from Senegal. Hidjeb explained that he was a "representative of the police," though this was quite an understatement: he was actually the director of the Renseignements Généraux, a branch of Algeria's brutal secret police, as well as Boumédiène's favorite assassin.*

Inside the terminal, Hidjeb guided Holder and Kerkow to Air Algérie's VIP lounge, where the somewhat dazed couple was offered glasses of orange juice and a platter of dates. Seeing that his guests were feeling comfortable, Hidjeb politely asked to take a look at the money—he wanted to make sure the entire $500,000 was there, just as the hijackers claimed.

Holder was reluctant to hand over the bag, but Hidjeb assured him that the money would be returned shortly. Holder acquiesced, and the ransom was whisked away by one of Hidjeb's aides.

Outside the VIP lounge, meanwhile, Cleaver and several other Black Panthers were on the verge of knocking down the locked doors—they wanted the money. Also champing at the bit was William Eagleton, the American diplomat charged with handling the affair. He was seething, telling anyone who would listen that the Pentagon was prepared to order a naval blockade of Algeria if the plane and the ransom weren't returned at once.

Hidjeb finally agreed to let Cleaver and the Panthers enter the lounge. Eagleton was turned away.

Cleaver's first reaction upon seeing the hijackers in the flesh was disappointment. He had expected a crew of four or five strapping Black Panthers, not a skinny brother in glasses and his white hippie girlfriend.

The hijackers, by contrast, were awed to be in Cleaver's presence.

---

*Hidjeb preferred to go by the nom de guerre Si Salah, a tribute to an Algerian guerrilla commander who had been executed by the French in 1961. He also went by the nickname "Salah Vespa," a reference to his knack for carrying out assassinations while riding a motor scooter.

Kerkow had long been fascinated by the Panther mystique, dating back to the symposium she had attended at the University of Oregon in 1970. Now here she was, face-to-face with the fugitive Minister of Information himself, having just pulled off one of the wildest capers in history. Whatever doubts she had felt back in New York now vanished, replaced by sheer giddiness.

When Holder looked at Cleaver, he saw the whole reason he had come to Algiers: to unite with a kindred spirit, a fellow threat to The System responsible for the war that had left him shattered. They were both dangerous, intelligent men; surely they were meant to become close allies in the struggle against all that was rotten in the world.

As the two men shook hands, Cleaver uttered his very first words to Holder: "So, where's the bread?"

Holder jerked back his hand, disheartened. So this was how the great Eldridge Cleaver saw him—not as a revolutionary equal but as a dollar sign. Their relationship was off to a rocky start.

Loudly protesting the fact that he had yet to lay eyes on the half-million dollars, Cleaver was hustled out of the room—though not before slipping Holder his phone number. In came a camera crew and several Algerian journalists, who upset Holder and Kerkow by sticking microphones in their faces. The reporters peppered the two hijackers with questions in broken English; the couple hid their faces in their hands, disoriented by the bright lights and the barrage of inquiries. "I got nothing to say," Holder mumbled while looking down at his lap. "Nothing at all."

The camera crew next moved into an adjoining room, where the Algerian police showed off the bag of money and the black Samsonite briefcase, which was popped open to reveal its contents: an alarm clock, a dog-eared copy of Madame Blavatsky's *The Secret Doctrine*, and an empty disposable-razors box.

Holder and Kerkow had pulled off the longest-distance skyjacking in American history without a single real weapon.

|||

THE CAMERA CREW'S last stop of the night was the Maison Blanche cafeteria, where the Western Airlines crew was filmed chowing down on a meal—their first food since New York. The five men were all smiles, for they had been informed that their fears of imprisonment were unfounded: Air Algérie was under government orders to refuel the Boeing 720H and let it depart the country at once. When reached in Senegal, President Boumédiène had decided not to risk a direct military confrontation with the United States; he preferred to fight his Western adversaries by funding proxies like the Vietcong and the Black Panthers.

As Newell and his crew ate their fill at the airport, Holder and Kerkow were riding through Algiers in the backseat of a government sedan. The driver was an English speaker named Mustafa, one of Hidjeb's most trusted operatives. He introduced the toadlike man in the passenger seat as No Nuts, explaining that the nickname stemmed from an unfortunate incident during the War of Independence.

Mustafa and No Nuts escorted the Americans to the Hotel Aletti, an Art Deco edifice overlooking the city's harbor. As they strolled through the hotel's casino, a murmur rippled across the baccarat tables—everyone knew of the hijacking. Several gamblers rose to applaud Holder and Kerkow, but the couple was too weary to appreciate the gesture. They had been traveling for well over thirty hours straight, under exceedingly stressful circumstances.

As they split a bottle of red wine and a plate of charcuterie at the hotel's dining room, Holder and Kerkow were informed that they would remain guests of the Algerian government for a few more days, as certain security checks were performed. Their money would be returned the following morning, after the necessary official paperwork had been completed.

Once they were tipsy and fed, Holder and Kerkow were taken

upstairs and ushered into a well-appointed room facing the Rue de Constantine; the hallway outside was lined with a dozen police guards. Mustafa and No Nuts bade them good night, and the exhausted couple collapsed onto the bed, still fully clothed—Holder with his bell bottoms and bare feet, Kerkow in her pink blouse and purple slacks. They wrapped their arms around each other as they drifted off to sleep, soothed by the sound of a warm breeze rustling the room's lace curtains.

12

"MY ONLY BOMB IS MY HUMAN HEART"

A NAKED BETH NEWHOUSE groggily stumbled to the front of her family's cabin, tucked away in the woods above the Coos River. It was too early on a Sunday morning for any of her friends to be paying a visit, so she had been particularly alarmed to hear the sound of crunching gravel outside. She peered through a window and saw a late-model sedan pulling up the driveway. It was the kind of car favored by undercover cops.

Newhouse ran back into the bedroom, where her boyfriend, Lee Davis, was fast asleep. "Oh my God, oh my God!" she shrieked as she scrambled to pull on a pair of jeans. "We're busted!"

Newhouse and Davis had been crashing at the cabin for a week, having driven up to Coos Bay to sell a load of Fast Eddie's marijuana. A few pounds of the drug were still in the trunk of their car. Newhouse feared that the local police had caught wind of their illicit trade.

Once dressed, Newhouse went to the front door to greet the cops, hoping to allay their suspicions with flirtatious pleas of ignorance. But the two men who emerged from the sedan were not members of the Coos Bay Police Department. One was Newhouse's father, Andrew, the town's most prominent attorney; the other was a friend of his, an FBI agent named Thomas Elliott, whose son had graduated from Marshfield High School the same year as Beth.

Now Newhouse was truly freaked out. She had transported large quantities of drugs across state lines—a federal crime. That had to be why the FBI was here.

But Elliott put her fears to rest at once. "You're not in any trouble," he assured her. "We need to talk. There's been a hijacking."

Over coffee in the cabin's kitchen, the FBI agent laid out as much of the story as he could: how Cathy Kerkow and Roger Holder had ended up on Western Airlines Flight 701; how Kerkow had refused to disembark in New York; and how the Algerians were apparently reluctant to hand over the couple. Elliott said that Holder had flown under an assumed name but had been positively identified by a seatmate who had seen his Army discharge papers. Kerkow, by contrast, had made no effort to conceal her identity while obtaining the Western tickets in Los Angeles.

Newhouse could not have been more stunned. She and Kerkow may have had loose morals, but they were far from hardened criminals. They were just ordinary hippie chicks, trying to enjoy their fleeting youth. The thought of Kerkow hijacking a plane and making off with a half-million dollars was too absurd to comprehend. And though Holder had always given her the creeps, Newhouse couldn't imagine him doing something so monumentally insane, either.

Elliott pressed Newhouse for details that might aid the investigation, but she couldn't provide much help. She did recall that Kerkow had asked her for money to buy airline tickets to Hawaii, but that was the extent of her useful information. She could only speculate that Holder had decided to hijack the plane on a whim, without Kerkow's knowledge. No other explanation made sense.

Newhouse's father asked Beth whether she might be willing to travel to Algeria to coax Kerkow into coming home. But she refused to go on such a mission, and not just because she had heard that Algeria was a dangerous place. She also knew that the courts were coming down hard on convicted skyjackers, handing out thirty-year sentences like candy. She couldn't bring herself to play a role in sending her best friend to prison for decades.

The rest of Coos Bay was just as dumbfounded as Newhouse to learn of Kerkow's crime. Kerkow's mother, Patricia, at first insisted that there must be some mistake, citing early news reports that erroneously described the female hijacker's hair as blond. But as it became clear that Cathy had, in fact, gone to Algiers with $500,000 in extortion proceeds, Patricia claimed that her daughter must have been duped: "From what I have been told, I cannot believe my daughter was actively involved in this in any way. It must have been an impulsive act on the other person's part. I can't imagine her taking part in planning something like this."

Many of Kerkow's Coos Bay acquaintances could only express astonishment when confronted by the many reporters who descended on the town. "The whole staff here was stunned, shocked," sputtered Elmer Johnson, the principal at Marshfield High School. "We just couldn't believe this was our Cathy. She was a good girl when we knew her here three years ago."

A few locals offered a less flattering portrait of Kerkow. One high school friend described her as "something of a swinger" who was no stranger to the pleasures of marijuana. "But she was very intelligent," the friend hastened to add, "and I cannot figure her smoking it on a plane in a hijack when she would want to be alert."

A former co-worker at a housewares store marveled that anyone so spacey could be involved in such an ambitious crime: "I didn't think she could follow orders well enough to be a hijacker."

Down in San Diego, meanwhile, Seavenes and Marie Holder were not surprised when the FBI showed up at their door on the morning of June 3: the previous evening, when news of the hijacking had aired on TV, Seavenes had casually remarked, "That sounds like something our crazy son would do."

The Holders cooperated fully with the investigation, telling the agents that Marie had driven their son and his girlfriend to the airport on Friday morning; Roger had told them of the couple's plans to homestead in Australia, though not the means by which they would get there. The Holders then guided the FBI to the Lauretta Street apartment that Kerkow had rented three weeks earlier. Agents tore the place apart, looking for clues to the hijackers' political agenda. They were also curious to learn whether Holder had any connection to the other skyjacker of June 2, who had been captured near Nevada's Washoe Lake around 5:30 that morning. That man, Robb Heady, had been a paratrooper with the 101st Airborne Division, and the FBI wondered if he knew Holder from Vietnam.*

But the FBI found nothing to shed light on Holder and Kerkow's motives, nor to indicate that their paths had ever crossed with Heady's. Aside from Kerkow's waterbed, all the agents discovered were clothes, astrology books, and several airline timetables.

The following day, at 12:35 p.m. Pacific time, the jury in the Angela Davis trial returned its verdict: not guilty on all charges. The usually stoic Davis burst into uncontrollable sobs upon hearing that her legal ordeal was over. "This is the happiest day because it means this is now out of the way so I can resume the struggle against oppression," she told the assembled press, shortly before greeting and embracing the jurors as they filed out of the courtroom.

Neither Davis nor any of her supporters mentioned a single word about the hijacking of Flight 701.

WHEN HOLDER AND Kerkow finally awoke on Sunday, June 4, they decided to go for a celebratory stroll along the bustling Algiers waterfront, where scores of brightly colored fishing boats bobbed in the pale blue water. But when they stepped outside their room, they were stopped by the police in the hallway, who were being overseen by Mustafa and No Nuts. Mustafa politely informed the Americans that they were not to leave the Hotel Aletti for the time being, for security

---

*In searching for Heady around Washoe Lake in the wee hours of June 3, local police noticed a parked car with a bumper sticker that read "Member of the U.S. Parachute Association." The cops staked out the vehicle until Heady showed up shortly before dawn.

reasons. They were free to make use of the casino or dine in the restaurant, but only if accompanied by at least two guards.

Holder asked about the money. Mustafa said it would be returned as soon as the couple had met with President Boumédiène; His Excellency was due back from Senegal on Tuesday, at which point the couple would be granted a private audience.

Holder and Kerkow returned to their room and tried to ring the Black Panthers, using the number that Eldridge Cleaver had slipped them at the airport. But the room's phone line was dead.

At the International Section's villa in Algiers's El Biar neighborhood, Cleaver was also getting stonewalled in his efforts to get his hands on the ransom: Algerian officials had rebuffed his numerous inquiries, explaining that the money had to be "processed." But that didn't stop the Panthers from making grandiose plans for the $500,000. When a reporter from the *Oregon Journal* called Pete O'Neal, Cleaver's top lieutenant, he got an earful about how the money would be spent: "When the brother and sister arrived, we spoke with them at the airport. They said the money they had liberated was earmarked for a number of causes. A substantial sum was to go to the Palestinian Liberation Forces and the bulk of it is for the Afro-American struggle, to be used to fight Zionism or American imperialism."

Even though the money was in limbo, Cleaver was ecstatic about the hijacking. The International Section had been losing visibility for months, as the novelty of the Algiers operation began to fade; journalists seldom came knocking anymore, looking to pay four hundred dollars or more per interview with the eminently quotable Cleaver and his gorgeous wife. Cleaver, whose literary talents included a nose for drama, knew he could regain relevance by tapping in to the American public's fascination with skyjacking.

The International Section therefore released an official statement hailing Holder and Kerkow as revolutionary heroes who had struck a major blow against the pig power structure. "Like our comrades in Vietnam, all the blacks and other oppressed peoples of the United States are undertaking a just war of liberation against the same capitalistic killers," the statement read. "[Hijacking] is a correct and just tactic to expropriate all that we can from the big capitalistic companies and corporations who extort billions from the people."

On the afternoon of June 6, just as they had been promised, Holder and Kerkow were driven from the Hotel Aletti to the presidential palace, a pristine Moorish villa guarded by saber-wielding soldiers in long white capes. They were met by Salah Hidjeb, the secret police chief who had welcomed them to Maison Blanche Airport three days earlier. He escorted the couple down a narrow marble hallway to a wood-paneled office with exquisite antique rugs. Beneath a gold-framed painting of praying Algerian peasants sat a stern-looking man with an aquiline nose and a bushy mustache. A dark cloak was draped around his slim-fitting suit. Though so skinny that his cheekbones nearly jutted through his flesh, he exuded the air of supreme authority.

President Houari Boumédiène rose to shake Holder's hand, though he ignored Kerkow. Without offering any further greeting, he began to converse with Hidjeb in Arabic so that the hijackers couldn't follow a word. After a few minutes of this discussion, Boumédiène signaled for Holder and Kerkow to be taken back to their hotel. He had decided their fates based on a single glance.

Bill Newell and his Western Airlines crew first realized the magnitude of the hijacking story while trying to leave Madrid. They had stopped in the Spanish capital on the night of June 3, to unwind with a few whiskeys and grab some much-needed sleep. At the airport the next day, as they made their way through the terminal, the pilots were stopped by a United Press International reporter and his photographer. "Take off your sunglasses," the reporter urged Newell as the photographer clicked away. "The people will want to see your eyes."

The businesslike Newell was annoyed by the intrusion, but he agreed to field a few questions. The reporter asked him to describe the male hijacker as best he could. "The hijacker was a highly intelligent man dissatisfied with his experiences in the Army," Newell replied.

"He said he wanted to go to Algiers because that was the only place he would be genuinely free."

By the time the crew got the Boeing 720H back to Los Angeles, the hijacking had become a media and political sensation, held up as evidence that the skyjacking epidemic now posed an existential threat to national security. By finding sanctuary in Algeria, Holder and Kerkow had inaugurated a whole new hijacker haven, one that actively supported the likes of the Vietcong. And the couple had also set a new American record for the amount of ransom paid by an airline, smashing the previous mark by nearly $200,000; the Flight 701 affair had made it seem as if there was no limit to how much skyjackers could extort. Everyone dreaded what was sure to come next: a wave of increasingly unhinged copycats who believed that they, too, could defy the odds and skyjack their way to happier circumstances.

Lt. Gen. Benjamin O. Davis, Jr., whom President Richard Nixon had picked to head the nation's antihijacking efforts two years earlier, publicly condemned Western Airlines for allowing Holder and Kerkow to escape. He argued that the Flight 701 fiasco proved that the airlines' policy of total compliance should be scrapped. "We must instill in all parties an increasing determination to resist hijack and extortionist demands to the fullest extent possible consistent with the safety of human life," he said. "Too often, hijackers have been afforded service and responsiveness that is not provided even the first-class traveler. Too often, funds have been raised and provided to extortionists in amounts and with a speed that approach the fantastic." Davis also urged the airlines to place greater trust in the FBI, stressing that the Bureau's agents were not "trigger-happy gunslingers" but rather seasoned professionals who would make every conceivable effort to avoid wounding passengers.

The Air Line Pilots Association (ALPA), by contrast, directed its ire at the federal government, arguing that the Nixon administration hadn't done enough to pressure Algeria into extraditing Holder and Kerkow. The labor union implored the president to order an air-service boycott of any nation that permitted its jets to land in Algeria—a measure that would put enormous pressure on allies such as Spain and France to suspend their daily flights to the North African country. ALPA also sent an open letter to Senator William Proxmire of Wisconsin, asking him to push for a total economic embargo of Algeria that would be lifted only if Holder and Kerkow were returned to the United States for prosecution.

When its entreaties to Washington did not elicit an immediate response, ALPA decided to take drastic and unprecedented action: the union called for a twenty-four-hour pilots' strike, to begin at two a.m. on June 19.

After announcing the strike, ALPA discovered that American pilots were not the only ones to be unusually disturbed by the Western Airlines hijacking: in a show of solidarity, the International Federation of Airline Pilots Associations, a coalition of unions in sixty-four foreign countries, declared that it would participate in the work stoppage. For a day, at least, global air travel would screech to a halt, all because of Holder and Kerkow.

The major American airlines filed suit against ALPA in multiple federal districts, arguing that the planned strike violated the public's inalienable right to a basic service. Several judges agreed with that logic and issued temporary injunctions barring the pilots from walking out. But the union vowed to press forward, claiming that its membership was undaunted by the threat of arrest. "When no governments seem willing to act, we, the pilots, who have responsibility for the passengers, have to do something," ALPA's president proclaimed.

The international strike seemed splendidly effective in its early hours, as air service was terminated throughout much of Europe; Paris-Orly Airport was completely shut down, while traffic at London's Heathrow plummeted by 60 percent. When day broke in the United States, however, American pilots awoke to the news that the injunction against the strike had been personally upheld by Supreme Court chief justice Warren Burger, who had issued his ruling shortly before midnight. Dispirited by the defeat in the country's highest court, the pilots' confidence wavered, and many made the eleventh-hour decision to show up for work. Thousands of flights were still grounded, including fourteen hundred by Eastern Air Lines alone. But pilots for Northwest Orient, Pacific Southwest, and United buckled at the last moment, and the disruption in the United States was not as severe as initially feared.

ALPA put on a brave face, terming the strike "very, very effective" in drawing worldwide attention to its members' plight. The union crowed about the fact that the day after the strike's conclusion, the United Nations unanimously passed a resolution calling for "all states to expand and intensify cooperative international efforts" to stop hijackings.

But the pundits scoffed at the UN's gesture. "That's about like coming out 100 percent for motherhood," observed one op-ed writer.

Two days after the resolution's passage, an introverted Navy veteran named Martin McNally hijacked an American Airlines Boeing 727 at the St. Louis airport. He did so using a submachine gun that he had carried on board in a trombone case. Seeking to break Holder and Kerkow's record for the highest ransom ever paid by an American airline, McNally asked for and received $502,000. He later jumped from the plane over a wooded area near Peru, Indiana, and hitchhiked back to his home in Detroit. He was arrested there five days later with just thirteen dollars in his pocket; he confessed that he had lost hold of the ransom while pulling his parachute's rip cord.*

In response to the McNally hijacking, ALPA sent up a trial balloon regarding a new protest idea: a boycott of all domestic airports where security practices were too feeble for the union's taste. But that plan was quickly dropped as untenable, given the courts' sympathy for the argument that air travel was a fundamental American right. Many

*The hijacking was almost stopped by a businessman named David Hanley, who was not a passenger on the plane. After watching live footage of the hijacking at a hotel bar near the airport, Hanley drove his Cadillac onto the tarmac and rammed the Boeing 727, destroying the wheels beneath its left wing. "Gee whiz, that guy must be nuts!" McNally exclaimed upon seeing the wrecked car wedged beneath the plane. Hanley survived the collision but suffered debilitating permanent injuries; McNally continued on with the hijacking by demanding another plane.

frustrated pilots began to wonder if the FBI was correct, and that violence was the only answer—even if it meant that passengers would get caught in the crossfire.

HOLDER AND KERKOW spent two weeks confined to the Hotel Aletti, completely shut off from the outside world. They were questioned for hours on end by Algerian intelligence agents, who incessantly asked about the couple's radical connections and political goals. The agents had a tough time following Holder's circuitous riffs about astrology, Angela Davis, and Hanoi. And they couldn't understand why the affable Kerkow had gotten mixed up in such a momentous crime.

Every night after their interrogations ended, Holder and Kerkow would retire to the hotel's casino to play roulette and dine on fresh lobster. They were always accompanied by Mustafa and No Nuts, who were under strict orders never to let the Americans leave their sight.

Finally convinced that Holder and Kerkow had acted alone and had no discernible politics aside from run-of-the-mill opposition to the Vietnam War, the Algerians informed the couple that they had been cleared for release. Holder and Kerkow had their doubts; they feared they might be taken to Maison Blanche and placed on a flight back to the United States. But true to their word, Mustafa and No Nuts drove the hijackers up the winding medieval streets of the Casbah and deposited them at the headquarters of the National Liberation Front, President Boumédiène's ruling party. Eldridge Cleaver and his lieutenants were waiting there to assume responsibility for the two young Americans. Holder and Kerkow had officially been granted asylum, and the International Section had bestowed upon them the title "Students of Revolution."

After the handover, the Panthers bickered over who should house the hijackers. Room was scarce at Cleaver's residence in El Biar, where the International Section's leader lived with his wife and two young children. Donald Cox, the Panthers' erstwhile field marshal and munitions expert, volunteered to put them up at his bungalow in the Bab el-Oued neighborhood, north of the city center. His motives for doing so were far from pure: he believed that whoever physically controlled the hijackers would ultimately control their money, which was still being held by the Algerian government.

Holder and Kerkow were overjoyed to discover that their new quarters were close to Pointe Pescade, a crescent-shaped beach once favored by the French colonial elite. They spent their first days of freedom on the sand, watching Algerian families frolic in the gentle waves. At night they played chess and smoked hashish with their friendly neighbors, a French economics teacher and his American wife. Despite its many glitches, Operation Sisyphus had finally delivered Holder and Kerkow to a Mediterranean paradise.

But the respite proved short-lived. On June 30, Cox heard upsetting news on a Voice of America radio broadcast: the money was gone.

In sizing up the hijackers at his palace, President Boumédiène had instantly pegged them as more akin to common thieves than revolutionaries. He wished to discourage such adventurers from seeking shelter in Algeria, strictly for business reasons. As much as Boumédiène loved to poke the West, he also depended on its vast appetite for oil and gas to keep his treasury flush—and, by extension, to fund his favorite third-world insurgents. In fact, the state-owned petroleum company, Sonatrach, was in the midst of secret negotiations to export natural gas to the United States. Rather than risk imperiling that deal, Boumédiène ordered that the money be returned.

The transfer took place on neutral ground, at a Bank of America in Paris. An Air Algérie official gave the money to a Western Airlines vice president, who had it counted on the spot. There was just $487,300 in the sack: Holder had left $5,000 as a tip for Newell's crew, and sticky-fingered Algerian police had evidently made off with another $7,700. The Western executive knew better than to complain.

Holder and Kerkow were sad to learn the money had been returned. While confined to the Hotel Aletti, they had fantasized about how best to spend their loot: sailing through the Strait of Gibraltar, funding a hospital in North Vietnam, building some sort of freaky statue in Coos Bay. Their dejection, however, was nothing compared to that of the Panthers; Cleaver and the others believed the Algerian government had given away what was rightfully theirs.

Donald Cox still dreamed of making money off the hijackers somehow. He had a reputation for being skilled at that sort of task: in 1970, for example, he had helped organize a celebrity-studded fund-raiser for the Panthers at the New York apartment of composer Leonard Bernstein. (Tom Wolfe famously lampooned the party in a *New York* magazine piece titled "Radical Chic.") Cox estimated that he could earn at least three thousand dollars by selling the hijackers' story to the American press; he thought no newspaper could resist the lure of an exclusive interview with Cathy Kerkow, the pretty girl-next-door turned badass revolutionary.

As Cox tried to peddle the hijackers' story, Holder grew to despise him. When he had selected Algiers as an alternate destination for Operation Sisyphus, the manic Holder had assumed that Cleaver and his acolytes were visionaries like himself, men whom fate had selected to alter the course of history. But Cox was now revealing himself to be little more than a hustler. Before long Holder could barely stand to be in the same room as the man who had once been in charge of teaching the Black Panthers to shoot. The animosity was mutual: Cox told several International Section colleagues that Holder was probably an FBI informant.

Kerkow, meanwhile, was grappling with nascent pangs of guilt. She was beginning to regret her failure to bid her family farewell. Her mother had been trying to reach her by telephone for weeks, aided by the office of Coos Bay's Republican congressman, John Dellenback. But the Panthers kept denying Patricia Kerkow's requests, and Cathy was barred from placing calls herself unless supervised by Cox. Instead, she wrote her mother a brief letter, stating only that she was doing well in Algiers. She offered no clue as to why she had helped hijack Flight 701.

Shortly afterward, in an attempt to convince the *Oregon Journal* to buy the hijackers' story, Cox put Kerkow on the line with a reporter named Rolla J. Crick. "I'm all right," she told Crick. "I don't have an explanation at this time. But I am concerned about my family. I think of them a lot."

Crick pressed Kerkow for details about her experiences in Algiers. But Kerkow was cagey, stating that she couldn't share much until a sufficient sum of cash had been wired to the International Section. The *Oregon Journal* turned down the deal, as did every other publication that Cox contacted. Even the most ethically tenuous newspapers couldn't stomach the thought of paying for access to skyjackers.

Having failed in his attempt to ply money from the media, Cox concocted a desperate Plan B. Kerkow had told him that she and Beth Newhouse had dealt marijuana in San Diego. Cox asked her to write a letter to her old friend, proposing an elaborate drug deal: the International Section would send Newhouse a large load of Algerian hashish in exchange for a shipment of guns.

When Newhouse received the letter in Coos Bay, where she was spending the summer, she could tell that it had already been opened and read by someone else—presumably the FBI. But even if her mail hadn't been monitored, there was no way she would ever involve herself in such an outrageous scheme. Newhouse got the sense that her friend was being manipulated by people who wouldn't hesitate to harm her.

One sentence in Kerkow's letter struck Newhouse as particularly sinister: "It's so easy to slip into darkness here."

CAPTAIN GENE VAUGHN wanted to make a statement. Something that would show the world that he and his fellow pilots were sick of ceding control of their planes to extremists and thieves. Merely killing the young man who had commandeered his Pan Am Boeing 747 would not suffice; Vaughn wanted to turn the hijacker's corpse into a warning, much as the English had once dangled the bodies of hanged pirates along the River Thames.

The focus of Vaughn's rage was Nguyen Thai Binh, a twenty-four-year-old college student from South Vietnam. Binh had graduated from the University of Washington on June 10, 1972, earning a bachelor's degree in fisheries management. He had intended to stay in the United States, but his visa had been revoked on June 7 due to his antiwar activism; he had been arrested for occupying the South Vietnamese consulate in New York. Seething over his expulsion as well as the carpet-bombing of North Vietnam, Binh had decided to hijack his flight home as an "act of revenge."

On July 1, the day before boarding Pan Am Flight 841 in Honolulu, Binh had mailed a letter to several antiwar groups, explaining the action he was about to take: "I know my voice for peace cannot be heard, cannot defeat the roared sound of B-52s, of the U.S. bombings. . . . My only bomb is my human heart."

Binh didn't reveal his intentions to the Pan Am crew until they were over the South China Sea. He passed a stewardess a note: "You are going to fly me to Hanoi and this airplane will be destroyed when we get there." When Vaughn refused to comply, Binh wrote a second note, which he spattered with a liberal amount of his own blood. "This indicates how serious I am about being taken to Hanoi," it read.

Vaughn went to the main cabin to meet Binh, a meek-looking young man who stood less than five feet tall. Binh showed off a foil-wrapped package that he said contained a bomb. Vaughn wasn't buying it; he had read all about Roger Holder's fake briefcase bomb and guessed that the diminutive Binh was trying to pull a similar stunt.

Vaughn knew that one of his passengers, a retired San Francisco police officer, had come on board with a .357 Magnum. He told the ex-cop to be prepared, for he would soon have an opportunity to end Binh's life.

Under the pretext of making a refueling stop, Vaughn landed at Saigon's Tan Son Nhut airport. Once the plane was at rest on the tarmac, Vaughn walked back to speak with the hijacker again. Binh was highly agitated, going on and on about how he would detonate his bomb unless the plane took off at once.

"I can't understand you too well," said Vaughn. "Let me come closer."

Binh leaned his head forward as Vaughn knelt down. Before Binh could repeat his demand, the captain grabbed him by the throat and thrust him to the floor. "Kill this son of a bitch!" Vaughn yelled as he pinned down the struggling Binh.

The cop came racing back with his weapon drawn. He shot Binh five times at close range, in full view of his fellow passengers.

Vaughn picked up Binh's lifeless body by the neck and legs and walked it to the Boeing 747's rear exit. He then heaved the 116-pound corpse onto the tarmac for all the world to see.

When he returned to the United States, Vaughn was greeted by a cheering crowd at the Phoenix airport. "I felt it was an offense to the human race and had to get the guy out of my presence," he explained to the mob of well-wishers. "A lot of time and effort has been spent on trying to prevent hijackings, but the only thing that will be effective is a mandatory death penalty for any hijacker, without loopholes."

The crowd applauded wildly. The widespread acclaim for Vaughn did not go unnoticed by the airlines or the FBI.

Three days after the killing of Binh, a hijacked Pacific Southwest Airlines jet landed at San Francisco International Airport. Operating from the same fourth-floor command center where they had watched Holder and Kerkow slip through their fingers a month before, the FBI agents assigned to the case resolved to keep the plane from leaving the ground. They had little trouble convincing Pacific Southwest that resistance to FBI intervention would be unwise, given the public's growing distaste for the coddling of skyjackers.

The jet had been hijacked by two Bulgarian immigrants, Michael Azmanoff and Dimitr Alexiev, who had boarded the Boeing 737 in Sacramento. They had seized the plane twelve minutes after takeoff, making three demands as they each held a stewardess at gunpoint: $800,000 in small bills, two parachutes, and the navigational charts necessary to get them to Siberia.

Upon landing in San Francisco to wait for the ransom, the hijackers were informed that their current captain was unqualified to fly to the Soviet Union. The airline offered to give them another pilot, one who had the experience necessary to curl around the Gulf of Alaska and cross the Bering Sea. Azmanoff and Alexiev had studied the Flight 701 hijacking, so they knew that a second crew had been used to reach Algeria. They accepted Pacific Southwest's proposal.

The pilot showed up on the tarmac nearly four hours later, wearing a Pan Am uniform and carrying the two requested parachutes. Per the hijackers' orders, he stopped a short distance from the boarding stairs to await further instructions.

A stewardess came down to meet him. "You are to take your clothes off right here, so they can see if you're armed," she said.

The pilot began to strip, starting with his slacks. The pants hit the tarmac with a metallic thud. The stewardess was suspicious. "You don't look like a flight captain," she said.

"I'm disappointed I don't look like a pilot," he replied as he continued to remove his clothes. "I'm an agent. Keep calm."

The stewardess noticed a flicker of motion near the plane's tail. She looked over and saw three men in white coveralls creeping beneath the plane's fuselage. Each held a shotgun. These FBI agents had sneaked up on the plane by taking a Coast Guard raft through San Francisco Bay.

Once the disguised agent had stripped down to his skivvies, he was given the go-ahead to board the plane—the hijackers hadn't spotted the .38-caliber pistol concealed in his pants pocket. A moment after the ersatz pilot passed through the door, the three shotgun-wielding agents stormed up the stairs and opened fire.

Alexiev, who was standing near the door, was the first to die; a shotgun blast tore open his chest before he realized what was going on. Stationed by the rear galley, Azmanoff wildly returned the FBI's fire. When he ran out of ammunition, he pulled out a hunting knife and threatened to kill anyone who approached. His stubbornness was rewarded with two bullets to the head, fired by the agent who had masqueraded as a pilot.*

But the FBI's celebration was muted, for its assault had incurred significant collateral damage. Two passengers were wounded, including the Chinese-American actor who played the cook on the TV show *Bonanza*. And one passenger, a sixty-six-year-old former railroad conductor, was killed by an errant bullet while sitting next to his wife.

This was precisely the sort of tragedy that Western Airlines' Bill Newell had tried to avert by refusing to indulge the FBI during the hijacking to Algeria. But there was no public condemnation of the Bureau's aggressiveness. The prevailing mood was that blood had to be shed to curtail the epidemic; the railroad conductor was thus viewed as an unfortunate martyr to a worthy cause.

In praising the killings of Alexiev and Azmanoff, one prominent figure suggested that an even more ghoulish form of violence was called for. "I'd recommend that we have a portable courtroom in a big bus and a portable gallows," said Ed Davis, chief of the Los Angeles Police Department, when asked to comment on the FBI's new audacity. "We [could] conduct a rapid trial for a hijacker out there and hang him, with due process of law, out there at the airport."

The day after the shoot-out in San Francisco, an AWOL soldier named Francis Goodell hijacked yet another Pacific Southwest plane as it neared Sacramento. He asked to be flown to San Diego, where he issued his demands: a $450,000 ransom that he would donate to two Palestinian organizations, a parachute, and an instruction manual on how to skydive.

Goodell was eventually frightened into surrendering by one of his

---

*The hijackers were later revealed to have had an accomplice, Lubomir Peichev, a former pilot for Bulgaria's flagship airline. The plan was for Azmanoff and Alexiev to land the Boeing 737 at a rural airstrip in British Columbia, where Peichev would be waiting with a small charter plane that he had hijacked. The trio would then fly back to a town near the U.S. border and ditch the second plane. Peichev abandoned his part of the operation after hearing about the shoot out in San Francisco; he was later convicted of conspiracy to commit air piracy and sentenced to life in prison.

hostages, a California Highway Patrol officer who described to him the grisly effects of a sniper's bullet on the brain. But this second hijacking in as many days convinced President Nixon that his personal intervention was once again required. Goodell's flight had passed directly over the president's head as he vacationed at his mansion in San Clemente, the so-called Western White House. Spooked by the thought of what could have happened if Goodell had been bent on assassination, Nixon asked his FAA administrator, John Shaffer, why the hijacker hadn't been selected by the agency's behavioral profile. Shaffer replied that the profile hadn't been applied—short-haul shuttle flights like the one that Goodell had hijacked were exempt from screening passengers.

Nixon ordered the FAA to close that loophole at once. But nothing changed: six days after behavioral screening became mandatory for all shuttle flights, two such planes were hijacked on the same day—one en route from Philadelphia to New York, the other as it flew from Oklahoma City to Dallas. The hijackers received a combined $1.15 million in ransom before their escapades ended in surrender.

On Capitol Hill, one prominent politician realized that the unthinkable had become unavoidable. On July 20 Senator Richard Schweiker of Pennsylvania introduced the Airline Passenger Screening Act, which would compel the airlines to make each and every passenger pass through a metal detector. "Nobody will board an airplane with a shotgun or knife jammed up their sleeve if my bill is adopted," he vowed.

An amended version of Schweiker's bill, beefed up to include such measures as the creation of a new Air Transportation Security Force, eventually passed the Senate by a vote of 75–1. But by the time it reached the House, the airlines' lobbyists had convinced numerous key representatives that universal electronic screening was unfeasible. And so as the bill made its way through committee, that particular mandate was stripped away. The two chambers of Congress were unable to reconcile their differences, and the bill died a quiet death.

13

"HOW DO YOU RESIGN FROM A REVOLUTION?"

HAVING FAILED TO profit from hosting Roger Holder and Cathy Kerkow at his Bab el-Oued bungalow, Donald Cox decided to give the couple the boot. In mid-July he informed Eldridge Cleaver that he was expecting visitors from America and therefore needed to clear space at his beachside home. The hijackers would have to find other accommodations.

Fortunately for Holder and Kerkow, their eviction coincided with one of Elaine Klein's frequent trips abroad. The daughter of a wealthy Connecticut dress shop owner, Klein had become a fervent supporter of Algeria's National Liberation Front while attending a Paris art school in the early 1950s. She later parlayed her activism into a job as press secretary for Algeria's first president, Ahmed Ben Bella, whom Houari Boumédiène overthrew in 1965. Unlike her boss, who would go on to spend the next quarter-century under house arrest, Klein had landed on her feet after Boumédiène's bloodless coup, finding work as a translator with the Ministry of Information. She had also become one of Cleaver's closest confidants, often acting as a liaison between the International Section leader and the Algerian government.

Klein had gone to Paris in June for an extended stay with friends, and she had left Cleaver the keys to her apartment in El Biar—a spacious flat on the Rue de Traité, right around the corner from the Black Panthers' headquarters on the Rue Viviani. Cleaver invited Holder and Kerkow to crash there until Klein's return. He also gave them an envelope stuffed with dinars so they could attend to their basic needs.

Holder and Kerkow blew the money on lavish meals in restaurants, where they always created a stir upon entering. Kerkow made few concessions to Algeria's culture of female modesty; she delighted in traipsing about in the same hip-hugging slacks she had worn during the hijacking, a scandalous look in a country where many women draped white veils across their mouths and noses. Ever the troublemaker, she got a rise out of watching male diners' faces contort with revulsion and lust as she and Holder picked their lobster tails clean.

Kerkow considered her provocations nothing more than a cheeky game, but Holder sensed that she was courting real danger. To guard against Algerian men who might take violent exception to his girlfriend's antics, he borrowed a .357 Magnum revolver from Cleaver's personal stash of weapons.

When they weren't feasting on seafood or haunting the café at the Hotel St. George, Holder and Kerkow were roped into political education classes with the Black Panthers. Influenced by his travels in Pyongyang and Hanoi, Cleaver had developed a geeky fascination with the minutiae of Marxist-Leninist theory, filling up audiocassettes with his rambling thoughts about the First International and Trotskyite revisionism. The discussions he led were thus rife with terms like *dialectical materialism* and *bourgeois nationalism*, to the befuddlement of Holder and Kerkow. The couple had never imagined that the revolution could be so deathly dull.

In addition to riffing on his vision for turning Babylon into a classless paradise, Cleaver made the diplomatic rounds in Algiers, trying to drum up support for one of his pet projects: convincing the United Nations to dispatch peacekeepers to America's inner cities. He also began to write a major speech that he planned to deliver on August 18, to commemorate the seventh anniversary of the Watts Riots. And whenever he could spare a few moments, Cleaver would shoot targets with his favorite pistol, a gift from an admiring Zairian politician.

But these pursuits could only temporarily divert Cleaver's attention from the grim reality at hand: with the hijackers' $500,000 gone, the cash-strapped International Section stood little chance of long-term survival. There were just too many mouths to feed and not enough revenue coming in.

Shortly after midnight on August 1, though, Cleaver's sagging spirits were lifted by a phone call from Donald Cox. A few hours earlier, while listening to his shortwave radio, Cox had heard a news report about a hijacked plane in Florida. "I didn't want to wake you up until I was sure which way they were headed," he told Cleaver. "They're coming to Algeria with $1 million."

THE NIGHT BEFORE they hijacked Delta Airlines Flight 841, the five adult residents of a rat-infested Detroit house held a religious ceremony to bless their impending crime. They poured a mound of dirt onto their living-room floor, on top of which they placed a white-skinned doll with a red-handled penknife stuck in its chest. This mock burial, which symbolized the hijackers' rejection of a racist America, was conducted beneath an advertising poster emblazoned with the slogan "Fly Delta's Big Jets."

The hijackers, all young African-Americans who had been roommates for less than a year, had varied reasons for wanting to leave the United States. Melvin and Jean McNair, a married couple from North Carolina, were on the run from the Army; Melvin, a former star athlete at Winston-Salem State University, had become opposed to the Vietnam War while stationed in West Berlin, and he had deserted when ordered to fight in Southeast Asia. George Wright and George Brown had both broken out of a New Jersey penitentiary in 1970: Wright had been serving a lengthy sentence for the murder of a gas station proprietor, while Brown had been doing five years for armed robbery. And Joyce Tillerson, a childhood friend of the McNairs, had become radicalized while working odd jobs at Oberlin College, where she first encountered the works of Marcus Garvey and Malcolm X.

The five had come together in Detroit to form a commune of sorts, a vegetarian household that eschewed alcohol, embraced marijuana, and avidly studied African mysticism. The commune was rounded out by three children, none of them older than three: the McNairs had a son and daughter, Johari and Ayana, while Tillerson had a daughter, Kenya.

Their decision to become skyjackers was precipitated by a conflict with Detroit's police department. In January 1972 George Brown had a violent run-in with a Detroit police unit known as STRESS (Stop the Robberies, Enjoy Safe Streets). STRESS, which planted cops disguised as bums in high-crime neighborhoods, was notorious for its brutality; during its two-year existence, its members killed seventeen people, all of them black. Brown survived his encounter with STRESS, but just barely: after being mistaken for a robbery suspect, he was shot six times.

Miraculously, Brown, who was living under the pseudonym Harold Singleton, was not identified as an escaped convict while recuperating from his wounds. Four months after the shooting, he was acquitted of robbery and assault charges at trial, a verdict that greatly embarrassed the police. As Brown left the courtroom a free man, several STRESS cops accosted him, promising that he and his housemates wouldn't live through the summer.

The commune's members agreed that they needed to flee Detroit before the police made good on their threat. They desperately wanted to emigrate to Africa, which they idealized as an enchanted land devoid of Western decadence. But without money or passports, such a move seemed an unattainable dream.

But then Holder and Kerkow demonstrated that there was a way to reach the Motherland free of charge and even make a tidy sum to boot. Duly inspired, the commune's members set about planning their version of the perfect hijacking.

The plane they seized on July 31 was a DC-8 bound for Miami. George Wright, dressed in the robes of a Catholic priest and armed with a .38-caliber pistol, confronted the pilot an hour before the flight's scheduled arrival. George Brown and Melvin McNair, with two .22-caliber revolvers between them, were responsible for keeping an eye on the passengers in the main cabin. Joyce Tillerson and Jean McNair watched after the kids, none of whom were old enough to realize what their parents were up to.

The hijackers said they wished to join their revolutionary brothers and sisters in Algiers, whom they planned to honor with $1 million in ransom. They asked that this money be delivered to the plane in Miami by a man wearing only a tight-fitting swimsuit, so that he couldn't conceal a weapon. The hijackers also demanded that this seminude deliveryman tie the cash to a rope that they would lower from the DC-8's front door.

The plan went off without a hitch, as Delta predictably hewed to its policy of total compliance. An FBI agent in bathing trunks carried a suitcase containing $1 million to the plane. The hijackers hoisted up the seventy-pound piece of luggage, then allowed the eighty-six passengers to go free. Flight 841 next proceeded to Boston's Logan International Airport, to pick up a qualified navigator for the long trip to Algiers. Aware that three children were on board, the FBI decided not to risk an assault in Boston; the so-called Hijacking Family was permitted to leave the United States without any interference.

Around eight a.m. on August 1, Cleaver learned that Flight 841 would be landing at Maison Blanche Airport at noon. He rushed there with several Panthers in tow, hoping to beat Salah Hidjeb to the money. But the Algerian military had the airport locked down tight, with tanks posted at every entrance; word had arrived that one of the hijackers was an escaped murderer, and the Algerians feared that his cohorts might be similarly prone to violence.

Like Holder and Kerkow before them, the Hijacking Family were initially given the warmest of welcomes. "We are your brothers," declared a smiling government official who ascended the boarding stairs to meet Melvin McNair. "You are home here." The hijackers were taken to the airport's VIP lounge, where the children were given glasses of cold milk. A member of President Houari Boumédiène's secret police kindly asked to inspect the money.

Upon discovering that the suitcase contained only $700,000, however, the Algerians dropped their kindly facade. They roughly searched the hijackers and their children, finding bundles of fifty- and hundred-dollar bills stuffed in underwear, brassieres, and even Ayana McNair's diaper. The hijackers were left with nothing as they were herded onto an Air Algérie bus bound for the Hotel Aletti.

As the bus sped toward central Algiers, Cleaver pulled up alongside it in his Renault 16. Sekou Odinga, one of Cleaver's lieutenants, leaned out the car's passenger-side window and yelled to the hijackers, "Don't give up the bread! Don't give up the bread!"

The bus screeched to a halt, as did its police escort. Eight men with submachine guns surrounded Cleaver's vehicle and screamed for the Panthers to make a U-turn. Cleaver and Odinga showered the Algerians with obscenities before finally departing. The Hijacking Family watched the hostilities with dismay; they had imagined that the Black Panthers and the Algerian police would be on friendly terms, united in their opposition to the depraved and imperialist West.

While the Hijacking Family's adults were interrogated at the Hotel Aletti, the Panthers convened in El Biar to discuss their next move. Cleaver was furious that he had once again been deprived of a fortune that, to his mind, belonged to the International Section. Worse yet, he was getting flak from back home—Panther officials in New York were constantly calling to demand a cut of the hijackers' loot.

Pete O'Neal, Cleaver's second in command, offered several bold proposals for bringing attention to the International Section's grievance: he suggested that the Panthers organize a sit-in at the National Liberation Front's headquarters in the Casbah, or march on the presidential mansion. But Cleaver ridiculed these ideas as sure to lead to disaster. "Where do you think you are—Harlem?" he scoffed. He knew that the Algerians, just ten years removed from a war that had killed a million of their countrymen, would not hesitate to massacre the Panthers in the streets. Cleaver instead decided to write an open letter to President Boumédiène, to lay out his case for why the International Section deserved the hijackers' $1 million. Cleaver had supreme confidence that his literary skills would win the day.

On August 5 all eight members of the Hijacking Family were released into the Panthers' custody. American journalists inundated the International Section's phone lines with pleas for access to Melvin McNair or George Brown, but they were all emphatically rejected by O'Neal, who acted as the organization's media coordinator. One enterprising young reporter, however, managed to get past O'Neal by making a different request: Bill Keller of *The Oregonian*, who asked to speak with Cathy Kerkow.*

It had been nearly three weeks since Rolla J. Crick of the *Oregon Journal* had chatted with Kerkow while she was cooped up in Bab el-Oued. The twenty-three-year-old Keller hoped that she would now talk more freely, having realized that her coyness with Crick had failed to pique commercial interest in her story.

Perhaps caught off guard by Keller's interest in the white girl rather than the more au courant Hijacking Family, O'Neal passed the phone to Holder, whom he chauvinistically considered Kerkow's boss. Kerkow listened over her boyfriend's shoulder as he began to respond to the reporter's questions.

Holder was cautious at first, warning Keller that any story *The Oregonian* ran would be "detrimental to our organization." But he loosened up as Keller gently probed his past: within minutes, Holder was recounting his family's tragic experience in Oregon ("We were the only niggers in Coos Bay"), his time as an Army deserter ("They didn't even know I was gone"), and his initial encounter with Kerkow that past January ("I was looking for another girl and when I knocked at the door she answered with soap in her eyes"). He also vehemently denied Keller's suggestion that Kerkow might not have been a willing participant in the hijacking of Western Airlines Flight 701.

---

*Keller is now best known for serving as the executive editor of the *New York Times* from 2003 to 2011.

"[Cathy] decided she wanted to do something about the mess the world's in rather than wait," Holder said. "She seemed to have her eyes wide open. She wasn't just coming along for the ride because she loves me. That's life imprisonment, man!"

When Kerkow finally took the phone, she sounded like a seasoned Panther rather than the sweet-yet-mischievous party girl who had left Coos Bay in her beat-up Volkswagen the year before. "Look around the country, man," she told Keller in an attempt to explain why she had turned to international air piracy. "Nothing's getting done by the so-called radicals there. They're getting stomped on and stepped on."

Kerkow went on the defensive when Keller asked whether she had put much thought into her decision to accompany Holder. "Would you jump into something like that without doing a lot of thinking?" she snapped. "I had a lot of people to think about, a lot of consequences to worry about. Well, here I am."

Unaware that Kerkow had not spoken to her mother since arriving in Algiers, Keller asked how her parents had reacted to the news that their daughter was now a wanted skyjacker. "What would your parents say if you did what I did?" she retorted.

"Yeah, and with a nigger, too!" Holder gleefully shouted in the background.

Unfazed by the hijackers' insolence, Keller tried a different tack, asking Kerkow whether she was happy with her decision to become a fugitive. Her mood turned pensive in a flash.

"There are a lot of different sides to that," she replied softly after a moment's thought.

And would she do it again?

"I couldn't say."

THE SWIMSUIT-CLAD FBI agent who had delivered the ransom to Delta Airlines Flight 841 became the latest icon of the failed War on Skyjacking. Every major newspaper in the country ran the same grainy, surreal photo of him lugging the oversize suitcase containing

$1 million. The accompanying stories described the Hijacking Family's success as a major setback both for the airlines and for the FBI, which had previously seemed on the verge of making real progress in the war. The twenty-four-hour pilots' strike of mid-June, the killings of Michael Azmanoff and Dimitr Alexiev in early July, the tighter security regulations for shuttle flights—all these supposed turning points now seemed worthless. By carefully planning their tactics and using their children to stave off the FBI, the Hijacking Family had proved that commercial airplanes were as vulnerable as ever.

In response to the second Algiers-bound hijacking of the summer, the FAA once again revised its security rules: airlines were now ordered to search all passengers who fit the FAA's behavioral profile, regardless of whether those selectees could present valid identification. Cynics noted, however, that this new policy would not have prevented the hijacking of Delta Airlines Flight 841, since none of the perpetrators had been picked for additional screening.

The day after the Hijacking Family landed in Algiers, Eastern Air Lines announced the launch of a groundbreaking experiment at New York's LaGuardia Airport: passengers on its shuttle flights to Boston and Washington, D.C., would have to pass their carry-on bags through an X-ray machine, the Philips Norelco Saferay. The Saferay had been in development since early 1968, but it had only recently received the FAA's blessing after the federal Bureau of Radiological Health had concluded the device posed little risk to humans. The machine scanned each piece of luggage with a paltry 0.2 milliroentgens of radiation for fifty nanoseconds, and its interior was lined with lead that absorbed the scattered X-rays. Lead curtains at each end of the Saferay's conveyor belt discouraged passengers and security personnel from foolishly sticking their hands inside.

Though convinced the Saferay would not damage its customers' health, Eastern worried that the electronic screening would significantly slow its boarding process. But a mere ten days into the experiment, the airline pronounced itself pleased with the results: Eastern stated that "the use of the device had no effect on departure times," despite the fact that the Saferay produced such fuzzy images that 10 percent of bags had to be checked by hand.

But Eastern made no immediate plans to purchase additional Saferays beyond the single one it had at LaGuardia. And despite the positive publicity surrounding the screening experiment, Philips Norelco could not persuade another airline to buy one of its $30,000 machines. Potential customers such as United and Pan Am said they first wanted Congress to give them $2 million for new security equipment. But a financing package that would allocate that amount was stuck in committee, as congressmen quibbled over how much pork they could tack on.

As Congress and the airlines dawdled, skyjackers continued to come up with clever ways of routing around airport security. On August 18 a forty-three-year-old man named Frank Markoe Sibley hijacked a United Airlines Boeing 727 as it boarded passengers in Reno. He did so by riding a bicycle through a gaping hole in the airport's perimeter fence. No one noticed that a man in a ski mask was pedaling across the tarmac until it was too late.

Sibley diverted the San Francisco–bound flight to Vancouver, where he asked for an exorbitant ransom: $2 million in twenty- and fifty-dollar bills; fifteen pounds of gold bars; two .45-caliber pistols; three submachine guns; twenty bottles of amphetamines; a set of walkie-talkies; a flashlight; a radio; a set of handcuffs; and, for some inexplicable reason, a jug of ammonia. Sibley also demanded that a newscaster from a local radio station, CJOR, read a lengthy statement he had prepared. "We are a well-disciplined paramilitary organization fed up with Nixon's broken promises and deceit which is clearly expressed by his secret buildup in Thailand, Laos, and Cambodia," the statement began, before going on to promise that United jets would continue to be hijacked until the last American soldier had left Vietnam.

Sibley was eventually undone at the Seattle airport, where he made the common skyjacker mistake of letting two FBI agents disguised as relief pilots come aboard the aircraft; the agents shot Sibley multiple times. It soon emerged that Sibley was a former American Airlines pilot who had flown secret CIA-backed supply missions over Laos during the mid-1960s. Wracked by guilt over his role in the war, he had steadily unraveled upon returning from Southeast Asia, losing a series of jobs as well as his statuesque German wife. He had hoped to unburden his conscience by donating United's cash and gold to a North Vietnamese orphanage.

"I'm not a criminal in the real sense of the word," a subdued Sibley would later claim at trial. He was sentenced to thirty years in prison.

ELDRIDGE CLEAVER SPENT several days working on his open letter to President Houari Boumédiène, striving for the right combination of firmness and flattery. On August 10 he called a press conference to present the finished product to the world. Minutes before facing the reporters, Cleaver showed the letter to Pete O'Neal, who was supposed to approve all of the International Section's official statements. O'Neal was alarmed by the bluntness of his boss's words and begged Cleaver not to release the letter. But the increasingly paranoid Cleaver was wary of O'Neal's motives; he suspected that his top aide was in cahoots with the Algerians. He decided to go ahead with the press conference.

Flanked by members of the Hijacking Family, Cleaver read the letter verbatim in his sonorous voice, addressing it to "Comrade Boumédiène":

> To carry out that struggle for the liberation of our people, as any and every revolutionary and freedom fighter fully understands, we must have money. There are no ifs, ands, or buts about that point. Without money to organize and finance the struggle there will be no freedom, and those who deprive us of this finance are depriving us of our freedom. This is clear. It is for this reason, and this reason alone, and not because of any humanitarian

> considerations, that the ruling circles of the United States are going crazy over the prospects of the one million and a half dollars recently expropriated by these American revolutionaries and freedom fighters, coming into the hands of the International Section of the Black Panther Party.
>
> The Afro-American people are not asking the Algerian people to fight our battles for us. What we are asking is that the Algerian government not fight the battles of the American government for the ruling circles that are oppressing the whole of the American people.

Cleaver considered himself quite shrewd for framing President Boumédiène's choice in such a manner. He had no inkling that his open letter would, in fact, be the International Section's ruin.

Boumédiène was deeply insulted by Cleaver's public gambit. He thought the letter insinuated that Algeria was a lackey of the West, eager to capitulate to American demands rather than defend its revolutionary principles. Nor did Boumédiène appreciate receiving political advice from a man he essentially considered a low-level employee, whom he paid five hundred dollars a month to serve as a symbolic irritant to the United States. Cleaver, the self-described "fat mouth," had talked his way into the bad graces of the only man whose opinion truly mattered in Algeria.

The following afternoon Holder and Kerkow were lounging in Elaine Klein's apartment when they heard a commotion outside on the Rue de Traité. They went to the window to see people rushing toward the Panthers' villa on the Rue Viviani. Holder and Kerkow went downstairs to join the excited crowd.

They reached the villa to find it surrounded by dozens of soldiers, who were holding the onlookers at bay. Police were streaming in and out of the compound, hauling away telephones, typewriters, and AK-47s. The entire leadership of the International Section had been inside the villa when the raid occurred; all were now under house arrest, as payback for Cleaver's public relations blunder.

Five days later Cleaver and O'Neal were summoned to Salah Hidjeb's office to explain their impudence. The two Panthers insisted that they had done no wrong, for they genuinely believed that the Hijacking Family's money belonged to them and that Algeria was betraying its ideals by handing it back to Delta.

The Panthers' lack of contrition enraged Hidjeb. He disparaged Cleaver and O'Neal as "palace revolutionaries" who were all talk, no action. He said if they wanted money for their struggle, they should have the guts to rob and kidnap on American soil, rather than lazily wait for hijackers to come to Algeria. And he blasted the Panthers as ingrates for embarrassing their generous hosts: "You should be thankful that the Algerian government has allowed you to live here in exile, to function openly, and to receive enough money to operate."

The stubborn Cleaver was not cowed by Hidjeb's tongue-lashing. He complained that the International Section could not accomplish its important work unless the Algerian government furnished it with "large sums of money to take care of business." And he demanded that the police return his favorite pistol, which had been seized during the villa raid.

Shortly after this contentious meeting, one of Hidjeb's operatives visited O'Neal and gave him an ultimatum: Cleaver had to relinquish day-to-day control of the International Section, or the Panthers were finished in Algeria. The Boumédiène regime insisted that O'Neal himself take over the reins; the Algerians considered him a more pliable partner than the headstrong Cleaver.

When Holder heard that Cleaver had acceded to the Algerians' demand and stepped aside in favor of O'Neal, he was aghast. *How do you resign from a revolution?* he thought. Donald Cox's zeal for money and Cleaver's logorrheic Marxist sermons had already soured Holder on the International Section. Now, having learned that the organization was at the mercy of Algeria's secret police, he lost all faith.

Holder's pessimism was justified by O'Neal's brief tenure atop the International Section. One of O'Neal's first acts as chief was to ask Hidjeb to supply him with passports for himself, Sekou Odinga, Larry Mack, and several other Panthers who had grown weary of life in Algiers. Hidjeb, who was keen to dismantle the International Section after his confrontation with Cleaver, was happy to oblige.

On September 16 O'Neal and his wife, Charlotte, left for Cairo without Cleaver's knowledge; they intended to resettle in Tanzania, another nation known for its hospitality to left-wing militants. O'Neal left behind a letter in which he named his successor as head of the International Section: Willie Roger Holder.

14

"THE OLYMPICS WASN'T ANYTHING"

THE SKYJACKING THAT heralded the end of the epidemic began in humdrum fashion. On the night of November 10, 1972, three days after President Richard Nixon's landslide reelection and twenty-three weeks after the hijacking of Western Airlines Flight 701, three African-American men took over Southern Airways Flight 49 as it made its way across central Alabama. The hijackers were armed with guns as well as three hand grenades, which they had purchased from a military surplus store in Birmingham; they had smuggled the weapons aboard in a folded-up raincoat. The ringleader, Louis Moore, put a stewardess in a chokehold and marched her to the cockpit, where he ordered the pilot to land in Jackson, Mississippi, for refueling. Moore then wanted to go to Detroit, where he had been working in restaurants and factories for the past few years.

Like the members of the Hijacking Family, Moore was at odds with Detroit's controversial STRESS police unit. After filing a complaint against STRESS for beating him outside a bar in late 1971, Moore claimed that the cops had threatened to kill his wife and children. He fired back by suing the city for $4 million; the city countered with a settlement offer of twenty-five dollars, a figure that Moore considered an affront. On October 13, 1972, Moore and one of his best friends, Henry Jackson, were arrested for sexual assault—a charge the two men alleged had been trumped up to punish them for opposing STRESS. They fled the city after posting bail, joined by Moore's half brother, Melvin Cale, a convicted burglar who had recently escaped from a Tennessee halfway house. The fugitive trio made a pact to teach Detroit authorities an unforgettable lesson.

As Flight 49 flew toward Michigan, Moore told the captain what the hijackers wanted in exchange for the twenty-six passengers: ten parachutes, ten bulletproof vests, and $10 million in cash, along with an official White House letter certifying the money as an irrevocable "government grant." Save for Arthur Barkley's absurd request for $100 million in 1970, this was the largest skyjacking ransom demand in history—double the amount that the West German government had paid the Palestinian hijackers of a Lufthansa flight that past February. Southern Airways, a commuter airline with a fleet of fewer than forty planes, couldn't possibly come up with such an extravagant sum.

Southern officials tried to negotiate with the hijackers, offering them a lesser amount and unhindered passage to the destination of their choice. But Moore and his cohorts refused to settle for a penny less than the full $10 million. The talks were getting heated when the hijackers learned that Detroit was too fogged in to permit a safe landing. Forced to improvise, they ordered the pilot to fly to Cleveland instead.

As the DC-9 veered southeast toward Lake Erie, the hijackers steadied their nerves by helping themselves to the plane's liquor cabinet. The three men knocked back forty miniature bottles of whiskey and vodka in short order. The infusion of alcohol turned their behavior erratic.

After picking up fuel in Cleveland, the intoxicated hijackers asked to be flown to Toronto. As the plane landed there, an elderly passenger suffered a nonfatal heart attack. Southern officials, who had managed to rush $500,000 to the Toronto airport, begged the hijackers to accept the money and release the stricken hostage. But their pleas were ignored: the hijackers ordered the plane to take off again, this time bound for Knoxville, Tennessee.

Moore, who had grown up in Knoxville, had one last gambit in mind. "This is going to be the last chance," he radioed Southern officials as Flight 49 soared over Lake Ontario. "If we don't get what we want, we're going to bomb Oak Ridge."

Moore was referring to Oak Ridge National Laboratory, twenty miles west of downtown Knoxville. The facility's centerpiece was a nuclear reactor powered by highly enriched uranium-235, a primary component of fission bombs like the one that had obliterated Hiroshima.

The Pentagon and White House were apprised of the potentially catastrophic situation as Flight 49 circled low over Oak Ridge, waiting for word from Southern that the full ransom was ready. At one point the drunken Moore decided to terrorize his hostages. "I was born to die," he slurred over the public address system. "And if I have to take all of you with me, that's all right with me."

Around noon on November 11, one of President Nixon's top advisers, John Ehrlichman, was patched through to Flight 49's cockpit. He tried to reason with Moore, explaining that it could take days, even weeks, for Southern to come up with $10 million. But Moore was not in a patient mood. "I'm gonna show you the Olympics wasn't anything—that Munich wasn't shit," he swore to Ehrlichman, referring to the September massacre of eleven Israeli athletes by Palestinian terrorists.

Southern scraped together every last nickel it could—$2 million in all. The airline had no choice but to gamble that the hijackers would be so overwhelmed by the sheer heft of the ransom—approximately 150 pounds—that they wouldn't bother to count it.

Flight 49 landed in Chattanooga around 1:30 p.m. to pick up the money. Just as Southern had hoped, Moore, Jackson, and Cale were too awestruck by the abundance of cash to realize they had been shorted by $8 million. The hijackers celebrated their new wealth by handing out wads of cash to passengers and crew members; the captain and co-pilot alone received $300,000.

But the ecstatic hijackers reneged on their promise to release the passengers in Chattanooga, fearing that the FBI would storm the plane as soon as the hostages were free. They instead demanded to be flown to Havana—they wanted a personal audience with Fidel Castro to beg for asylum.

But the hijackers were unaware that Castro had no love for criminals. As Flight 49 headed south over the Gulf of Mexico, the Cuban leader was briefed on the hijackers' threat to cause a minor Armageddon in Tennessee. He personally traveled to José Martí International Airport to ensure that such maniacs never set foot on Cuban soil.

Upon arriving in Havana, the hijackers were bluntly told that neither they nor their hostages would be allowed to exit the plane. Flight 49 was forced to take off once more and head back to the United States, eventually landing at an Air Force base in Orlando, Florida. That was where the FBI decided to make its stand.

As the DC-9 refueled for the sixth time since the hijacking began, six FBI agents opened fire on the plane, aiming to take out its landing gear. The hijackers panicked and yelled at the captain to take off immediately; in the confusion, Jackson shot the co-pilot in his left arm. Though its tires were shredded and its pressurization system was destroyed, the plane somehow managed to get airborne, clearing the base's perimeter fence by just a few feet. The hijackers could think of no better plan than to head back to Cuba, where they had been so rudely rebuffed just hours earlier.

Around a quarter past midnight on November 12, nearly twenty-nine hours after Louis Moore had first wrapped his arm around a frightened stewardess's neck, Flight 49 began its second descent toward José Martí. Cuban airport workers had tried to cover the runway with foam to create a cushion for the jet's denuded landing gear, but they had run out of material before finishing the job. The Southern crew prepared for a crash landing by opening the plane's emergency exits, creating a mighty gust of wind that sucked fifty- and hundred-dollar bills out of the cabin. When the DC-9's rubber-free wheels hit the runway asphalt, a mass of orange sparks lit up the Cuban night.

The plane screeched to a jarring stop. Disoriented passengers choked on thick black smoke as they scrambled down the inflatable slides that extended from the exits; once safely on the José Martí tarmac, they collapsed onto their backs and gasped for air. Everyone had survived the ordeal, even the elderly man who had suffered a heart attack in Toronto.

Moore, Jackson, and Cale were nabbed by Cuban soldiers as they ran through the grass that lined the runway. Their nightmare was just beginning: enraged that the hijackers had returned to Havana knowing full well that they were personae non gratae, Castro vowed to treat them with maximum cruelty: he promised Flight 49's captain that the hijackers would spend the rest of their lives "in four-by-four-foot boxes."*

Back in the United States, the FBI was roundly condemned for its attempt to disable the jet in Orlando. One of Florida's senators termed the assault a "stupid blunder" that had nearly caused the deaths of more than two dozen innocents. The FBI had erred not only by failing to cripple the plane, the critics charged, but also by firing on the DC-9 as it was connected to a fuel truck; a lethal conflagration would have ensued if one of the hijackers' grenades had exploded near a pool of spilled gasoline. L. Patrick Gray, the FBI's acting director, took personal responsibility for the fiasco, though he argued that his agents had at least prevented the hijackers from reaching a more distant destination such as Algeria.

But the controversy over the Orlando shoot-out was only a sideshow. The far more troubling issue was the skyjacking epidemic's new twist: the potential use of airplanes as weapons of mass destruction. In the face of such lunacy, the airlines could no longer claim that the crisis deserved anything less than the most extreme response possible.

---

*The three hijackers were imprisoned in Cuba until 1980, when they were returned to the United States along with twenty-seven other American citizens. An overjoyed Melvin Cale told reporters at the time that an American prison would seem like "a country club, a paradise" compared to what he had experienced in Cuba. He, along with Louis Moore and Henry Jackson, served an additional seven years in the United States.

|||

ELEVEN YEARS HAD passed since the August 4, 1961, Senate hearing at which the notion of universal physical screening had first been raised. On that day the head of the FAA had rejected the idea as so impractical that it didn't merit even a moment's consideration. The airlines had subsequently adopted that dismissive position as their own, defending it with a zealousness that bordered on the pathological. As the skyjacking epidemic's outbreaks increased in both frequency and severity, the airlines went to great lengths to avoid having to check every passenger's body and luggage. They narrowly escaped that fate in the summer of 1972 by derailing Senator Richard Schweiker's Airline Passenger Screening Act. But after Southern Airways Flight 49 was nearly hurled into a nuclear reactor, the airlines realized that their campaign against universal physical screening was doomed. The risks of porous security had become too grave for even their closest political allies to ignore.

On December 5 the Nixon administration declared an emergency FAA rule: starting five days after the new year, airlines would be required to screen every single passenger with metal detectors, as well as inspect the contents of all carry-on bags. Furthermore, all of the nation's 531 major commercial airports would have to post a local police officer or sheriff's deputy at each boarding gate, to deal with any passengers who were found to be in possession of weapons.

"We are now encountering a new breed of hijackers," said Lt. Gen. Benjamin O. Davis, Jr., the nation's skyjacking czar, at a press conference unveiling the sweeping new security regulations. "They are people unequaled in their ruthlessness and their wanton disregard for human life. Where a simple screening of passengers might have deterred hijackers in the earlier stages of this period of aerial piracy, we must now be ready to forcefully stop them at the boarding gate."

Ardent civil libertarians were outraged by the Nixon administration's unilateral move. They believed that universal physical screening ran afoul of the Fourth Amendment's prohibition against unreasonable searches, a view not wholly unsupported by a handful of court decisions. A federal judge in Los Angeles, Warren Ferguson, had recently ruled in favor of a drug defendant whose stash had been discovered after he was selected by the FAA's behavioral profile. Ferguson's passionate opinion made him a hero to those who feared that basic rights would be disregarded in the name of stopping skyjackers:

> In cases involving areas of great public concern it is easy to succumb to the expediency of the moment and, contrary to the Constitution, adopt the principle that the end justifies the means. All reasonable men are aware that airport hijacking and traffic in narcotics have reached serious proportions. This problem, however, as all other great problems of the past and the future, must be solved in the context of our Constitution or else the principles upon which this nation was founded will have disappeared in a cloud of fear.

But dissenters were in the minority among legal scholars. Warrantless searches can be deemed reasonable if the government can demonstrate that it has a compelling enough interest at stake. Given that skyjackers had come close to turning greater Knoxville into a radioactive wasteland, it was easy to see how expanded airport screening might meet that test.

The main controversy over universal physical screening was not its questionable legality but rather who would foot the mammoth bill, estimated to be as high as $300 million annually. Though airlines and airports grudgingly accepted that they would have to splash out millions for new metal detectors, they loudly protested the notion of paying for security personnel to operate the equipment. The airlines lobbied hard for the creation of a Department of Transportation police force, whose officers would screen the half-million Americans who flew each day. The Nixon administration, by contrast, was adamantly opposed to any government expansion: its officials argued that airports should be treated no differently than bus depots or train stations, which operated safely without federal assistance.

As the January 5, 1973, start date for universal physical screening drew near, the Nixon administration also made progress on another significant antihijacking initiative, one that had been considered a pipe dream since the epidemic's earliest days: an extradition pact with Cuba.

By pinging sporadic messages through the Swiss embassy in Havana, the Cuban and American governments had spent years secretly discussing the possibility of such an agreement. The stumbling block had always been the Castro regime's insistence that the United States extradite Cuban refugees who had reached Florida on stolen boats, a political impossibility for any White House occupant. Though regular dialogue about the matter had continued throughout the 1960s, the discussion had ceased in December 1970, after the U.S. State Department unwisely chastised the Cubans for their relaxed negotiating pace. Like so many men who wield absolute power, Castro did not like to be criticized for operating on a schedule of his own choosing.

The State Department's diplomatic faux pas shuttered the negotiations until October 30, 1972, when the Cubans abruptly notified the United States that they were ready to bend on the refugees issue. Castro had finally tired of receiving skyjackers from all over the Western Hemisphere; he had decided that the few thousand dollars he earned by returning each plane were outweighed by the risks of dealing with violent and deranged foreigners. According to Cuban diplomats, Castro had been particularly spooked by an incident involving a Nicaraguan plane that had been hijacked by four youths who hoped to attend the University of Havana. While taking over the jet, they had shot the son of a high-ranking Nicaraguan government minister, and they had later wounded Costa Rica's minister of security during an ill-fated refueling stop in San José.*

The State Department responded to the Cubans' overture by asking Havana to submit a draft agreement. American officials suspected that this request would end the matter, for the Cubans had previously proven reluctant to take the initiative. But after the Southern Airways Flight 49 drama, the Castro government became convinced that time was of the essence: it submitted its proposal for the antihijacking pact to the Swiss embassy in Havana on November 25.

The Cubans agreed to give the United States the option of granting political asylum to boat hijackers who had committed no other crimes while fleeing to Florida, an accommodation that the American government had been seeking for years. The State Department volleyed back a list of proposed revisions, mostly minor linguistic tweaks that stressed that while both nations could prosecute skyjackers themselves, rapid extradition was the preferred course of action. To the department's surprise, the ordinarily obstinate Cubans were receptive to that adjustment.

"The Cuban preliminary reaction to the possibility of returning guilty parties is interesting in that they inquired about procedures rather than reject the option," one of the American negotiators wrote to Secretary of State William P. Rogers on December 12. By the end of the month, the signing of the agreement—the first formal pact between the United States and Cuba since Castro's revolution—seemed like a foregone conclusion. Once that happened, potential skyjackers would know for certain that nothing but misery awaited them in Havana. All fantasies of tasting true freedom in Castro's "paradise" would disappear for good.

With the landmark Cuban agreement nearly complete, State Department officials began to wonder whether they could strike

*Two of the four hijackers were killed during this airport shoot-out, which was personally directed by sixty-five-year-old Costa Rican president José Figueres Ferrer. The president, widely known as Don Pepe, tried to fire on the plane with a submachine gun, which his bodyguards had to wrest out of his hands.

a similar deal with the world's second most notable hijacker haven: Algeria.

AFTER PETE O'NEAL absconded to Cairo, leaving Roger Holder in charge of the International Section, the remaining Black Panthers began to flee Algiers en masse. Larry Mack and Sekou Odinga left for Egypt on September 23, though not before selling several cameras, tape recorders, and mimeographs that they had pilfered from the Rue Viviani headquarters. Donald Cox soon followed, leaving his bungalow in Bab el-Oued vacant; Holder and the other hijackers moved in, seizing the opportunity to give themselves easy access to the beach at Pointe Pescade.

Eldridge Cleaver put on a brave face when addressing the defections, telling anyone who would listen that the International Section was far from finished. "There are some good things cooking, politically speaking, that might jump off soon," he wrote to a friend in Zambia. "If they do, a lot of problems will be solved." But in reality he felt powerless and adrift, as the Panthers became pariahs among their former allies in Algiers. Once a fixture at embassy cocktail parties, Cleaver no longer received invitations to meet with the North Korean and North Vietnamese diplomats who had been his most avid supporters. Sovereign nations couldn't risk offending President Houari Boumédiène, who had lost all affection for the Panthers after Cleaver's insulting press conference.

Harassed by Algerian intelligence agents wherever he went, Cleaver was forced to become a homebody. He passed the time by immersing himself in Buwei Yang Chao's 1949 best seller *How to Cook and Eat in Chinese*. "This marks the first time in my life that I have gotten down and related to cooking," Cleaver wrote in his journal that October. "I like the rational, systematic way that the Chinese move on cooking. And the results are so rewarding!" Cathy Kerkow would sometimes come to Cleaver's home on the Rue de Traité to help him whip up oily stir-fries; Cleaver, however, disapproved of her penchant for improvising rather than sticking with the recipes.

Holder, meanwhile, was botching his job as the International Section's new boss—perhaps just as Pete O'Neal had intended. As his comrades from Vietnam could attest, Holder's intelligence was rivaled only by his eccentricity; he tended to strike people as an odd duck, a trait that did not serve him well in trying to forge relationships with conservative Algerian officials or humorless diplomats from the Soviet realm. Furthermore, Holder had no concrete plans for the International Section, just vague aspirations to change the world. Frustrated by the minutiae of the organization's day-to-day affairs, he quickly lost interest in his duties.

Holder did, however, become significantly more paranoid upon assuming the International Section's top post. He began to speak of CIA agents who were following him through the streets of Bab el-Oued, or Panther rivals who were lying in wait at the Hotel St. George's café. The nervous spells that had plagued him in Vietnam returned, and hashish now did little to combat his anxiety. The manic energy that had borne him through Operation Sisyphus and the early months in Algiers was replaced by worry and gloom.

Holder's mental state only worsened in December, when Eldridge Cleaver informed the International Section's remaining members that they were in grave danger. After reading news reports about the Nixon administration's antihijacking agreement with Cuba, Cleaver had heard rumors that a top State Department official was in Algiers to discuss a similar pact with the Boumédiène regime. He told everyone that it was time to close up shop in Algeria, before they were all arrested and shipped back to the United States to face prosecution.

Cleaver had already started to make preparations for his own exit, working with his friend Elaine Klein to orchestrate a circuitous trip to France. His wife, Kathleen, meanwhile, was attempting to get a fake passport and driver's license from a Panther associate in California, a man code-named Comrade T who specialized in such delicate tasks. The idea was for her to travel incognito to France with the children, then reunite with Eldridge and retreat into the underground. Once they were established in France, the Cleavers would arrange for the escape of those left behind in Algiers.

The three parents among the Hijacking Family, Melvin and Jean McNair and Joyce Tillerson, were faced with a difficult choice: take their young children on the run or send them back home. After much agonizing, they opted for the latter: they contacted an old acquaintance in North Carolina, who came to Algiers to gather Kenya, Johari, and Ayana. The McNairs and Tillerson were devastated to lose their children—as Melvin watched the car containing his son and daughter drive off to Maison Blanche Airport, he felt as if his heart had been sliced out of his chest. But he also knew he had made the right decision—he couldn't subject his kids to any more madness than he already had.

At seven a.m. on New Year's Day, as most of Algiers slept, Eldridge Cleaver slipped out of the country in his Renault 16. Nine hours later, he arrived at the Tunisian border town of Nefta—the first stop on his clandestine journey to France. He had not told anyone at the International Section about his departure ahead of time, for fear of having word leak to Salah Hidjeb and Algerian intelligence.

The once-celebrated International Section now consisted of seven American skyjackers who hadn't even been Black Panthers before arriving in Algiers.

The Algerian government continued to support the group with a five-hundred-dollar monthly stipend, but all other sources of revenue dried up. Stripped of its communications equipment, the villa in El Biar became useless and fell into disrepair; it was eventually repossessed by the National Liberation Front. Huddled together at Donald Cox's former bungalow in Bab el-Oued, the struggling hijackers could only wait for help from Cleaver once he surfaced in France. But weeks flew by with no word about his fate.

HOLDER'S PANIC ATTACKS grew more frequent as winter turned to spring. He started to believe that he and Kerkow were certain to be killed in Algiers, by any number of foes both real and imagined: Salah Hidjeb, the Panthers, the CIA, the Vietcong. Convinced that such a fate was unavoidable, he decided to follow through on the promise he had made to Kerkow while planning Operation Sisyphus.

"Let's get married," he blurted out one day as he and Kerkow lay together on the beach at Pointe Pescade. "At least that way we can be buried together."

Kerkow lovingly ran her fingers through Holder's tight Afro. "Rub a nigger's head for luck," she said with a devilish grin. And with that playful jest, she rose and waded into the surf, reveling in the stares of male beachgoers as she splashed water over her immodestly covered frame.

She never did respond to Holder's proposal.

15

"MONSIEUR LECANUET, ANYONE CAN STEAL . . ."

WHEN THE FIRST airport security queues began to form on the morning of January 5, 1973, no one was quite sure how the public would react. The conventional wisdom was that many travelers would never stand for being treated like criminal suspects and so would loudly protest when asked to place their keys in plastic trays. Eager to catch such moments of rage, reporters staked out the walk-through metal detectors that now prevented unfettered access to all of the nation's boarding gates.

Those reporters were disappointed by the day's lack of conflicts. The skyjackers had become so brazen that even the most privacy-conscious travelers had come to accept the need to sacrifice convenience for peace of mind. And so even though the airport security gauntlets took an average of fifteen minutes to navigate, scarcely anyone complained about the hassle. "Somebody's got to put a stop to this hijacking," one Alabaman told the Associated Press as a guard picked through his carry-on bag at New York's LaGuardia Airport. "If this will do it, glory be!"

Because it was still unclear whether drugs seized during these inspections were admissible in court, guards were instructed to search only for weapons. They discovered an abundance: handguns, knives, swords, batons, screwdrivers, fish saws, even a black widow spider stored in a mason jar. The weapons' owners were not always arrested: many pleaded ignorance regarding the new security rules and were allowed to stow their potentially lethal items in their checked luggage.

To cut down on the screening delays, many airports soon decided to forbid all but ticketed passengers from passing through security, thereby ending the tradition of families bidding farewell to loved ones at boarding gates. The airlines also began to purchase hundreds of X-ray machines, which were rolling off the assembly lines of engineering firms for which the antiskyjacking push represented a golden opportunity. These companies boasted that their machines could screen a carry-on bag in three seconds, seven to ten times faster than any human inspector.

To the surprise of the Justice Department, which was prepared to defend universal physical screening all the way to the Supreme Court, no significant legal challenges to the FAA's new security rules emerged. The most notable case triggered by the new regulations questioned not the constitutionality of the searches but rather the safety of the X-ray equipment: consumer crusader Ralph Nader filed suit against the FAA, claiming that the machines manufactured by two companies, Bendix Corporation and Astrophysics Corporation, leaked radiation. Nader was correct: both companies' machines failed to protect their openings with lead-lined curtains, and their X-ray emitters were not properly shielded. But the FAA acted with atypical haste to establish technical guidelines for future machines, and there was little public outcry over the fact that untold thousands of travelers had been dosed with harmful amounts of radiation.

The airlines and the Nixon administration, meanwhile, amicably resolved their dispute over how to pay for the tightened security. The idea for a new Department of Transportation police force was scrapped, as was the notion of making the airlines use salaried personnel to operate metal detectors and X-ray machines. The airlines were instead permitted to contract their security to private firms—a unique arrangement in the developed world. They funded these contracts through a combination of fare increases and a government-approved surcharge that averaged thirty-four cents per ticket. Customers did not seem to mind shouldering the fiscal burden; despite the higher ticket prices, the number of airline passengers would increase by a healthy 7 percent in 1973.

By February 15, the day Secretary of State William P. Rogers finally signed the long-anticipated extradition pact with Cuba, the United States had gone more than six weeks without a hijacking—the nation's longest such stretch since 1967, the year the epidemic had begun to accelerate toward its peak. The streak continued through the spring, then the summer, then the fall, even as the epidemic persisted in parts of the world that had yet to adopt universal physical screening. Planes were commandeered in Libya, Venezuela, and even France, where the wife of a Parisian film producer was slain after hijacking a Boeing 747 and demanding that all French cars sit idle for a day. But in all of 1973, not a single such incident occurred in American airspace. Nor were any commercial flights successfully hijacked in 1974. (One charter plane was taken to Havana in December 1974, but the Cuban government promptly extradited the skyjacker back to the United States.)

The longer the skyjacking lull lasted, the more the epidemic receded from the public imagination—and, by extension, from the escapist fantasies of the despondent and deranged. The essence of skyjacking's allure had always been the theatricality of the crime; a seized plane was a mammoth stage, the nation below an audience rapt in suspense over how it would all end. But like so many theatrical fads, skyjacking did not age well: once images of ransom deliveries and tarmac shoot-outs disappeared from the airwaves, the crime quickly assumed a dated feel. What lingered in people's minds was not the skyjackers' audacity, but their futility.

And so the most desperate Americans sought new ways to cast themselves as the heroes of their own warped redemption tales. The years that followed Watergate and the fall of Saigon would be filled with plenty of high-profile mayhem committed by men and women at their wits' ends—kidnappings, car bombings, and assassinations of politicians and celebrities alike. But almost none of the era's madness would occur in America's skies.

ON THE NIGHT of January 6, 1975, two years and a day after American aviation security changed forever, two Paris policemen spotted something unusual along the River Seine: a tall, skinny black man wandering about the Quai de l'Hôtel de Ville in a daze, as if thoroughly drunk. This was not a part of town with many Senegalese or Ivorian residents, and the man did not look like a typical wide-eyed tourist. The police approached him and asked to see his identification; when he could not produce any, they escorted him to their headquarters on the Île de la Cité for further questioning.

Roger Holder held nothing back during his interrogation. He stated his real name and admitted that he had been living in France illegally "for quite some time," though he couldn't say precisely how long. He gave the police the address of his current residence, a sixth-floor apartment on the Rue Blomet in the Fifteenth Arrondissement. Without prompting, Holder also revealed that he was wanted by American authorities for hijacking a plane to Algeria.

The French police thought this all sounded preposterous, for the genial and spacey man before them did not seem dangerous in the least. Besides, what sort of international fugitive would blab so freely? The cops surmised that this man who claimed to be a hijacker was a harmless kook whose sole crime was overstaying his visa. They let Holder go the next day, after photographing him and extracting a promise that he would return with his passport by week's end.

Almost as an afterthought, a police supervisor notified the American embassy on January 8 that someone who called himself Roger Holder had been briefly detained. The Americans were outraged that the police had not held this man until his identity could be verified; they demanded that he be rearrested at once.

The embarrassed Paris police rushed over to Holder's apartment, but the occupants had apparently packed suitcases and fled just hours earlier. The bedroom closets still contained numerous articles of male and female clothing. In the living room, the cops discovered a movie projector, a stack of pornographic films, and several models of trains, airplanes, and helicopters in various states of assembly.

Roger Holder and Cathy Kerkow had hung on in Algiers longer than anyone else. The Hijacking Family left in May 1973, finding their way to France with the aid of Eldridge Cleaver, who had resurfaced in the Latin Quarter of Paris. But Holder and Kerkow remained at the Bab el-Oued bungalow, living off meager handouts from the Algerian government and bumming around the beach at Pointe Pescade. They grappled with boredom and got on each other's nerves.

Though the International Section had disintegrated, Holder still believed he was in peril from unseen foes. He became prone to babbling about a mishmash of disturbing topics: atrocities from Vietnam, the secret operatives who were tracking his every move, his regrets over leaving his twin daughters in San Diego. By the fall of 1973, caring for Holder had become a full-time occupation for Kerkow, who found the job too difficult to manage. She reached out to Cleaver for help.

Though Cleaver had been in France for less than a year, he already had many friends in the country. The Black Panthers had always been popular among French intellectuals, who shared the Panthers' dim view of the United States. There were thus many artists and scholars eager to support exiles like Cleaver. Julia Wright Hervé, the daughter of *Native Son* author Richard Wright, was always willing to assist Panthers with money or shelter, as was her mother, Ellen, who became Cleaver's literary agent. And the celebrated French writer Jean Genet, who had traveled to the United States in 1970 to speak on behalf of imprisoned Panthers co-founder Bobby Seale, offered to provide Cleaver with introductions to highly placed politicians.

Through these connections, Kerkow arranged for herself and Holder to escape from Algiers. A Black Panther in San Francisco sent them American passports that identified the couple as Leavy and

Janice Ann Forte; someone very skilled at forgery had affixed the hijackers' photographs to the documents. In January 1974 Holder and Kerkow used those passports to follow in Cleaver's footsteps, wending their way through Tunisia, Switzerland, and southern France before finally arriving in Paris, where they crashed in a sympathizer's apartment near the Rue Beaubourg.

A man the couple knew from Algiers—the French economics teacher who had once been their neighbor in Bab el-Oued—pulled some strings to get Holder into the Borde Clinic, an experimental psychiatric institute located in a stately château about two hours south of Paris. The clinic employed a Marxist-inspired approach to treatment, whereby patients were expected to help run the facility, handling jobs ranging from gardening to cooking to administration. It had a long and distinguished history of treating traumatized war veterans.

While Holder settled into his therapeutic routine, Kerkow moved into the apartment on the Rue Blomet, the pied-à-terre of a prominent physicist who was active in left-wing politics. Other French activists provided her with a modest allowance so that she needn't look for work. Kerkow was delighted with her comfortable new circumstances, not least of all because she was finally free of Holder. The object of her youthful infatuation had become a burden over the preceding year; she pined for a future that consisted of more than just watching her boyfriend unravel.

Though just twenty-two years old when she arrived in Paris, Kerkow bore little resemblance to the naïve masseuse who had left San Diego in 1972. The hardships of Algiers had melted away her juvenile exuberance. She now radiated a weary sophistication, her beauty tinged with a glint of icy reserve. The aimless party girl from Coos Bay had become a survivor.

Unlike Algerian men, who'd had a difficult time relating to Kerkow's overtly sexual vibe, the male denizens of Paris knew exactly how to respond to her signals. As she explored the city, Kerkow discovered that she rarely needed to pay for meals in cafés; admirers sitting a few tables away picked up the checks. She started dating men who bought her shoes and dresses from swanky *grands magasins*; soon enough she developed a keen eye for fashion, abandoning her previous taste in hippie garb for clothes more befitting a young woman of means.

But Kerkow's happy interlude was brief: in the autumn of 1974 Holder joined her in Paris. His time at the Borde Clinic had gone well enough, but he had grown weary of the asylum's languid pace of life. The clinic let patients come and go as they pleased, so Holder had decided to take a break and soak up some Parisian atmosphere. He trusted that Kerkow would help him stay on an even keel during his sabbatical.

His nerves dulled by a daily regimen of four tranquilizers, Holder spent long hours wandering the streets with a vacant look in his eye and a cigarette dangling from his lips. He perked up when passing by corner stores with large glass windows; he suspected that his enemies spied on him from such vantage points.

When he did spend time at the apartment on the Rue Blomet, Holder would build models he obtained through a mail-order catalog. The hobby allowed him to retreat to his adolescence in California, a halcyon age when his life had not been such a disorienting mess.

KERKOW HADN'T BEEN terribly concerned when she woke up alone on the morning of January 7, 1975, for she knew that Holder occasionally walked all night. She expected that he would return shortly, thirsty for coffee and mumbling about the rubber groves near Loc Ninh. But when Holder finally appeared after a full day's absence, he spoke of something more disturbing than his memories of Vietnam: a police interrogation at which he may have exhibited a lack of discretion.

Kerkow knew they had to run. And at this point in their relationship, she alone was responsible for making such decisions.

She once again contacted Eldridge Cleaver, who by that time was living openly in Paris with his wife and children. Cleaver had earned this privilege by forging a personal relationship with France's president, Valéry Giscard d'Estaing, whom he had met through the politician's mistress; as a personal favor to that woman, Giscard had given Cleaver political asylum. Now comfortably ensconced in a two-story house on the Left Bank, Cleaver had lost much of his militant edge; he had turned against Marxism, for example, and had come to believe that the 1974 impeachment of President Richard Nixon signaled that all was not entirely rotten in "Babylon." Though Cleaver was reluctant to risk his privileged status in France, he still felt obliged to help the hijackers; he provided Kerkow with a list of useful contacts.

As Holder and Kerkow bounced from one Paris safe house to the next, the FBI sent agents to the San Diego home of Seavenes and Marie Holder, to show them a photograph of the man they believed to be their now-twenty-five-year-old son. The agents wanted the Holders to sign an affidavit confirming Roger's identity so the United States could prepare an extradition request for France's Ministry of Justice. But the Holders refused; as much as they had been devastated by Roger's actions, they could not bring themselves to bear witness against him. Instead they claimed that Roger was still in Algiers, and that the man in the photo was their older son, Seavenes Jr., then an Army soldier posted in West Germany. Their charade was in vain, however, for the FBI had also obtained Holder's fingerprints from the French.

On January 23, having eluded capture for over two weeks, Kerkow wondered whether the danger might have passed. She surveyed the area around the Rue Blomet apartment and saw no sign of the police. So she and Holder settled back into their home that night, confident that the authorities had lost interest in the case.

But Kerkow had underestimated the police, who had asked one of the couple's neighbors to monitor the apartment. Early the next morning, as Holder exited the building to begin one of his interminable walks, he was instantly surrounded by cops. Kerkow was hauled out of bed and handcuffed, pleading all the while that her name was Janice Ann Forte. But once she and Holder were whisked into the Ministry of Justice at the Place Vendôme, Kerkow realized there was no longer any point in lying. It was instead time for her to call upon the most important contact on Eldridge Cleaver's list—the only man in France who could save her from spending the next two decades in an American prison.

As a novice lawyer in the mid-1950s, Jean-Jacques de Felice had desired nothing grander than a modest career helping juvenile delinquents. He set up an office in the dingy Parisian suburb of Nanterre, where the majority of youthful offenders were Algerian immigrants. He couldn't help but notice that many of his clients' fathers were incarcerated for aiding Algeria's National Liberation Front, which was then orchestrating both peaceful protests and systematic bombings throughout France. De Felice was intrigued by these men, whom he began to visit in French prisons. Soon enough he was traveling to Algiers to meet with anticolonial fighters whom the French had sentenced to death by guillotine. Those death-row encounters altered the course of his life.

"What always strikes me about these imprisoned and chained men is their almost mythical acceptance of their fate," he wrote of his meetings in Algiers. "I come out of prison not overwhelmed and demoralized, but rather comforted by their quiet strength."

De Felice thereafter became France's leading legal provocateur, dedicated to defending anyone whose interests ran contrary to those of the establishment. He defended Algerians accused of bombing French trains and cafés; Italian migrant workers threatened with deportation; the indigenous peoples of French Polynesia; peasants stripped of their property rights by developers; and anyone else whose cause brought discomfort to the powerful.

When Eldridge Cleaver had first arrived in Paris in early 1973 and needed advice on how to seek asylum, de Felice was naturally the first lawyer to offer his assistance. Though de Felice hadn't been able to help him much, Cleaver had been impressed by the attorney, whom he described as "the embodiment of French concern for human rights." He had advised Kerkow to seek de Felice's counsel should she ever wind up in French custody.

De Felice met the hijackers at Fleury-Mérogis Prison in late January, a few days after their arrest. A preliminary hearing on the American extradition request had already been scheduled for February 7, which gave the lawyer scant time to prepare. But after listening to Holder's convoluted account of Operation Sisyphus, de Felice knew precisely the legal tactic he would employ.

On the day of their first hearing, Holder and Kerkow were escorted to the imposing Palais de Justice in central Paris, where reporters had gathered for their first glimpse of the skyjacking lovers. The press was drawn to the poised and pretty Kerkow, who had opted for a crowd-pleasing outfit: a sleek violet dress complemented by knee-high purple boots.

Holder, Kerkow, and de Felice waited in an anteroom as the judge prepared for the proceedings. They were about to be ushered into the courtroom when Holder's arms and legs began to twitch violently. He fell to the floor in a semiconscious heap as guards rushed in from all directions.

After several anxious minutes, Holder improved enough to explain that he was prone to such episodes, especially when deprived of his daily allotment of tranquilizers. Since he did not appear well enough to handle the pressures of open court, he was taken to a vacant office to rest. Kerkow walked into the courtroom as the sole defendant, radiating an aloof cool that caused a stir among the spectators.

Due to Holder's poor health, the judge decided to limit the day's business to formalities. He asked Kerkow to sign a form verifying her identity and then advised her of the serious charges listed in her American arrest warrant: air piracy, kidnapping, and extortion.

Kerkow caught the court off guard by replying to the judge in impeccable French: "This warrant for arrest concerns me, but I have nothing to say for the moment."

As the hearing drew to a close, a guard beckoned Kerkow to follow him. "Come here," he said. "Your friend is having a new crisis."

Cathy Kerkow in Paris, 1975.
INTERPOL

Kerkow was brought to the office where Holder was being kept. He was curled up on the floor, trembling and moaning his refusal to sign his identity papers.

Kerkow knelt by her boyfriend of over three years and gently stroked his shaking hands. "Everything's going to be all right," she whispered in his ear. "Everything's going to be all right."

Secretary of State Henry Kissinger advised his relatively new boss, President Gerald Ford, that extraditing Holder and Kerkow was essential to maintaining America's hard-won gains in the War on Skyjacking. "U.S. government views [this] case as very important for many reasons, including the precedential value of a successful extradition of a hijacker from France, a country with so much influence on 'Third World countries,'" the State Department's legal team stressed to Kenneth Rush, America's ambassador to France, in a February 18 memo.

That memo also highlighted the State Department's principal concern about the case: that de Felice would argue that the hijacking had been a political act. The 1909 extradition treaty between the United States and France contained a clause of great interest to defense lawyers:

> A fugitive criminal shall not be surrendered if the offence in respect of which his surrender is demanded be of a political character, or if he proves that the requisition for his surrender has, in fact, been made with a view to try or punish him for an offence of a political character.

> If any question shall arise as to whether a case comes within the provisions of this article, the decision of the authorities of the Government on which the demand for surrender is made shall be final.

Proud of its revolutionary tradition, France had long proved willing to exercise its rights under this clause, which appeared in numerous bilateral extradition treaties to which the nation was a party. As a result, France had become a favorite home base for extremists from around the world. In 1974, for example, the French had declined to arrest the four Basque assassins of Spanish prime minister Luis Carrero Blanco, stating that extradition would be an impossibility because the crime was "so obviously political." Prominent members of West Germany's Red Army Faction and Italy's Red Brigades called Paris home at that time, as did the Venezuelan terrorist-for-hire Ilich Ramírez Sánchez, better known as Carlos the Jackal. And of course, President Giscard had personally secured asylum for Eldridge Cleaver, who was still wanted for attempted murder in California. The State Department feared that a nation so protective of radicals would have a soft spot for Holder and Kerkow.

Ambassador Rush, a former Union Carbide executive known for his tact and loyalty, expressed these concerns to a top official at France's Ministry of Justice. Rush offered to supply the ministry with a dossier of evidence supporting the Americans' contention that the hijacking was "purely criminal." Kissinger's legal team had already sent the ambassador an FBI document stating that neither Holder nor Kerkow had been members of the Black Panther Party prior to the hijacking. Rush assured the French official that his colleagues in Washington, D.C., could round up plenty more damning evidence if need be.

The official said that wouldn't be necessary—any more material would, in fact, be "gratuitous" and likely to harm the Americans' case. He gave Rush every indication that the extradition process would be trouble-free.

De Felice, meanwhile, was taking advantage of the French public's growing fascination with his female client. On March 3, before another preliminary hearing at the Palais de Justice, de Felice arranged for Kerkow to chat with a small group of sympathetic journalists. Calm and cheerful, wearing a well-tailored jacket and glasses with huge ovoid frames, Kerkow spoke of her deep appreciation for France's history of sheltering political refugees and of her hope that she and Holder might become part of that rich tradition. "One is always an optimist," she said in her surprisingly good French. "If we are not extradited, I think they will let us stay in France."

Four days later de Felice held a press conference at which he laid out the narrative he planned to present to the judge—an embellished and streamlined tale that elided the more incoherent elements of Operation Sisyphus. De Felice stated that Holder was a war hero who had deserted the Army after becoming disillusioned with America's mission in Vietnam. Traumatized by the horrors he had witnessed, he had joined the "black liberation movement" upon returning to the United States. He had orchestrated the hijacking solely as a protest against the Vietnam War, and he had fully intended to give the $500,000 ransom to the Vietcong. He had changed his destination to Algiers only upon learning that the hijacked jet would have to refuel at American military bases en route to Hanoi, something that he found morally odious. Kerkow, de Felice added, had been active in the antiwar movement, which was why she had elected to take part in the hijacking.

De Felice concluded his press conference by announcing that several of France's leading artists and intellectuals had formed an ad hoc committee to oppose his clients' extradition. He waved a copy of an open letter that the committee had addressed to President Giscard, which characterized the hijacking as "without a doubt a political act directly linked to the Vietnam War." The letter was signed by three of the nation's most famous men: Alfred Kastler, a Nobel Prize–winning physicist; Claude Bourdet, founder of the left-wing *Le Nouvel Observateur* newspaper and a hero of the French Resistance; and Jean-Paul

Sartre, the father of existentialism, who believed that America's actions in Vietnam had constituted a genocide.

The formal extradition hearing was held at the Palais de Justice on March 17. The judge opened the proceedings by grilling Holder about his motives for the hijacking. "I wanted them to give me Angela Davis," Holder replied, to the noticeable exasperation of de Felice. The lawyer's entire strategy hinged on portraying the hijacking as an antiwar gesture; introducing Davis into the narrative could only complicate matters. De Felice was relieved when the judge cut short his examination of Holder and shifted his attention to Kerkow, a more focused and eloquent witness. Kerkow was perfectly on message with her characterization of the hijacking as "something we felt we needed to do because of the war."

After de Felice presented his case, it was time for the French government's representative, the *avocat general*, to speak. Everyone in the packed courtroom expected him to make the argument that his superiors at the Ministry of Justice had approved: that hijackings involving extortion were, by definition, criminal rather than political, and so France was legally obligated to extradite the defendants.

But swayed by the strong public sentiment in favor of Holder and Kerkow, the *avocat general* went rogue. "There is no formal evidence to disprove the political nature of this act," he proclaimed. He blasted the U.S. State Department for providing the court with "incomplete" information regarding the alleged crime, noting that he had received no statements from witnesses to the hijacking. Therefore he felt it was his duty to advise the court to deny the extradition request.

The judge thanked the *avocat general* for his input and announced that he would render his verdict on April 14. He stressed that he would not consider any additional evidence while making his decision.

Kissinger was enraged to hear of the case's unexpected turn. France was a signatory to the Hague Hijacking Convention of 1970, which meant the nation recognized hijacking as a serious crime that merited severe punishment. He could not fathom why the French would undermine that treaty and imperil America's antihijacking efforts to protect the likes of Holder and Kerkow.

"Department deeply distressed at development of Holder case," one of Kissinger's legal advisers wrote to Ambassador Rush on March 21. "It is precisely what department was afraid might happen. . . . It is ludicrous that we are now faced with a *fait-accompli* as a result of the relationship between the *avocat general*, the Ministry of Justice, and the court."

After much pleading from Rush, the Ministry of Justice agreed to review any evidence that the Americans might have to support the notion that Holder and Kerkow were common criminals rather than political activists. If the ministry deemed that evidence convincing, there was a chance the judge in the case could be persuaded to take a look.

At the State Department's behest, FBI agents fanned out across the United States to reinterview crew members from the hijacked Western Airlines flight. William Newell, captain of the Boeing 720H that had flown to Algiers, testified that the hijackers had made no overtly political statements during the long journey from San Francisco to North Africa. But Jerome Juergens, captain of the Boeing 727 that Holder had seized en route to Seattle, told a more problematic story. "Holder stated in his initial demands that he wanted to fly to Hanoi, but [he] did not explain his reasons for wanting to go to Hanoi," Juergens said to his FBI inquisitor. "Holder did mention that he wanted to go to Hanoi on more than one occasion, but I do not recall exactly how many times."

When he received the dossier of evidence, Ambassador Rush agonized over whether to remove Juergens's affidavit before forwarding the file to the Ministry of Justice. He worried that the French would disregard the entire dossier once they saw that Holder had indeed mentioned Hanoi during the hijacking. But Rush ultimately decided that honesty was the best policy. "If it ever were to become known that we had withheld it, it would be very damaging and could seriously hurt our credibility in this and further cases," he wrote to the State Department.

Rush's noble decision had precisely the effect he feared: the Ministry of Justice dismissed the dossier as too feeble to foist upon the judge.

ON APRIL 14, Holder and Kerkow were once again taken from Fleury-Mérogis Prison to the Palais de Justice, to hear the court's verdict on the extradition request. Knowing that his words would be carefully parsed in Washington, D.C., the judge meticulously described how he had arrived at his decision. He discussed Holder's desertion from Fort Hood in 1970, which he interpreted as a protest against the entire war rather than a reaction to a personal slight. The judge said he agreed with de Felice's contention that the hijacking had been Holder's attempt to "absolve himself for participation in the war," a view substantiated by the fact that Holder had meant to donate the ransom to the Vietcong.

As for Kerkow, the judge said he believed her claims that she had been "a militant in antiwar movements . . . motivated by passionate feelings about Vietnam." The Algerians had recognized this, he continued, which was why they had granted the couple political asylum in June 1972—a precedent that had factored into his deliberations.

"Neither party acted out of a desire for vengeance against individuals, no one was physically hurt, and no financial gain was won," the judge noted as he concluded his speech. With all that in mind, he could not in good conscience send Holder and Kerkow back to the United States, where he felt they would face persecution for expressing their deeply held political beliefs. The only comfort he could offer the Americans was a promise to consider trying the couple in France; until the court made that decision, Holder and Kerkow would remain in custody at Fleury-Mérogis.

The apoplectic State Department responded in the only way it could: with an irate cable to Ambassador Rush, instructing him to use all available means to cajole the French government into overriding the court's decision. The cable's author took the opportunity to lampoon the judge's logic:

> Court's point regarding fact that no one was hurt is pertinent, as the reason no one was hurt was that everyone on board cooperated in face of threats to kill everyone on board. The fact that subjects reaped no financial gain was simply because government of Algeria seized the ransom and returned it to U.S. Fact still remains that individuals' lives were held at bay for ransom.

The ambassador, of course, could not afford to be so acerbic in his dealings with French officials. Six days after receiving the angry cable from Washington, Rush held a posh luncheon at his residence on the Rue du Faubourg Saint-Honoré, to which he invited France's minister of justice, Jean Lecanuet. As the guests took a break between courses, Rush drew Lecanuet aside and expressed the Ford administration's bitter disappointment over the rejection of the extradition request. He said his bosses were particularly troubled by the judge's gullibility regarding de Felice's narrative.

"Monsieur Lecanuet, anyone can steal money and later say he did it for political motives," said the ambassador.

Lecanuet politely brushed aside Rush's critique. "Our hands are tied by the court's ruling," he explained apologetically, before adding that France was still very much interested in helping the United States combat the "hijacking menace."

A week later Rush pleaded his case to Christian Le Gunhec, director of the criminal affairs division at the Ministry of Justice. Unlike the diplomatic Lecanuet, Le Gunhec seemed offended that an American would dare question the French impulse to protect those motivated by conscience.

"Le Gunhec took considerable pains to explain that court decisions of this kind were influenced by philosophical concepts going back to the French Revolution," Rush noted in his summary of the meeting. "Judgments tend to be based more on subjective considerations than on careful sifting of evidence." Such an approach to justice, Le Gunhec had emphasized, is "difficult for Anglo-Saxons to understand."

16

OMEGA

As was so often the case, the Paris bureau of the Associated Press was still buzzing as sunset neared on May 6, 1977. It was a Friday night, the end of an eventful week during which the French capital had played host to landmark reconciliation talks between the United States and Vietnam. President Valéry Giscard d'Estaing had departed that morning for a major economic summit in London, where his American counterpart, Jimmy Carter, would be making the first international trip of his presidency. The AP crew had reams of copy to edit and file before they could begin their weekends.

Around eight p.m., however, the bureau's work was interrupted by an unannounced visit from Roger Holder. It took a moment for the journalists to register the identity of their surprise guest; nearly two years had passed since Holder's highly publicized release from prison, and his celebrity had dimmed considerably over that span. But his attire was that of a man who still ran with a chic crowd: a white sweater coat, a tight black turtleneck, and a pair of old-frame sunglasses that he insisted on wearing indoors. Holder could easily have passed for a bohemian expat at work on his long-gestating novel.

Holder had decided to visit the AP bureau after learning of President Carter's visit to nearby London. He hoped to use the wire service to make the president aware of his desire to return home, as well as the reasons why he believed he deserved leniency.

"I would like to go back alone, solo, and turn myself in," Holder told a reporter at the start of what would become a two-and-a-half-hour interview. "I want no armed guards. I just want the Carter administration to know what my objective is. . . . If they review my whole military record they will see what I did was patriotic."

IN JUNE 1975, a month and a half after learning that they would not be extradited to the United States, Holder and Cathy Kerkow had been put on trial in Paris—not for hijacking, but for possessing false passports. After being found guilty of that minor offense, they were each fined several hundred francs and sentenced to time served, which meant that they were to be released from Fleury-Mérogis Prison at once. Because the couple still faced possible trial on the hijacking charges, the court placed restrictions on their freedom of movement: they were not to leave Paris without permission, and they were required to check in with a magistrate twice a month.

When they emerged from custody, Holder and Kerkow discovered that their company was a sought-after commodity in certain Parisian circles. As living symbols of resistance to American tyranny, they were treated as honored guests at swank functions attended by intellectuals, artists, and journalists from *Le Nouvel Observateur.* At dinner parties and cocktail receptions, the couple received warm congratulations from their prominent supporters: the diminutive and elderly Jean-Paul Sartre, for example, made Holder uneasy by lavishing attention on Kerkow, with whom he appeared quite smitten.

Holder and Kerkow soon drifted into the orbit of some cinematic luminaries who were active in leftist politics. The actor Yves Montand, a former lover of both Edith Piaf and Marilyn Monroe, embraced them, as did his wife, Oscar-winning actress Simone Signoret. Kerkow struck up a particularly close friendship with Maria Schneider, star of the erotic 1972 drama *Last Tango in Paris,* in which she was infamously degraded by a corpulent Marlon Brando. The two women were virtually the same age, and they bonded over having endured similarly searing experiences: both had been forced to deal with international notoriety while barely out of their teens, and both had trusted charismatic men too much.

Even as they enjoyed flitting about the rarefied echelons of Parisian society, Holder and Kerkow were struggling through the final dissolution of their romance. After spending months apart in separate wings of Fleury-Mérogis, they had reunited to discover that the fading spark between them had vanished entirely. And though Holder always introduced Kerkow as his wife, they were now on strictly platonic terms. They openly dated others, with Kerkow finding success among moneyed movie industry types who showered her with fancy clothes and jewels. Holder, meanwhile, romanced a beautiful but neurotic young actress named Danielle, who sported an avant-garde haircut similar to David Bowie's.

Roger Holder on the Champs-Élysées, May 1977.

AP PHOTO

Rubbing shoulders with the glitzy set did nothing to halt Holder's bouts of anxiety, however. He now fixated on the distress he had caused his family back home, especially his twin daughters. It pained him to realize that he had missed the girls' entire childhoods while fighting in Vietnam and dodging the law. He began to wonder whether it was time to stop running.

On April 22, 1976, Holder suffered one of his worst panic attacks yet, a seizure that frightened Kerkow so much that she rushed him to the Pitié-Salpêtrière Hospital in the Thirteenth Arrondissement. The next evening, as he recuperated in the hospital's psychiatric center, Holder placed a call to the American embassy. He told an officer there that he wished to be transferred to the American Hospital of Paris, then be sent back to the United States "immediately" to reunite with his family.

The embassy officer replied that although he couldn't arrange for the hospital transfer, he might be able to secure Holder a travel visa and a one-way ticket home. He advised Holder to come visit the embassy as soon as he was released from Pitié-Salpêtrière so they could iron out the details.

Holder showed up at the embassy four days later. He raised the possibility of serving a reduced sentence should he return to the United States voluntarily, but he was told that no such deal was possible—the Justice Department was not predisposed to strike bargains with fugitive skyjackers. Holder said he would need to consult with Jean-Jacques de Felice before moving forward, and he promised to return to the embassy within forty-eight hours to discuss the matter further.

But Kerkow convinced Holder not to go back. As much as she disliked playing Holder's nurse, she shuddered at the thought of him being trapped in an American prison. But more important, she worried that his departure might affect her own status in France. Kerkow was having the time of her life hobnobbing with the glitterati; she was living a life that exceeded the wildest fantasies of her Coos Bay adolescence. She didn't want to give the French government any excuse to bring her happiness to an end.

Right after Holder's brief flirtation with surrender, Kerkow announced she was moving into her own apartment, paid for by a movie producer paramour. She promised to check on Holder regularly and to never be more than a phone call away. But after four and a half arduous years, she was finished being Holder's companion. Kerkow had a future of her own to pursue, and Holder was not part of her ambitious plans.

THE ASSOCIATED PRESS reporter who interviewed Holder on the night of May 6, 1977, could barely get a word in edgewise. Holder had given careful thought to the logistics of his return to the United States, though many of his ideas were clearly the products of a manic mind. He stated, for example, that he would like to prove his patriotism by coming home on June 14—Flag Day, as well as his twenty-eighth birthday. Though he acknowledged that he would have to stand trial for air piracy, he proposed pleading guilty to a lesser charge, for which he would serve his sentence not in prison but as a "civilian adviser to the Military Assistance Command Group, dealing primarily with the Third World." He added that he was granting the interview not only to reach President Jimmy Carter but also to alert his parents and children to his impending return, so that "they could take whatever steps they have to take to shield themselves."

The reporter finally managed to ask what Kerkow thought of all this, to which Holder gave a surprising answer: he hadn't seen Cathy for over a month, and he worried that one of his many enemies—the French police, perhaps—had caused her to come to harm. He expressed regrets over putting Kerkow in such a dangerous situation, and he vowed to "make it up" to her family in Oregon.

In reality, Kerkow was doing quite well for herself in Paris, enjoying her wealthy boyfriends' attentions and avidly accumulating fine garments. She had failed to check on Holder only because her sisterly sense of obligation to him was growing fainter by the day.

As could be expected, no one from the Carter administration contacted Holder to discuss the deal he proposed to the Associated Press. But one person did take action upon reading the published interview: Eldridge Cleaver.

Despite his comfortable circumstances in France, which included a vacation apartment near Cannes, Cleaver had quickly wearied of life in exile. Suffering from writer's block, he had switched creative gears and tried to establish himself in the world of fashion, designing a pair of men's pants that featured an external pouch for the genitalia—a codpiece, more or less. "All these designers are concentrating on the bottom, you know?" Cleaver explained to a group of curious Harvard students who came to visit him in Paris in 1975. "They're all accentuating your 'boo-boo,' you know? They're not concentrating on those areas that really differentiate a man and a woman. This is what I'm trying to get away from."

When Cleaver failed to move his pants past the prototype stage, he sank into a deep depression. He was disturbed by his children's growing preference for speaking French instead of English, and by how his son, Maceo, loved soccer but didn't know the first thing about American football. Many of Cleaver's activist friends were gaining real power back in the United States, becoming mayors, state legislators, even congressmen. "So I contacted these old friends and said, 'Hey, remember me? How about helping me get back home?'" Cleaver would later recall. "Surely, if the astronauts can come back from the moon, I could stroll through California again."

But no one could make Cleaver's attempted murder charge disappear. His friends advised him to "settle down and become a black Frenchman and enjoy all those French pastries." Despondent over the prospect of living the rest of his life in France, Cleaver retreated to his Cannes apartment and contemplated suicide.

Then, one night in the summer of 1975, as he looked out at the Mediterranean Sea from his balcony, Cleaver saw an image of himself cast across the luminous moon. As he stared at this image, it slowly morphed into a parade of the revolutionary heroes he had rejected: Fidel Castro, Mao Zedong, Karl Marx. Then, once the last Communist icon vanished, the lunar image turned into a figure whom Cleaver hadn't thought of in years: Jesus Christ.

Cleaver burst into tears, rushed inside the apartment, and opened his neglected Bible to the 23rd Psalm. In that moment, the man who had once yearned to burn down the White House became a born-again Christian.

That November, confident that God would solve his legal problems, Cleaver flew back to New York, where he was arrested by the FBI. He was eventually bailed out not by his former Black Panther allies, who had denounced him as a traitor, but by an evangelical insurance tycoon. As he awaited trial, Cleaver made numerous appearances at revival meetings to testify that he and his wife, Kathleen, were now full-fledged "companions to the Lord."*

When he read Holder's interview, Cleaver decided to do the Christian thing and help a man in need—even though that man had long despised him as a revolutionary poseur. With the help of his new evangelical friends, Cleaver reached out to Representative John Buchanan of Alabama, who had been a Baptist minister before entering politics. He hoped the congressman could secure a passport for Holder, then convince the Justice Department to offer a plea agreement that would take into account Holder's combat-related trauma. But Buchanan discovered that the French government, which was still planning to try Holder for hijacking, was afraid to cooperate; even if Holder left on his own accord, the administration of President Valéry Giscard d'Estaing worried that French voters would accuse it of engaging in "disguised extradition."

Still, Cleaver refused to give up. In October 1977 he flew to Paris and escorted Holder to the American embassy, to appeal for assistance in dealing with the reluctant French. Cleaver asked a consular officer to supply him with a letter "stating [that] Holder, if released from French judicial control, [would] be provided with travel documents for return to [the] U.S. to face charges there and to take care of personal and legal affairs." Cleaver thought that if he presented this letter to the French magistrate who was preparing the hijacking case, Holder would be permitted to leave.

But the embassy rejected Cleaver's idea, concluding that "it would be untimely to inject embassy into French judicial process, even indirectly." The consular officer suggested that Holder go to the magistrate himself and explain his desire to go home. Perhaps the magistrate could be swayed by the emotional heft of a personal request.

---

*Cleaver's religious evolution was just beginning at this point: he would later have public flirtations with both Mormonism and Sun Myung Moon's controversial Unification Church.

Holder promised to give the officer's proposal careful thought. But he never followed through.

SNOW WAS COMMON all over Paris in February 1978, with three successive blizzards bringing the city to a frigid standstill. Unable to wander the streets without getting chilled to the bone, Holder camped out in his new apartment on the Rue Vaneau; the place was owned by Count Denis de Kergorlay, a generous young aristocrat who helped fund the humanitarian group Doctors Without Borders. Though he was surrounded by his beloved models of aircraft and trains, Holder was feeling every bit as miserable as the weather outside: all his efforts to return home had failed, and he was dreading the French hijacking trial that seemed inevitable.

When the buzzer rang, he had no clue who the caller might be. But he was too lonely to turn down company; he hurried downstairs to greet his visitor.

Holder could barely recognize Cathy Kerkow, whom he hadn't seen in months. Her dress was more elegant than ever, her neck and wrists draped with jewelry that must have cost a small fortune. She exuded the confidence of a woman accustomed to being treated with great deference. The naïve teenager who had come to San Diego in a beat-up Volkswagen was now just a ghost.

Holder and Kerkow made small talk for a while, discussing film director Roman Polanski's arrival in Paris a few weeks earlier; Polanski was also a fugitive from American justice, having come to Paris to avoid a prison term for sexual assault. They joked about the advice they should offer Polanski on coping with the threat of extradition.

Then Kerkow cut to the chase: "I can't be in this situation we're in anymore."

Holder asked what she meant.

"Being here, waiting for this trial," she replied. "I have to go and find a way to take care of all of this. I have to go."

Holder couldn't understand what she was trying to say. Kerkow had previously made it clear that she would never return to the United States. But what else could she have in mind? They were, after all, forbidden to leave Paris, much less France. What was her plan for wriggling free of their limbo?

Kerkow could tell that Holder was unsettled by her words, which she had purposefully left vague; since he had blurted out his true identity to the Paris police three years earlier, she knew better than to trust Holder with secrets. She tried a more soothing approach.

"Listen, I'm going to go away for a few days, to Geneva with friends. We can talk more about this when I get back, all right?"

Does she want me to beg her to stay? Holder thought as Kerkow fished around in her purse for something. *Does she expect me to get down on my knees?*

She handed him a small box; it contained an expensive Omega watch. Holder was nearly moved to tears by the gift. "I'm sorry I haven't been able to do anything to help you," he said as he draped the watch over his wrist. "But, look, I never treated you bad, right? Never called you a bitch."

Kerkow just smiled and asked Holder if she could use his phone to call a taxi. She had to run and meet someone else.

They waited inside the building's front door until the cab arrived. They chastely embraced, and Kerkow again assured Holder that she would contact him after her return from Switzerland. They would discuss the future then.

And with that Kerkow ventured out into the icy February night, knowing full well that she intended to break her promise.

17

TWEETY BIRD

THOMAS CRAWFORD WAS still bleary-eyed from a good night's sleep when William Newell rang. Newell was one of Western Airlines' top executives now, having been promoted to vice president of flight operations just a few months earlier, at the start of 1980. Crawford couldn't imagine why such a big shot would be calling a lowly pilot like himself at seven-thirty in the morning.

"I just wanted to make sure you were all set to go to Paris," said Newell.

Crawford, who was scheduled to fly from Los Angeles to Washington later that day, was confused: "Captain, as of ten seconds ago I had no idea I was going to Paris."

"Awwww, jeez. Really? No one informed you?"

"No, no. No one."

"Hrrrmmm. Okay, look, you have a passport, yeah?"

"Yeah, sure."

"All right, good. Then listen, Tom, I'm going to need you to pack a bag and come out here to the airport right away. What we'll do is we'll buy you a full-fare ticket to Orly on TWA. We need you in Paris no later than tomorrow morning. The trial's supposed to start on Thursday."

The reason for the hurried trip now dawned on Crawford. Five years earlier he had heard that the two hijackers of Flight 701—one of whom he had tricked into giving up his demand for Angela Davis—had been apprehended in Paris. The time had evidently come for the couple to stand trial, albeit in France rather than the United States.

The French magistrate handling the case had asked Western to supply two witnesses from the first plane, the Boeing 727 that Roger Holder had seized on approach to Seattle. Jerome Juergens, the flight's captain, had committed suicide in 1978, so Crawford had been picked to represent the cockpit crew. Gina Cutcher, the stewardess who had spilled bourbon on Holder's Army dress uniform, had also been called to testify.

At the Los Angeles airport, a Western official handed Crawford a thousand dollars in traveler's checks and a first-class TWA ticket to Paris. When Crawford arrived in the French capital on June 11, 1980, a car from the American embassy whisked him to a hotel, where Cutcher was also staying. The two witnesses were instructed not to venture outside, for they might be targeted by rabble-rousers seeking to disrupt the trial. An armed guard was posted outside their adjacent doors as they slept that night.

The next morning Crawford and Cutcher were taken to the embassy, where a legal attaché briefed them on what to expect. She apologetically explained that the court was unlikely to mete out harsh punishment, since the French were so sympathetic to Americans who had opposed the Vietnam War.

The legal attaché also informed Crawford and Cutcher that there would only be one defendant on trial.

As a condition of her bail, Cathy Kerkow had been required to check in with a French magistrate on the first and third Monday of every month. When she missed her appointment on February 20, 1978, the magistrate was not overly concerned—he chalked up the absence to inclement weather. Nor did he see fit to panic when Kerkow failed to appear on March 6, March 20, April 3, or April 17. It was not until Kerkow's sixth consecutive no-show on May 8 that the magistrate decided to alert the French National Police.

When informed that Kerkow had vanished, the American embassy in Paris launched an inquiry into her whereabouts. The investigation yielded a confidential tip that she had gone to Switzerland—not to hide, but rather to obtain a new passport.

Getting into Switzerland would have been easy enough for Kerkow, despite her lack of identity documents. The underpaid and overworked guards at the Geneva border crossings were lax about checking papers. A well-dressed young woman like Kerkow, presumably traveling as a passenger in a car with French license plates, would arouse no suspicion.

The embassy feared that Kerkow had then traveled on to Zurich or Bern, the two cities where American citizens could apply for passports. Though the State Department warned traveling Americans that it was difficult to obtain replacements for lost or stolen passports, the reality was quite different—especially in tranquil countries like Switzerland. Consuls often failed to scrutinize the sob stories told by stranded Americans. They would only check the applicant's name and description against a master list of "lookout cards," which identified fugitives and personae non gratae. But bizarrely, Kerkow was not part of that list: her lookout card had expired in November 1977, and the State Department had mistakenly neglected to renew it.

Kerkow would probably be asked to furnish some proof of American citizenship—a copy of a driver's license or birth certificate, for example. But the embassy in Paris knew that such documents could be easily obtained by a woman with Kerkow's connections; all it would take was the complicity of another American woman in her mid to late twenties, or the assistance of a modestly skilled forger. As long as Kerkow could convincingly field basic questions about her borrowed background, a consul in Bern or Zurich would be unlikely to give her a hard time. And Kerkow was adept at using her words and smile to deceive.

Embassy officials in Paris alerted their colleagues in Switzerland to keep an eye peeled for any women fitting Kerkow's description. Yet they knew this was probably a futile request: Kerkow had been gone for at least three months, and replacement passports valid for five years were often issued within forty-eight hours. With the financial backing of her wealthy film industry friends, she could have fled almost anywhere in the world—even the United States.

THERE WAS NO shortage of drama in Holder's life after Kerkow disappeared. His actress girlfriend Danielle, the one with the David Bowie haircut, gave birth to a son who she claimed was Holder's; she committed suicide shortly thereafter, and her grieving family absorbed the child. Holder, meanwhile, decided to check into a psychiatric clinic in the Parisian suburb of Rambouillet, to receive fresh treatment for his worsening anxiety and paranoia. He failed to inform his supervising magistrate about his hospitalization, however, and the French National Police declared him a fugitive, resulting in the indefinite delay of his hijacking trial.

When Holder returned to Paris in May 1979, he moved back into the Rue Vaneau apartment owned by Count Denis de Kergorlay, one of his most prominent French supporters. Holder relied on his friends' largesse to survive, though he also found sporadic work. He briefly manned the door at a transvestite bar in the Marais district; he later swept floors at a university, in the vain hope that the job might lead to admission to the school's aeronautical engineering program. He also cycled through several brief affairs with women who were initially charmed by his intelligence and charisma but quickly wearied of nursing him through his psychological crises.

Through it all, Holder couldn't shake his longing to see his twin daughters, Teresa and Torrita. Like so many once-reckless men who start to glimpse middle age, Holder had come to regret his youthful selfishness. He had once planned to donate his hijacking ransom to the Vietcong, in order to assuage his guilt over his role in the war;

now he felt a commensurate amount of guilt over how the hijacking had turned him into a derelict father. And so throughout late 1979 and early 1980, Holder visited the American embassy every few weeks to beg for a passport and a plane ticket home. But his pleas were always greeted with the same response: the French were now dead set on prosecuting him for the hijacking, and they wouldn't let him leave the country before his trial had taken place.

On the eve of that long-awaited trial in June 1980, Jean-Jacques de Felice assured Holder that he had nothing to fear. He was certain because of his previous success in defending the Hijacking Family, Holder's fellow travelers from Algiers.

In May 1976 four of that group's members—Melvin and Jean McNair, Joyce Tillerson, and George Brown—had been arrested in Paris, where they had been secretly living for three years. Still livid over France's refusal to extradite Holder and Kerkow the year before, the American government pressured the country's Ministry of Justice for a more agreeable result this time: the State Department threatened to ignore future French extradition requests should the hijackers not be returned to the United States.

The Ministry of Justice received the message loud and clear. At the October 1976 extradition hearing, the French government was represented by the same *avocat general* who had recommended that Holder and Kerkow be allowed to stay in France. This time, however, he took the exact opposite position, arguing that the Hijacking Family had never made any political statements while flying to Algiers. Holder, by contrast, had been a "wounded, decorated veteran suffering ill health as [a] consequence," whose stated desire to reach Hanoi had been tantamount to an antiwar protest.

But the *avocat general* was no match for the spirited de Felice, who portrayed his clients as "symbols of repression" who had exercised their "sacred right" to struggle against institutional racism. He vividly described the daily hardships of life in America's ghettoes, as well as the contempt that most Americans felt for France. The court was duly moved and declined to extradite the Hijacking Family.

Two years later, at the hijackers' trial in Paris, de Felice called a parade of witnesses who detailed the horrors of American bigotry. The defense experts spoke of police brutality, the failure of desegregation, and the prevalence of malnutrition among black children. De Felice himself characterized the proceedings as "a trial on American history" and asked the court to find his clients innocent. He did not get his wish, at least not exactly: the McNairs, Tillerson, and Brown were convicted on all charges. But citing "extenuating circumstances," the court sentenced the hijackers to just five years each, with credit for time served. Within six months of the verdict, all of the Hijacking Family's members had been released from prison and granted permission to settle in France.

De Felice expected a similarly favorable outcome in Holder's case, though not the same level of media attention. The Hijacking Family's trial had been a spectacle, attended by movie stars who had read the hijackers' popular memoir, *Nous, Noirs Américains Évadés du Ghetto*. Holder's celebrity, by contrast, had largely evaporated by 1980. His cause was no longer touted by the likes of Jean-Paul Sartre and Yves Montand but rather by a handful of activists from the fringes of French politics—aging veterans of the 1960s protest movement who were beginning to seem like relics, much like skyjacking itself.

By the time Gina Cutcher and Thomas Crawford arrived at the Palais de Justice on the afternoon of June 12, 1980, a dozen protesters had gathered on the boulevard opposite the building's main entrance. Two of them held a crude banner urging the court to honor the French tradition of *Liberté, Égalité, Fraternité* by exonerating Holder.

Inside the courtroom, another twenty or so of Holder's supporters sat in the public gallery; their scruffy manner of dress irked Crawford as he walked to the witness stand. *Typical non-tax-paying, worthless pieces of crap,* Crawford thought as he began to answer the judge's straightforward questions about the hijacking. He was struck by how quickly the judge excused him from the stand and brought on Cutcher; it seemed as if the court were just going through the motions.

After Cutcher testified about the hijacking's initial moments, Holder took the stand. The judge asked him to explain his motives, to which Holder responded with a rambling monologue that cited his resentment toward the Army, his spiritual impetus to help Angela Davis escape to North Vietnam, and even the dissolution of his marriage to the unfaithful Betty Bullock. The judge then asked Holder whether he would like to apologize for having terrorized so many innocents. But Holder refused to play along, instead continuing to riff about his ill-fated military career.

The judge grew exasperated, burying his head in his hands as Holder went on and on about his last days in Vietnam and his ensuing desertion. "What I am looking for is some remorse," the judge finally interjected. "If you could do it all over again, what would you do differently?"

Holder, who had been resting his elbows on his knees as he spoke, sat up straight once the judge's words had been translated into English. Yes, of course he had regrets—much deeper regrets than he could express in any two-sentence apology. But with the gallery packed with the last of his admirers, Holder could not let the court diminish his life's most memorable achievement.

"My only regret," he said, "is that I did not smash that plane into the ground."

Holder's supporters roared their approval, until the judge had to order them to pipe down. Holder did not bat an eye at the cheers.

The court reconvened the next day for the verdict. Holder was found guilty of hijacking and kidnapping, but with extenuating circumstances. He was given a five-year suspended sentence, which meant that he wouldn't spend a single day in prison. But the sentence came with one onerous condition: Holder could not leave France until his term was up. His exile would have to continue until at least 1985.

And so the day before his thirty-first birthday, Holder walked out of the Palais de Justice a free man, though one confined to France. He did not feel the slightest tinge of joy.

HOLDER DID NOT stay long in Paris after the trial. His friend and benefactor, Count Denis de Kergorlay, had recently inherited an eleventh-century château in the Norman village of Canisy. He invited Holder to move into one of the castle's many splendid rooms.

Life at the château was merry and freewheeling, with a steady stream of intriguing characters stopping by for weeks or months at a time. The folksinger Joan Baez was one of the count's most frequent guests: at communal meals lubricated by fine wines, she would listen intently to Holder's graphic tales from the Vietnam War, a conflict she had prominently opposed. Holder was also fond of telling Baez that he had once hated her guts, back in the late 1960s when she was urging young men to resist the draft.

By day, Holder would typically stroll the château's forested grounds for hours, then hole up in his room to work on his memoirs. When he did venture off the estate, he often went to a nearby oyster farm, where he performed odd jobs. He also befriended a local physician who restored vintage airplanes, a skill that Holder was eager to learn.

Everyone in Canisy thought of Holder as delightful company, even though he barely spoke a word of French. They loved his hearty American laugh and his enthusiasm both for lewd jokes and for James Baldwin novels. But Holder's outward bonhomie masked his true feelings of near-suicidal depression. There were only two things he desired at that point: to see his twin daughters again, and to cleanse his mind of Vietnam. The artists and the idle rich who passed through the château could not help him reach either goal.

In October 1981 Holder burned his unfinished memoirs in the fireplace of his room—dozens of handwritten pages went up in smoke. Shortly thereafter he left the château without saying goodbye and checked himself back into the psychiatric clinic in Rambouillet. The count, who had treated Holder like a member of his own family, never heard from him again.

Holder spent over a year at the Rambouillet clinic, where his therapy focused on helping him deal with his memories of combat. He was discharged in early 1983 and returned to Paris, where he begged old friends for money. One of those friends invited him to a dinner party, where Holder met a sharp-tongued journalist named Violetta Velkova, a six-time divorcée a dozen years his senior. The leftist Velkova, who was paralyzed on one side of her body due to a stroke, instantly fell for Holder, whom she adored for having embarrassed the United States in such dramatic fashion. The two instantly became lovers as well as colleagues; Holder took charge of lugging his new girlfriend's photography equipment and typewriter from one assignment to the next.

In 1984 Velkova took Holder to the southeastern town of Apt to meet her father, Janika, who had been a Partisan resistance fighter in Yugoslavia during World War II. Janika coaxed Holder into proposing marriage to his daughter by buying him a brand-new Citroën. The betrothed couple then settled in the city of Aix-en-Provence, north of Marseilles, where Holder got a job stocking shelves at a hardware store.

But the relationship between Holder and Velkova had more downs than ups. They fought bitterly at times, and their disputes often ended with Holder living in his car for days. Still plagued by debilitating anxiety attacks, he drifted in and out of hospitals and jails: he was arrested at least twice in Aix-en-Provence, once for his involvement in a brawl, the other time for possession of hashish.

Through it all, Holder never lost track of time. He always knew that his five-year confinement to France was scheduled to end on June 13, 1985. He counted down the months, then the weeks, then the days.

On the morning of June 14, 1985, just hours after his suspended sentence expired, a bedraggled Holder celebrated his thirty-sixth birthday by walking into the American embassy in Paris and applying for a passport. No one there recognized him or his name; the embassy's staff had turned over completely in the five years since his trial. But when Holder's application was telexed to Washington, D.C., it was flagged by the State Department's new computerized lookout system. The FBI soon contacted its French equivalent, the Direction de la Surveillance du Territoire (DST), to inquire about the logistics of getting Holder back on American soil.

Though even the most fervent of Holder's former boosters had forgotten him, the French government was still reluctant to let him go; if the story came to light, President François Mitterand could be slammed for turning his back on France's tradition of sheltering political firebrands. But Holder's misdemeanor arrests in Aix-en-Provence provided the DST with a convenient excuse: the French could say they agreed to expel Holder because he had violated the terms of his sentence. Holder was taken into custody and placed in a psychiatric facility, to wait until the necessary diplomatic paperwork had been completed.

That process took an entire year, during which Holder languished in a Paris hospital, where he was pumped full of Thorazine and other powerful psychotropic drugs. Finally, on the morning of July 26, 1986, four DST agents escorted him onto a TWA flight bound for New York's John F. Kennedy International Airport—the same airport where, fourteen years earlier, Holder and Kerkow had bid farewell to the United States en route to Algiers. The moment he stepped off the plane, Holder was arrested by the FBI and taken to the Metropolitan Correctional Center in Chinatown. He was so heavily medicated that he could barely register that his long-standing wish to return home had finally come true.

Holder was fortunate to attract the interest of Lynne Stewart, an attorney who specialized in representing clients accused of using violence to further their political aims. She had recently defended Richard Williams, who had been convicted of murdering a New Jersey state trooper as part of the United Freedom Front, a Marxist group known for bombing the offices of IBM.* Respected and reviled in equal measure for her feistiness, Stewart agreed to take on Holder's case pro bono.

---

*Stewart would later represent Sheikh Omar Abdel-Rahman, who was convicted of conspiracy to commit terrorism in 1995. In 2005, Stewart was herself convicted

Holder spent nearly two years in detention as Stewart tried to secure a favorable plea bargain. That such a deal was even possible was a testament to how much times had changed: the skyjackers of the early 1970s now seemed almost quaint, vestiges of a bygone era that American society had come to view with an odd sense of nostalgia. Cocaine and the Soviet Union were the designated bogeymen of the Reagan Era, not Black Panthers and disillusioned Vietnam vets. The federal government had lost its zeal for imprisoning skyjackers for decades on end.

Roger Holder under arrest at John F. Kennedy International Airport, July 1986.
AP PHOTO/DAVID BOOKSTAVER

Like the judge who had presided over the trial in Paris, the American prosecutors wanted Holder to express contrition for his acts. But as he explained in a letter to Stewart, he still had no interest in complying with that modest demand. "As for my personal feelings about the hijacking, I can say that I don't feel that I did any or too much wrong," he wrote. "There are a lot of things that happened in Vietnam that many Americans do not know about and in 1972 I felt that some bold and daring actions needed to take place to wake us all up to the apathy towards the many deaths taking place."

On March 18, 1988, Holder pleaded guilty to two counts of

of passing messages from the imprisoned Abdel-Rahman to his Egyptian followers; she is currently serving a ten-year prison sentence.

interfering with a flight crew—a much less serious crime than either air piracy or kidnapping, the two top counts of his original indictment. He was sentenced to four years in prison, to be served at a medium-security facility in North Carolina.

Holder's stay there was brief: in August 1989 he was transferred to a halfway house in San Diego, to begin his transition back to normal society. His initial probation report noted that he was "a polite man with a tendency to please" who had a "sincere wish to make a life for himself."

ONE OF HOLDER'S first acts in San Diego was to arrange a reunion with his twin daughters, who were now twenty-two years old. The meeting was brokered by Holder's mother, Marie, who had raised Teresa and Torrita as her own. The pressures of doing so had contributed to the breakup of her marriage to Seavenes—the couple had divorced in 1975, and Seavenes had passed away in April 1986, just three months before Roger's return to the United States. In his final years, Seavenes had used his influence to have Roger's Army discharge upgraded from "undesirable" to "general under honorable conditions"—a small but touching act of paternal love.

The moment he laid eyes on his daughters, Holder could tell they were disappointed. He felt as if they had expected him to be a chiseled paragon of masculinity, like something out of one of the era's B-grade action films. But with his sleepy eyes and gangly limbs, the man who had abandoned them to rescue Angela Davis was anything but imposing.

They think I look like Tweety Bird, Holder thought as he looked at his daughters' crestfallen faces. Their ensuing conversation was icy; a meaningful reconciliation was not to be.

Holder had kept up a correspondence with Violetta Velkova, his French ex-fiancée, during his time in prison, and they began to speak regularly after he entered the halfway house. Once he was released from custody in the spring of 1990, Holder invited Velkova to come live in San Diego; they married at the county clerk's office that December. The newlyweds moved in with Holder's older brother, Seavenes Jr., now a divorced alcoholic who occupied a dreary, motel-like apartment wedged between an elementary school and a freeway junction. Holder covered his share of the rent with money from his Social Security disability checks; a psychiatrist at the halfway house had diagnosed him with post-traumatic stress disorder, characterizing the combat-related ailment as "the root cause of his psychological problems."

Holder promised both Violetta and Seavenes Jr. that he would find work to supplement his disability payments. But Holder wildly overestimated his value to employers. He initially hoped to parlay his military experience as a flight engineer into a job at an aerospace company, but such firms had no interest in hiring a confessed hijacker. He also investigated the possibility of attending law school, even though his only academic credential was the high school equivalency diploma he had earned in prison. The only job Holder could land was at a hospice, where he earned six dollars an hour mopping floors and emptying bedpans; he quit after a few weeks.

Frustrated by his lack of career options, Holder yearned for the days when the eyes of the world were upon him. A psychotherapist whom Holder saw as a condition of his parole noted that he was "stuck in the 1970s, perhaps with some idea of reliving the times and reconciling his part in history." In conversations with strangers and acquaintances, Holder spun colorful yarns about his adventures while on the lam. But few people believed that a disabled, unemployed ex-convict had ever walked the halls of Algeria's presidential palace or quaffed champagne with Jean-Paul Sartre.

On May 12, 1991, Holder attended a Joan Baez concert at a San Diego amphitheater. He talked his way backstage after the show, and Baez greeted him with a hug and warm words. But rather than lift Holder's spirits, this encounter with his old friend from Canisy reminded him just how far he had fallen. Holder began to loathe himself for doing nothing to change the world.

To blot out his misery, Holder resorted to a steady diet of alcohol and marijuana. He soon flunked a drug test administered by his parole officer, who warned Holder that he was in danger of landing back in prison. But Holder kept on using, often buying weed from a man with whom he shared an intimate connection: Marvin Bullock, the brother of his adulterous ex-wife, Betty.

Several people advised Holder against hanging out with Bullock, whose rap sheet listed twenty-five arrests, primarily for selling and possessing drugs. But Holder was too wrapped up in self-pity to heed his friends' counsel. He smoked and drank with Bullock, who was a receptive audience for his tales of Algiers and Paris. During one of these two-man parties in June 1991, a stoned Holder mentioned something startling: he wanted to hijack another plane and donate the ransom to the African National Congress, Nelson Mandela's political party.

Holder could not have picked a worse confidant: Bullock had been a police informant for fifteen years.

Bullock immediately tipped off his handler at the California Department of Justice, Special Agent Michael Coleman. Given Holder's history, Coleman could not dismiss the hijacking proposition as mere fantasy. He alerted the FBI and ordered Bullock to wear a wire to his subsequent encounters with Holder.

On June 18 Holder and Bullock met to discuss the hijacking further. Holder drew the same bomb diagram he had shown the crew of Western Airlines Flight 701, and he described his proven method for tricking people into thinking that he had armed accomplices. Bullock urged Holder to consider using a real bomb this time, pointing out that the authorities were unlikely to be fooled by the same ploy twice. Holder said he would think it over.

Three days later Bullock told Holder that he knew a guy who sold AK-47s and plastic explosives. "I'm more interested in the plastic explosives," said Holder. "I'm gonna make body bombs . . . Try to beat him out of as many blasting caps as you can."

The conversation then turned to where Holder could take the hijacked plane. Holder said that it would be important for him to declare his political objectives during the flight, as this would strengthen his case for asylum wherever he landed. He mentioned Germany or the Middle East as possible destinations, adding that he had befriended members of the Red Army Faction and the Palestine Liberation Organization while living in France.

On the morning of June 26, Bullock swung by Holder's apartment and told him that he had arranged a lunch meeting with the arms dealer—a Mexican named Dave who had ties to the Tijuana underworld. For the first time, Holder became suspicious of Bullock's eagerness. He declined to attend the lunch, explaining that he didn't yet have enough money to buy the explosives. But Bullock wouldn't take no for an answer: "We got to go ahead and go through with this thing. 'Cause I got this hooked up and everything, man. I don't want to back out."

A few hours later the two men drove to the Brigantine Seafood Restaurant, a popular tourist spot on Shelter Island. As soon as Holder entered the Brigantine's brick-walled dining room, he knew that something was amiss. Dave was already there, occupying one of the semicircular booths near the bar. He wore a blazer despite the summer broil. He didn't strike Holder as the sort of man who knew his way around military-grade explosives.

At the square table opposite the booth, four clean-cut men in preppy vacation garb were sipping Cokes and iced teas. Holder pegged them for undercover cops.

After settling into the booth, the apprehensive Holder refused to remove his sunglasses or order any food. Dave—a California Department of Justice agent whose real name was David Torres—was the one to break the ice.

"Marvin brought you to me because you need some things, yes?"

Holder only nodded. The less he said, the better.

Torres said that he had reviewed the diagram that Holder had made for Bullock, and he praised its sophistication. He assured Holder that his associates in Tijuana would have no problem supplying the materials necessary to build the device. They just had to discuss the issue of money; Torres said he wanted five hundred dollars for a brick of C-4 explosives.

Holder sheepishly admitted that he was flat broke. But even if he had a few bucks to spare, how did he know that Dave's price would be best? "I want to look around, see what else is on the market," he said warily.

But Torres started to get pushy. "I'm sure we can work something out," he insisted, stressing that he would be happy to accept a small deposit, then wait for the balance until the project was complete.

Holder felt cornered. He stammered a bit as he said that he could probably scrape together one hundred dollars by the following week.

Torres seemed pleased. He was just curious about one thing.

"Now, tell me—what is it that you want to blow up?"

"Nothing really," Holder replied cagily. "Just doing some ballistics."

Torres asked several more times what Holder planned to do with the explosives, but Holder never let down his guard. At the meeting's end, the two men agreed to discuss the matter further over the phone, using the code word "boat putty" to refer to explosives.

Two days later Holder noticed a suspicious van parked down the street from his apartment. He sneaked out the back and drove his fifteen-year-old Pontiac Grand Prix to Santa Barbara for the weekend. The men in the van, agents with the California Department of Justice, did not inform their superiors that Holder had given them the slip.

Holder finally called Torres on July 1. He said he was backing out of their deal because he had already bought some "boat putty" from a source in Santa Barbara.

The following afternoon, concerned that Holder might have gotten his hands on some C-4, the FBI raided his apartment and placed him under arrest. The agents found no weapons, though they did discover a bulletproof vest. They also seized the first thirty-one pages of a new memoir that Holder had been writing. Its tentative title was *Terror by Fiat.*

|||

ELEVEN MONTHS WOULD pass before Holder got his day in court. He was first sent back to New York to face charges that he had violated his parole by conspiring to hijack a plane. He was represented pro bono by Susan Tipograph, a friend and colleague of Lynne Stewart. Tipograph had famously defended William Morales, the alleged leader of Puerto Rico's Armed Forces of National Liberation, as well as Black Liberation Army members responsible for killing two policemen during a 1981 armored-car robbery.* She was drawn to Holder's background with the Black Panthers.

At Tipograph's request, Holder was sent to a federal prison hospital in North Carolina to receive a psychiatric evaluation. He was examined by three doctors, who diagnosed him with a range of possible ailments: post-traumatic stress disorder, drug and alcohol dependence, panic disorder, bipolar disorder, even paranoid schizophrenia "with grandiose and persecutory delusions." All agreed, however, that Holder was competent to stand trial.

On June 2, 1992, Holder was finally brought before Judge Eugene Nickerson of the U.S. District Court for the Eastern District of New York. The prosecutor in the case, assistant U.S. attorney Jason Brown, was stunned by the skyjacker's feeble appearance. Like Holder's daughters, Brown had expected an intimidating figure, the sort of man whose physique and demeanor would inspire fear among a flight crew. But Holder was frail and bookish, and he looked a decade older than his nearly forty-three years.

This guy, this docile guy, is supposed to be some big-time political terrorist? Brown thought.

Based on what he had heard on the tapes of Holder's conversations

*One of the robbers was Sekou Odinga, who had been a member of the Black Panther Party's International Section. He had been one of the last Panthers to leave Algiers, fleeing to Egypt in September 1972 after Holder was named head of the organization.

with Marvin Bullock and David Torres, Brown knew he had a tricky case on his hands. Bullock, in particular, had egged Holder on to an unseemly degree. Shortly after the meeting at the Brigantine, for example, Holder had clearly told his ex-brother-in-law that he no longer wished to do business with Torres—"I'm out of it," he had said emphatically. But Bullock had countered that the explosives were already en route from Mexico, and that both he and Holder would be in serious trouble if they reneged on their commitment. This threat had caused Holder to backtrack just enough to keep the sting operation going.

Brown gamely argued that Holder was still a threat to public safety, but Tipograph's claims of entrapment were more persuasive. "Each time Holder resisted participating with the informant and the undercover agent, they pressured him to participate in or admit to the crime," Judge Nickerson wrote in his ruling. "There is no credible evidence that Holder ever discussed any plans to commit a terrorist act with anyone other than these government agents. . . . Nor has [the government] shown that Holder himself had the criminal intent to have violated a condition of his release by conspiring to commit a terrorist act."

Judge Nickerson ordered that Holder be released at once and allowed to return to San Diego. But he also cautioned Holder that the legal system would not be so lenient if he ever again flirted with the idea of recapturing past glory.

18

ERASED

THE FINAL PRICE tag for ending America's skyjacking epidemic exceeded the airlines' wildest fears. In 1977, after a few quiet years in the nation's skies, a University of Chicago economist named William Landes attempted to quantify the cost of the calm. Based on data culled from the airlines and the FAA, Landes calculated that the cost of deterring a single hijacking was as high as $9.25 million—or put another way, $219,221 per passenger spared the agony of becoming a hostage. "Although the mandatory screening program is highly effective in terms of the hijackings prevented," Landes concluded, "its costs appear enormous."

But there was little the aviation industry could do aside from grouse about the fiscal inconvenience. The American public seemed to rather like hijack-free travel; airline ridership increased by 25 percent between the start of universal physical screening and the publication of Landes's study. And the government is always loath to rescind security measures once they've been put in place.

The metal detectors and X-ray machines were by no means foolproof. In the last years of the 1970s, a few skyjackers slipped through the system: a disturbed Army veteran tried to hijack a United Airlines jet to Memphis, only to surrender at the Denver airport after the pilots jumped from the cockpit; a former mental patient was arrested in Portland after threatening another United plane with a fake bomb and demanding that the airline pay his outstanding debts; a seventeen-year-old girl with road flares strapped to her chest commandeered a TWA flight en route to Kansas City, in a futile attempt to free an imprisoned skyjacker who had been her mother's lover.

Then, in the early 1980s, there were two minor outbreaks that were reminiscent of the epidemic's earliest phase: thirteen planes went to Havana in 1980, and another twelve in 1983. But these outbreaks were explicable anomalies rather than portents of a skyjacking revival. Nearly all the perpetrators were Cubans who had come to the United States during the Mariel Boatlift of 1980 and had decided to return home after struggling to find work or running afoul of the law. They mostly targeted small commuter flights in South Florida, so there was little anxiety in the country at large. And once Fidel Castro started to send these hijackers back to the United States to face prosecution, the outbreaks abated and the "virus" failed to spread. After the brief spike of 1983, the number of skyjackings once again dwindled to one or two per year, carried out with comic ineptness by the mentally unwell.

The contagion lost its power partly due to America's growing trepidation of the Muslim world, where hijacking remained a favored tactic of militants. The Iran hostage crisis, which lasted from 1979 to 1981, convinced millions of Americans that radical Islam was a paramount threat. That mind-set was only reinforced two years later, when Islamic Jihad suicide bombers killed 241 American servicemen in Beirut. Then in 1985 members of Hezbollah seized a TWA flight bound from Cairo to London, seeking the release of hundreds of their imprisoned brothers-in-arms. The hijackers murdered a U.S. Navy diver who was on the flight, and they held dozens of passengers hostage for two weeks. The episode's iconic photograph depicted the plane's fifty-eight-year-old American pilot, a ruggedly handsome Korean War veteran, leaning out the cockpit window while one of his swarthy young captors held a gun to his head. In the American imagination, that photo forever rebranded skyjacking as an alien crime; the virus could not get its hooks into a population that now equated hijacking with the ambitions of a despised and enigmatic foe.

After 1991 skyjacking disappeared entirely from America's aviation landscape: over the next nine years, not a single commercial flight was seized in American airspace. As the skyjacking threat grew more remote with each passing year, airlines came to view security as an expensive nuisance ripe for trimming. They doled out contracts to private firms that submitted absurdly low bids; those firms, in turn, routinely provided less personnel than promised, or hired screeners whose only training consisted of watching twenty-minute instructional videos. By 2000 the average salary of an airport security officer was just $12,000.

The airlines saw no reason to update their hijacking policies, which remained unchanged from the mid-1960s. Crew members were still instructed to offer hijackers their complete cooperation, on the assumption that such compliance would ultimately save lives. A hijacked crew's main directive was to connect their captors with officials on the ground so that negotiations could commence. The airlines had every confidence that open dialogue would always lead to peaceful resolution.

No one in a position of authority fathomed a scenario in which skyjackers would have no interest in using their hostages as bargaining chips.

A MOMENT AFTER pressing Roger Holder's buzzer for the first time, I noticed that his apartment building's security gate was ajar. I nudged it open right as Holder was rounding the stucco wall at the entranceway's rear. He was wearing a purple shirt unbuttoned to the sternum, dark-blue Levi's, and black cowboy boots embroidered with floral patterns. He was taller and skinnier than I had imagined, with legs that loped in deep, graceful strides. His sleepy eyes and broad nose were much more prominent in real life than in photographs.

"I'm sorry, your—your gate here was already open," I stammered, unsure of what to expect from an aging skyjacker dressed like a Reagan-era lothario.

Without saying hello, Holder inspected the gate's bolt and knob, which seemed to operate to his liking. "Well, you always did remind me of a burglar," he said, before beckoning me toward his ground-floor apartment with a flick of his head.

Holder's place was cramped but tidy, with a collection of antique baskets nailed to the breakfast nook's wall. Though the living room's one window was open to the street, the air reeked of cigarette smoke; an abalone-shell ashtray was overflowing with Pall Mall butts. After offering me coffee and a deflated croissant, Holder showed off his Dell desktop computer and asked if I could help him set up the printer he had recently acquired; he was eager to get serious about finishing his memoirs.

Locating Holder had been a frustrating affair. After his release from federal custody in 1992, his name seldom showed up in public records—he was never arrested, never bought property, never seemed to hold a job. For many months, all I could unearth was a string of disconnected phone numbers and invalid addresses. His lawyers in the United States and France, his comrades from Vietnam, his Black Panther associates from Algeria—no one knew what had become of him. I only managed to find him thanks to a series of happy accidents—a bureaucrat's failure to redact a Social Security number, Holder's decision to update his voter registration, a letter that reached its mark despite being addressed to the wrong apartment.

Holder hadn't left much of a paper trail because his life after 1992 had been remarkably sedate. When he returned to San Diego after the government's conspiracy case fell apart, he discovered that Violetta Velkova had gone back to France and his brother Seavenes Jr. had moved to Sacramento. He used his disability payments to rent a tiny flat and occasionally worked as a day laborer. Seeing that Holder was struggling to get by, a shady acquaintance offered to employ him as a male escort, a job that paid far better than painting houses. Holder declined.

In November 1993 Holder attended a Thanksgiving dinner hosted by a friend of a friend. A fellow guest named Joy Gentilella, a health aide and mother of five originally from New England, offered him a ride home. Gentilella had just gotten out of a bad marriage and wasn't looking to start anything new. But she was drawn to Holder's keen intelligence and off-kilter sense of humor. That weekend she and Holder went on their first date, an excursion to the beach. By Christmas, Holder had moved in to Gentilella's place—the first of several apartments the couple would share over the years.

The loving Gentilella took care of all the couple's financial needs, leaving Holder free to fill his days much as he had in Paris and Canisy: he chain-smoked Pall Malls during long strolls, built model helicopters, and jotted notes for his memoirs. Sometimes he brought vagrants home, to feed them and regale them with his musings on geopolitics. He drank a fair bit, too, to tamp down the anxiety that often overran his thoughts, but he never lost control—he was too afraid of disappointing Joy, who eventually took Holder's surname even though they never married.

Holder tried several times to patch things up with his daughters, but he could never get past their bitterness; whenever he approached them to make amends, Teresa and Torrita would remind him that he had chosen Angela Davis over his own flesh and blood.* But Holder did reconcile with his mother, Marie: when she fell gravely ill in 1994, she moved in with Joy and Roger. She remained with them until her death the following year, having achieved some small insight into her second son's eccentric life.

Holder left the TV blaring as we sat down to talk that late-August morning in San Diego. As we chatted, he smoked in a curious manner, keeping three Pall Malls in play at all times; he would take a drag off one, stub it out, then move on to the next. "I quit for a long time, but I started back up last year," he said apologetically, aware that the room's tobacco haze was making my eyes water.

We spoke for many hours, stopping only to refill our mugs with

*Torrita has had legal problems of her own: in 2008, for example, she was sentenced to fifteen months in prison for robbing a San Diego bank.

coffee and heaping spoonfuls of sugar. We went through his story step by step, starting with his happy childhood memories of accompanying his father to the Norfolk shipyards. Whenever we came to a painful moment—the grisly death of his friend Stanley Schroeder in Vietnam, his first wife's betrayal—Holder would remove his eyeglasses and thoughtfully rub his chin and mouth before proceeding. But he was seldom shy about answering questions that conjured up raw emotions: he spoke frankly about his regrets over the way things had ended with the Army ("I've never been able to forgive myself for that"), the carnage he had seen and caused in Vietnam ("Death was mostly what I did"), and his lasting disdain for Eldridge Cleaver and the International Section ("The only thing I saw with the Panthers was that all of them were afraid to die for how they felt").

While explaining his opaque motives for the hijacking, Holder expressed deep resentment toward Angela Davis. In a May 1996 interview with *Essence* magazine, Davis had discussed his attempt to free her: "During my trial, someone hijacked a plane, demanded to be flown to Algeria and demanded that I be released and brought to the airport, wearing a white dress and carrying ten parachutes or something like that. The judge put us all under house arrest inside the courthouse. They thought that this was my way of escaping before the verdict came down."

Holder had interpreted Davis's recollection as a slight. She seemed to think he was a fool, unworthy of having his name enshrined in her memory. Where was her appreciation for all he had sacrificed?

I asked, of course, a good deal about Cathy Kerkow. The first time I mentioned her name, Holder smiled crookedly as he swore that he wasn't responsible for her disappearance—"I didn't leave her in some closet in France, I can tell you that much." Holder was obviously accustomed to being accused of having murdered Kerkow, something that upset him greatly given his lingering feelings for his Operation Sisyphus accomplice.

"Cathy, she was definitely on the ball," he said. "She was

beautiful—too beautiful, too beautiful. About the hottest piece of ass you've ever seen! And this chick, she had a brain on her, and she knew how to use it. She even did all her own sewing. She was the kind of woman a man wouldn't mind working seven days a week for. . . . I wish she was available so I could spend the rest of my life taking care of her."

When I returned the next morning to continue the conversation, I arrived in Holder's neighborhood a few minutes earlier than planned. As I pulled off the freeway onto North Park Way, I was surprised to see Holder sitting beneath an ash tree in an empty drugstore parking lot, savoring a Pall Mall and staring off into space. This was, I would learn, one of his favorite pastimes, a crude form of meditation during which he revisited more glamorous days. No one who passed Holder's humble curbside perch would ever guess that this reedy, pensive man had once hijacked a plane to Algiers.

Later that day Holder shared some pages from his fragmentary memoir, now titled *Eli and the 13th Confession.* (He improbably claimed not to know that this was also the title of a famous Laura Nyro album.) He hadn't managed to write many chapters that lasted more than a few paragraphs—concentration was not his strong suit. He had, however, completed a prospective table of contents. The chapter about his relationship with Kerkow was to be called "Season of the Witch," a title that seemed at odds with the loving sentiments he had expressed the day before.

I asked Holder whether this meant that Kerkow had been a malevolent force in his life. He had once viewed their Coos Bay connection as a sacred sign that they were meant to do something spectacular together; did he now consider it an omen that he should have steered clear?

As was his custom when confronted with a difficult question, Holder removed his eyeglasses and rubbed his face. Then he walked to the living room window and peered outside cautiously; he seemed to be concerned that an eavesdropper might be crouching on the building's shabby lawn. As he scanned the grass below, I noticed that the tag on his Levi's listed a slender waist size of 30, yet the jeans were still slipping down his withered frame.

"You know, I still haven't gotten over all this," he muttered as he returned to his seat and tried to light a stubbed-out Pall Mall. His hands were shaking, and he had trouble with the lighter's flint wheel. He appeared to be fighting back tears.

I decided to take a more direct approach: "If you could go back and make the choice again, do you think you would still go through with the hijacking?"

For the first time since we had met, Holder turned visibly angry. "There's no way to determine that, sir!" he barked as he jammed his unlit cigarette back into the ashtray. He had refused to let either a French judge or American prosecutors strip him of his personal mythology; there was no way he was going to express contrition to the likes of me.

After his dark mood passed, though, Holder sounded a slightly more confident note about the hijacking's righteousness: "I just did something everybody else was too scared to do."

At the end of my week in San Diego, as JetBlue's check-in kiosk was printing out the boarding pass for my flight home, I received a call from Joy Holder. "I know Roger didn't say anything about this," she said, "but I thought you should know this, that you should understand—I don't know how much longer Roger has."

She explained that Roger had undergone triple bypass surgery in 2009, and that the procedure had almost killed him. He had subsequently been diagnosed with two inoperable brain aneurysms. His doctors had told Joy that Roger would be lucky to last a year.

So that's why he had started smoking those Pall Malls again. There was no reason not to.

Over the next few months Holder and I talked regularly. He was floored when I told him about the September 2011 arrest of George Wright, the fifth member of the Hijacking Family, who had been living in Portugal under the pseudonym Jose Luis Jorge dos Santos;

Holder asked me to keep him apprised of developments in Wright's fight against extradition.* He also wanted me to put him in touch with two other members of the Hijacking Family, Melvin and Jean McNair, who now operate an orphanage in Caen, France. He hadn't spoken to them in over thirty years.

But a rekindled friendship with the McNairs was not to be. Just before Christmas in 2011, Holder was hospitalized in poor health. On February 6, less than two weeks after his release from the hospital, Joy came home from work one evening to find him sitting in their living room, holding a butcher's knife. "I don't want to live anymore," he said.

Joy took away the knife and told Roger to get some rest in the adjoining bedroom—they would make a psychiatric appointment in the morning.

A few hours later Joy heard a loud thud. She rushed into the bedroom to discover Roger lying facedown on the carpet, the apparent victim of a burst aneurysm. He was sixty-two years old.

Holder's obituary in *The San Diego Union-Tribune* was literally just a single line, noting only the dates of his birth and death and the funeral home responsible for his body. Joy honored Roger's last request by having him buried in a military cemetery.

SEVERAL YEARS AGO the Coos County Historical Society decided to honor Patricia Kerkow as one of the town's pioneering women. She certainly deserved the award after so many decades of distinguished service to the community. She had raised four children by herself while working at such important local institutions as Southwestern

---

*A Portuguese court declined the U.S. extradition request in November 2011, on the grounds that Wright was a legitimate Portuguese citizen despite his longtime use of an alias. Wright had obtained his citizenship through circuitous means: in 1980, he moved from Lisbon to the African nation of Guinea-Bissau, a former Portuguese colony, where the government granted him political asylum. When he later married a Portuguese woman, he was able to seamlessly transfer his citizenship from Guinea-Bissau to Portugal.

Oregon Community College, the Weyerhaeuser pulp and paper company, and the Coos Bay Police Department. Kerkow also organized trips for ElderWise, served on the board of the First Community Credit Union, and managed the office of a Methodist church. The whole town regarded her with the utmost respect.

Kerkow was grateful for the historical society's recognition, but she made a request before agreeing to take part in the celebration: she asked that no mention be made of her fugitive daughter, and that any materials related to the hijacking of Western Airlines Flight 701 be removed from the society's archives.

Coos Bay has heeded Patricia Kerkow's evident wish to induce collective amnesia about Cathy. The town reveres another figure from the Marshfield High School Class of 1969, runner Steve Prefontaine, who perished in an auto accident at the age of twenty-four; tales of his splendid athletic feats and tragic death still pepper the conversations at Coos Bay's stores and taverns. But mention his track teammate Cathy Kerkow to a lifelong resident, and you'll elicit nothing more than a blank stare. Even men who grew up playing street football with Kerkow's brothers have no recollection of her existence, let alone her crime.

The FBI has not entirely forgotten about Kerkow, but its investigation stalled long ago. In the years following Kerkow's 1978 disappearance, agents would periodically contact her parents, on the off chance they had heard from her and might be providing her aid. But the FBI eventually became convinced that Kerkow would never reach out to her family; the parental interviews ended in the late 1980s. (Kerkow's father, Bruce, passed away in 2001.)

Beth Newhouse, Kerkow's best friend and roommate in San Diego, last heard from the FBI in 1991. She was living in a Seattle suburb at the time, working for Alaska Airlines and raising two children with her straitlaced husband; her wild youth was long behind her. Newhouse was distressed to be reminded of Kerkow after so many years; she worried that Alaska would fire her if the airline learned of her connection to a wanted skyjacker.

The FBI agent was surprisingly forthcoming about the sorry state of the investigation. He confessed that he and his colleagues were stumped; their only recent lead was a tip that Kerkow had become so fluent in French that she could pass for a native, and that she may have mastered other European languages, too. The agent begged Newhouse for any scrap of information she could provide.

But Newhouse had nothing to offer aside from a suggestion that Kerkow might have died while on the run. It was the only explanation she could muster for why her best friend had never tried to contact her again after proposing that ludicrous hashish-for-guns swap in 1972.

Newhouse's hypothesis is one of the few plausible theories regarding Kerkow's fate. If Kerkow did succeed in obtaining an American passport while in Switzerland, as the State Department seems to believe, she could have skipped off to any corner of the globe. But given her taste for the finer things in life, Kerkow would not have settled in a country where creature comforts are scarce. Contrary to persistent rumors, then, she did not flee to Havana, where a small community of fugitive American skyjackers still live openly. Nor did she follow in the footsteps of other International Section members by moving to Tanzania or Guinea-Bissau, where her skin color would have made her too much of a curiosity.

Kerkow could have slipped back into the United States with a valid passport, but it is difficult to imagine that she would have returned without asking friends or family for help—something she never did, according to both the FBI and confidants like Newhouse. Besides, forced exile had proven to be a blessing for Kerkow, a woman who had always been vaguely dissatisfied with her given circumstances—a condition inherited from her musician father, who had turned his back on cloistered Coos Bay. She never gave any indication that she pined for her rejected life.

The likeliest scenario is that Kerkow returned to France after obtaining false documents in Switzerland, then melted into French society under an assumed name. Perhaps she married a wealthy boyfriend, who arranged for her to obtain French citizenship and relocate to a provincial town where she would attract little notice. The French police could not be trusted to track her down; they had, after all, been totally unaware of her move from Algiers to Paris until Roger Holder foolishly blabbed his true identity. After a few years of adjusting to her new milieu, Kerkow would have become indistinguishable from those around her.

There is also a possibility that Kerkow opted for a more nomadic and exciting life abroad. She could have journeyed from Switzerland to West Germany, Italy, or even the Netherlands, all places where her movie business friends worked in the late 1970s, making soft-core films about sexual liberation. As the FBI noted to Newhouse, Kerkow's language skills were so sharp that she could have thrived almost anywhere in Europe.

Then there are darker outcomes to consider: a misadventure with drugs; a catastrophic illness; a car accident in the Alps that produced an unclaimed body. Any such tragedy would explain why Kerkow never tried to contact figures from her Oregon days.

But I prefer to imagine Cathy Kerkow as having achieved the sort of radical reinvention that eluded most of her fellow skyjackers—a version of the American dream that some can attain only by leaving America behind. I picture her as a dignified French woman in her early sixties, her once-lustrous hair now short and streaked with gray. She and her retired husband occupy a well-appointed house in a sleepy hamlet a few hours' drive from Paris, where they also own a pied-à-terre. They have always been a very private couple, though Kerkow has told a few neighbors that she moved to France as a small child, after her late American father was transferred by his company. Her grown children, now with families of their own, were baptized at the local church; they know nothing of their mother's criminal history and clandestine rebirth.

This Kerkow of my daydreams rarely pauses to reflect on how a rash decision made in the bloom of youth led to such unexpected bliss. But every so often, her thoughts can't help but wander to the pain she caused those left behind: the brothers she helped raise, the bohemian father who pursued his own path, the mother who sacrificed so much for her children. And in those fleeting moments, she understands that however much we might wish to sever ourselves from the past, ties of blood and memory remain. Even the most rebellious soul cannot be immune to that human truth.

Acknowledgments

To adequately express my gratitude to each and every person who made this endeavor possible would require a good ten thousand words, if not more. Rather than bore you in such a manner, let me instead apologize to all deserving parties who go unmentioned in the note below. I respectfully ask that you understand my predicament, and I beseech you to drop me a line if you feel slighted; I will do my best to make things right at the Queens Boulevard drinking establishment of your choice.

My greatest thanks must go to the men and women who invited me into their homes to share memories of the events in question: Roger Holder, Joy Holder, Elizabeth Olson, William Newell, Thomas Crawford, Jan Thompson, Edward Richardson, and Rosemarie Wilson. Without their boundless generosity, this slice of American history might have forever been lost.

Several other angelic folks went above and beyond to enrich my research: Louis DeWitt, Russ Mitchell, Randy Dotinga, Denis de Kergorlay, Jay Farr, Dennis Krummel, Susan Tipograph, Regina Youngren, Carlyn Juergens, Hannah Cooney, the Coos Bay Public Library, Ronald Dellinger, Marla Waarvick, Carole Friske, Donna Jones, Dick Deeds, Richard DeLorso, Billy Hamblin, Lindsey Sherline, and Miriam Chotiner-Gardner at Crown.

I never would have finished this labor of love without the aid of editors and colleagues who patiently supported my work these past few years. I owe an enormous debt to the entire *Wired* crew, particularly my wise overseers Robert Capps, Caitlin Roper, and Jason Tanz. Evan Ratliff and The Atavist provided me with an opportunity to hone my narrative chops in the most awesome way imaginable. And special thanks to Spike Lee, a peerless artist who gave me a master class in storytelling.

Though I have been writing for a living since the last millennium,

I am still not adept at dealing with the job's inevitable frustrations. Without the benevolence of friends and family, who were always quick to offer reassuring words when needed, my laptop would now be in a landfill: Ta-Nehisi Coates and Kenyatta Matthews, Ryan "Ulf" Nerz, Nathan Thornburgh, Jason Fagone, Jeff "Daddy Like" Kulkarni and the Fresh Produce team, Doug Merlino, Robert Galligan, Tom Folsom and Lily Koppel, Bird by Bird, Jonathan Green, Pat Walters, Loukas Barton, Michael Kunizaki, Matthew Williams and Zoe Vice, Ben Robbins, Nick Thompson, Thomas Beug, Molly Blooms, the Microkhan commentariat, and Jacki and David (oenophilic Angels fans nonpareil). An extra-gargantuan dollop of appreciation goes to my mother and father, who could not have been more supportive upon realizing that I wished to spend my life writing tales; I can only hope to provide my own progeny with the same amount of loving encouragement.

My advocates in the business realm, Zoë Pagnamenta and Matthew Snyder, have tirelessly labored on my behalf. I am lucky to have such brilliant and diligent pros in my corner.

It is difficult for me to imagine working with any book editor aside from Vanessa Mobley, who has helped me spin straw into gold a zillion times. She is a true genius with words and structure, as well as a saint for putting up with my frequent bouts of self-doubt. I can hardly wait to start another project under her aegis.

The last paragraph can only belong to my beloved Courtney, the Grand Empress to my Genghis. Many moons ago, when I followed her off the 1 train at 23rd Street, I opened the conversation by asking, "So what are you doing in my neighborhood?" The answer, of course, was that she was there to change my life.

Notes

Prelude

1 *no interest in food*: Willie Roger Holder, interview by author, Aug. 2011.

1 *discuss now is money*: Willie Roger Holder, interrogation by FBI, Jul. 2, 1991, handwritten notes (obtained through Freedom of Information Act request).

1 *generous payment plan*: Judge Eugene H. Nickerson, memorandum and order, *United States of America v. Willie Roger Holder*, May 29, 1992, National Archives and Records Administration, Central Plains Region, St. Louis, Mo.

1 *get things moving*: Special Agent David Torres, California Department of Justice, affidavit, Jul. 2, 1991 (FOIA).

1 *"want to blow up?"*: Nickerson, memorandum and order.

1. "Keep Smiling"

3 *in twenty-five minutes*: Ronald Dellinger, interview by author, Aug. 2010.

3 *polka-dot scarves*: Carole Friske (formerly Clymer), interview by author, Aug. 2010.

4 **forgot about his voucher**: Regina Youngren (formerly Cutcher), interview by author, Aug. 2010.

4 *"Read these"*: Regina Cutcher, written statement to FBI, June 2, 1972, private collection of William Newell.

6 *"don't stop!"*: Both notes were obtained from the FBI through a Freedom of Information Act request.

6 **In here**: Youngren interview.

6 *headed for the cockpit*: Regina Cutcher, written statement.

6 *wobbled even more*: Marla Waarvick (formerly Smith), interview by author, Aug. 2010.

6 *an urgent matter*: Donna Jones, written statement to FBI, June 2, 1972, private collection of William Newell.

7 *"need to read these!"*: Regina Cutcher, written statement.

7 *what he was doing*: Thomas Crawford, interview by author, Oct. 2010.

7 *"he wants us to do"*: Regina Cutcher, written statement.

7 *less than a month*: Edward Richardson, interview by author, Aug. 2010.

8 *hijacked in the United States*: FAA, Civil Aviation Security Service, "Hijacking Statistics for U.S. Registered Aircraft (1961–Present)," April 1, 1975, https://www.ncjrs.gov/pdffiles1/Digitization/28885NCJRS.pdf.

8 *strictly by coincidence*: Ned Glick, "Hijacking Planes to Cuba: An Updated Version of the Birthday Problem," *American Statistician* 24, no. 1 (Feb. 1970), 41–44.

8 *any organic pathogen*: Robert T. Holden, "The Contagiousness

of Aircraft Hijacking," *American Journal of Sociology* 91, no. 4 (Jan. 1986), 874–904.

9 ***commandeered the era's planes***: "On Return from Cuba, an Arrest for '68 Hijacking," *New York Times*, Oct. 11, 2009.

10 ***in American history***: At the time, some news reports contended that the Western Airlines Flight 701 hijacking was only the second longest in American history, behind the hijacking of Braniff Airways Flight 14 on July 2, 1971. However, this claim was clearly erroneous. The Braniff plane was hijacked in Houston, then taken to Monterrey, Mexico; Lima, Peru; Rio de Janeiro; and Buenos Aires, for a total distance of 6,846 miles as the crow flies. The Western Airlines hijackers, by contrast, logged 7,262 miles in the air. It is not clear why some reporters made this mistake, but it may have been due to a misunderstanding as to the exact location of Monterrey.

11 ***life without parole***: "Fruitless War Against Crime in the Air," *Life*, Dec. 29, 1972, 82–83.

2. Coos Bay

12 ***water in her wake***: Willie Roger Holder, interview by author, Aug. 2011; "Hijack Suspects 'Expect to Be Killed Off,'" *Oregonian* (Portland, Ore.), Aug. 8, 1972.

12 ***their standard magic***: Holder interview.

12 **know him from somewhere**: Ibid.

13 ***there could be trouble***: Elizabeth Olson (formerly Newhouse), interview by author, May 2011.

14 ***knew it very well***: Holder interview.

14 ***Art Deco centerpiece***: Author's visit, May 2011. Special thanks to the Coos Historical and Maritime Museum for its materials regarding the region's twentieth-century history.

15 ***dredging company by trade***: *Polk's Coos Bay and North Bend City Directory, 1958* (R. L. Polk & Co., 1958), 130.

15 ***jazz organist instead***: Holder interview; Olson interview; "What's Happening: Nightlife," *Daily News* (Port Angeles, Wash.), Jun. 28, 1974.

15 ***on the rocks***: Olson interview.

15 ***Seavenes Holder***: Seavenes Holder, U.S. Navy service record (service no. 8344312), National Personnel Records Center, St. Louis, Mo.

15 ***a Navy lifer***: Ibid.

15 ***fond of pointing out***: Holder interview.

15 ***the western Pacific***: Seavenes Holder service record.

16 ***room all to himself***: Holder interview.

16 ***the Holders were black***: Rosemarie Wilson (formerly Holder), interview by author, Apr. 2012.

16 ***pigmentation any further***: Ibid.

17 ***to protect himself***: Holder interview.

17 ***might lose a testicle***: Wilson interview; "Portrait of a Hijacker," *Bulletin* (Bend, Ore.), Aug. 19, 1972. The *Bulletin* piece misidentifies the victim as Roger rather than Danny.

18 ***further racial harassment***: "Editorial," *Empire Charleston Builder* (Coos Bay, Ore.), Sept. 28, 1959.

18 ***Coos Bay any further***: Wilson interview.

19 ***less than three months***: Holder interview; Willie Roger Holder, *Eli and the 13th Confession* (unpublished memoir), 10–11, private collection of Joy Holder. Please note that the pagination for *Eli and the 13th Confession* is haphazard; Holder skipped over many numbers,

repeated others, and failed to number each and every page.

19 ***chase bohemian dreams***: Olson interview.

19 ***make ends meet***: *Polk's Coos Bay and North Bend City Directory, 1965* (R. L. Polk & Co., 1965), n.p.

19 ***beneath her placid surface***: Dennis Krummel, interview by author, Jun. 2011; Jay Farr, interview by author, May 2011; Olson interview; Holder interview.

20 ***meals to elderly shut-ins***: *Mahiscan 1965* (Marshfield High School yearbook), Coos Bay Public Library, Coos Bay, Ore.

20 ***made straight B's***: "Skyjack Suspect an All-American Girl," *Oregonian* (Portland, Ore.), Jun. 6, 1972.

20 ***the town's leading attorney***: Olson interview.

20 ***friend and classmate Prefontaine***: *Mahiscan 1968*, Coos Bay Public Library, Coos Bay, Ore.

20 ***hamburgers at Dairy Queen***: Krummel interview.

21 ***well outside their league***: Ibid.; Olson interview.

21 ***the coolest parties***: Olson interview.

21 ***a sawmill in Prineville***: "Ms. Kerkow Recalled as 'Hippie Type,'" *Bulletin* (Bend, Ore.), Jun. 8, 1972.

22 ***operate the cash register***: "Coos Girl's Hijack 'Unbelievable,'" *Oregon Journal*, Jun. 7, 1972; Olson interview.

22 ***shrimp in the spring***: "Skyjack Suspect an All-American Girl"; "Miss Kerkow Recalled as 'Hippie Type'"; Olson interview.

22 ***stuffed in her purse***: Olson interview.

22 ***as she had hoped***: Krummel interview.

23 ***for southern California***: Olson interview.

23 ***La Jolla's yachting elite***: Ibid.

23 ***Patricia would be appalled***: Elizabeth Newhouse (later Olson), interview by FBI, Jun. 4, 1972 (obtained through FOIA request).

23 ***run-down Hillcrest neighborhood***: FBI Special Agent in Charge, San Diego Field Office, memo to headquarters, Jun. 7, 1972 (FOIA).

24 ***rubbed and tugged***: Olson interview.

24 ***at a doctor's office***: Ibid.

24 ***touching the topless dancers***: Ibid.

24 ***suburban Spring Valley***: FBI Special Agent, San Diego, memo to headquarters.

24 ***only as Fast Eddie***: Olson interview.

25 ***to lewder diversions***: Holder interview.

25 ***still just seventeen***: Willie Roger Holder, U.S. Army service record (service no. 18910865), private collection of Joy Holder.

25 ***Teresa and Torrita***: Wilson interview.

25 ***ACR's contingent in Vietnam***: Willie Roger Holder service record.

25 ***to his infant daughters***: "California Marriage Index, 1960–69," Ancestry .com.

26 ***the elusive enemy***: CIA, *Intelligence Memorandum: Pacification in the Wake of the Tet Offensive in South Vietnam*, March 19, 1968, declassified, Vietnam Center and Archive, Texas Tech University, http://www.vietnam.ttu.edu/virtualarchive/items.php?item=0410688004.

26 ***hail of AK-47 fire***: Department of Defense, *The United States Army Presents: The 11th Armored Cavalry Regiment* (film), http://archive.org/details/gov.dod.dimoc.30249.

26 ***as long as possible***: Holder interview.

26 ***such improvised devices***: Jonathan Shay, *Achilles in Vietnam: Combat Trauma and the Undoing of Character* (New York: Scribner, 1991), 34.

27 *ten cents a joint*: Peter Brush, "Higher and Higher: American Drug Use in Vietnam," *Vietnam* 15, no. 4 (Dec. 2002).

27 *shake his survivor's guilt*: Holder, *Eli and the 13th Confession*, 6–9. The comrade of Holder's who suffered the brain injury actually survived; the man who died was Sgt. Emile Cole, a twenty-eight-year-old native of Baton Rouge, La.

28 *a sign of weakness*: Holder interview; Virtual Wall, casualty report for Pfc. Stanley A. Schroeder, www.VirtualWall.org/ds/SchroederSA01a.htm.

28 *atop his M113 perch*: Photograph, 11th Armored Cavalry's Veterans of Vietnam & Cambodia website, http://www.11thcavnam.com/rogues/rogues2.html.

28 *raising his daughters*: Wilson interview.

28 *Bullock's betrayal*: Holder interview; Photograph of Holder at Bien Hoa Airbase, 1969, private collection of Richard DeLorso.

28 *just east of Saigon*: Willie Roger Holder service record.

28 *with guns blazing*: First Lt. Peter B. Howson, "The Top Tigers," *Hawk*, Aug. 1969, 16–18.

29 *bullets found their marks*: Holder interview.

29 *Frantz Fanon*: Ibid; Wilson interview.

29 *fire in the field*: Billy Hamblin, interview by author, Apr. 2011.

29 *"business is good"*: "Firefly," *Hawk*, Nov. 1969, 12–13.

30 *spying for the North*: "Mystery of the Green Berets," *Time*, Aug. 15, 1969.

30 *vain and callous men*: Holder interview.

30 *demotion to private*: Ibid.

31 *wander into minefields*: "Soldiers Suffering Marijuana Reaction," *Palm Beach Post*, Oct. 13, 1969.

31 *"fabric of American society"*: "Song My GI's May Have Been on Marijuana," *Lodi* (Calif.) *News-Sentinel*, Dec. 4, 1969.

31 *"the first popular war"*: "Military Battles Against Drugs," *Spartanburg* (S.C.) *Herald Journal*, Jan. 2, 1972.

31 *search soldiers' footlockers*: "Cookie, Smidgen, Hunt Mary Jane Across Vietnam," *Herald* (Rock Hill, S.C.), Aug. 28, 1969.

31 *faithfully they had served*: "Military Battles Against Drugs."

31 *handed the maximum sentence*: Willie Roger Holder service record.

31 *because of their skin*: Joe Kolb, "Long Binh Jail Riot During the Vietnam War," *Vietnam*, Dec. 2004.

31 *"he gets nine months"*: Stewart Kellerman, "Soul Session in Vietnam," United Press International, Apr. 25, 1971.

31 *death with a shovel*: Kolb, "Long Binh Jail Riot."

32 *the Comancheros*: Willie Roger Holder service record.

32 *Fort Hood, Texas*: Ibid.; Holder interview.

33 *track him down*: Holder interview.

33 *masquerading as White*: FBI, background report on Willie Roger Holder, compiled Jun. 3–Jul. 31, 1972 (FOIA).

33 *dancing Hueys*: Holder interview. Holder told me that he used LSD exactly eight times.

34 *sweet young things*: FBI, background report on Holder.

34 *admitted his true identity*: Ibid.; Holder interview.

34 *something spectacular*: Holder interview.

3. "I Don't Want to Be an American Anymore"

35 ***describe truck thieves***: James A. Arey, *The Sky Pirates: The Complete, Authoritative Story of Aerial Hijacking, Describing What Has Happened and Why* (New York: Charles Scribner's Sons, 1972), 49–53. Conventional wisdom holds that the world's first skyjacking occurred in Peru in 1931, when revolutionaries commandeered a mail plane. But the story is apocryphal: it stems from an October 1961 *Family Weekly* article written by the purported victim of that hijacking, Byron D. Richards. As Richards admits in the somewhat pulpy story, he was given several days in which to decide whether to drop leaflets for the revolutionaries; he ultimately scared them into rescinding their request by claiming that the "hijacking" might cause the American military to invade.

36 ***these Cuban planes***: Ben Funk, "Mr. Harris's War with Castro," *This Week*, Oct. 14, 1961.

37 ***giant teenager to death***: "Airline Pilot Kills 15-Year-Old Boy Who Tries to Hijack His Airplane," *Tri-City Herald* (Pasco, Wash.), Jul. 7, 1954.

37 ***letter of the law***: Edward McWhinney, *Aerial Piracy and International Terrorism: The Illegal Diversion of Aircraft and International Law* (Dordrecht: Martinus Nijhoff, 1987), 79.

37 ***passage to Cuba's capital***: "Airliner Over Keys Hijacked and Returned," *Lodi* (Calif.) *News-Sentinel*, May 5, 1961.

37 ***Caribbean rival's treachery***: "Hijacker: Cuba Suspected Spying," *Miami Herald*, Nov. 7, 1975.

38 ***unlikely to be repeated***: "Airways 'Pirate' Is Puzzle," *Lewiston* (Me.) *Daily Sun*, May 3, 1961.

38 ***did eventually take place***: "Gift for Castro," *Time*, Aug. 4, 1961.

38 ***blinded for life***: "'Wild' Gunman Shoots Two on Airliner," *Pittsburgh Press*, Aug. 1, 1961.

41 ***lurid hijacking yarn***: The account of the Continental Airlines Flight 54 hijacking is primarily based on three sources: testimony in *Bearden v. United States of America*, Fifth Circuit Court of Appeals, Jun. 14, 1962; "Jet Hijack Hero Feared Youth Most," *St. Petersburg Times*, Aug. 5, 1961; and "The Skywayman," *Time*, Aug. 11, 1961.

41 ***"planned hijacking of aircraft"***: "Stop Flying Fools Is Kennedy Plea," *St. Petersburg Times*, Aug. 5, 1961.

41 ***"from the air lanes"***: *Congressional Record: Senate 1961* (U.S. Congress, 1961), 15411–14.

42 ***raise the issue again***: "Seek Federal Law Against Air Hijacking," *Daily Iowan*, Aug. 5, 1961.

42 ***independence against France***: "Wife Sees Hijacker as Nervous Worrier," *Spokane Daily Chronicle*, Aug. 10, 1961.

42 SKYJACKED TO HAVANA: "Pan Am Jet Skyjacked to Havana," *New York Daily Mirror*, Aug. 10, 1961.

42 ***a capital offense***: "Senate Votes Death Penalty in Air Hijackings," *Blade* (Toledo, Oh.), Aug. 11, 1961.

42 ***on September 5, 1961***: "Kennedy Signs Bill Stiffening Penalties for Plane Hijacking," *Lewiston* (Id.) *Morning Tribune*, Sept. 6, 1961.

42 ***by firing squad***: "Plane Hijackers Fall to Firing Squad in Cuba," *Mexia (Tx.) Daily News*, Sept. 17, 1961.

43 ***sections of their newspapers***: Clark Whelton, *Skyjack* (New York: Belmont/Tower Books, 1970), 36–37.

43 ***lack of political sovereignty***:

"Youth Forces Plane to Land," *Des Moines Register,* Sept. 2, 1965.

43 ***location and modus operandi***: "2 U.S. Sailors Menace 13 on Hawaii Plane," *Chicago Tribune,* Oct. 13, 1965.

43 ***disappointment in Havana***: "Airline Pilot Declines Trip to Cuba, Uses Fire Ax to Call Exile's Bluff," *Blade* (Toledo, Oh.), Oct. 27, 1965.

44 ***relaxed emigration policy***: "Gemini Team Beat Hijack," *Ottawa Citizen,* Nov. 18, 1965.

44 ***"hold his self-respect"***: "Texas Boy Still in Jail," *Reading Eagle,* Nov. 20, 1965.

44 ***"seemed like the answer"***: Elizabeth Rich, *Flying Scared: Why We Are Being Skyjacked and How to Put a Stop to It* (New York: Stein and Day, 1972), 97–98.

45 ***"freedom at least once"***: Anthony Bryant, *Hijack* (Fort Lauderdale, Fla.: Freedom Press International, 1974), 12.

45 ***to retrieve each plane***: "Aerial Hijacking: Big Business," *Press-Courier* (Oxnard, Calif.), Sept. 28, 1969.

45 ***evidence to the contrary***: Bryant, *Hijack,* 31–50.

45 ***forty pesos each***: "'Take Me to Cuba': Often They're Sorry," *Age* (Melbourne, Australia), Nov. 16, 1972.

45 ***flesh was stripped away***: Bryant, *Hijack,* 85–88.

46 ***he lost an eye***: "Sorry Now: Hijacker Says Cuba Is Living Hell," *Evening Independent* (St. Petersburg, Fla.), Apr. 27, 1977.

46 ***hanged himself in his cell***: "American Hijackers Find Life Drab in Unsympathetic Cuba," *Lewiston* (Me.) *Daily Sun,* Nov. 29, 1971.

46 ***dressed as a cowboy***: "'Cowboy' Rustles Jet for Flight to Cuba," *Pittsburgh Press,* Feb. 22, 1968.

46 ***study Communism firsthand***: "Plane Hijacker Seeks Asylum, Cuba Radio Says," *Press-Courier* (Oxnard, Calif.), Feb. 19, 1968.

46 ***delicately seasoned* frijoles**: "Nervous Hijacker Homesick for Cuba," *Sarasota Journal,* Dec. 4, 1968.

46 ***"I see no reason"***: "FAA Says There's No Way to Prevent Plane Hijacks," *Bulletin* (Bend, Ore.), Jul. 5, 1968.

47 ***extra vacation days***: David Phillips, *Skyjack: The Story of Air Piracy* (London: George G. Harrap & Co., 1973), 74. It was customary for airlines to give hijacked employees an extra week of paid vacation.

47 ***willing to find out***: "Historical Air Traffic Statistics, Annual 1954–1980," Research and Innovative Technology Administration, Bureau of Transportation Statistics, http://www.bts.gov/programs/airline_information/air_carrier_traffic_statistics/airtraffic/annual/1954_1980.html.

47 ***$360 million in 1967***: "Airlines View Earnings Decline," *New York Times,* Dec. 5, 1968.

47 ***his government post***: "Pan Am's Lobbyists Help," *Ocala Star-Banner,* Sept. 29, 1966.

47 ***"invasion of privacy"***: "FAA Says There's No Way to Prevent Plane Hijacks."

47 ***James Eastland of Mississippi***: "Pistol-Wielding Man Talked Out of Hijacking Airliner," *Spartanburg* (S.C.) *Herald Journal,* Jul. 14, 1968.

48 ***against capitalist decadence***: "Idea Proposed to Curtail Hijacking of Airliners," *Dispatch* (Lexington, N.C.), Jul. 11, 1968.

48 ***"lives of all on board"***: "'We've Got Another Hijacking' and Action Begins to Have Plane and Passengers Released," *New York Times,* Dec. 20, 1968.

49 ***"can't make Cuba"***: "Pilot Cards

Avoid Hijacking 'Babel,'" *Pittsburgh Press*, Jan. 26, 1969.

49 ***return of stolen planes***: "Hijacking Routine," *Lodi* (Calif.) *News-Sentinel*, Jan. 28, 1969.

49 ***"or rum daiquiris, sir?"***: "It Happened Last Night," *Middlesboro* (Ky.) *Daily News*, Mar. 21, 1968.

49 ***"there are no tragedies"***: "Handling Hijackings," *Pittsburgh Press*, Dec. 10, 1968.

50 ***"Czech peasant blouses"***: "What to Do When the Hijacker Comes," *Time*, Dec. 6, 1968.

50 ***tactic in their struggle***: "19 Years on the Run: A Hijack Suspect's Life," *New York Times*, Jul. 27, 1988.

50 ***war as a motive***: "Deserter Jacks Plane to Cuba," *Beaver County* (Ore.) *Times*, Jan. 25, 1969.

51 ***three-year-old son***: "Little Boy in Hijack Try Home," *Sarasota Journal*, Jan. 14, 1969.

51 ***can of bug spray***: "Pilot to Help Dutchess Teen Who Tried Hijack," *Evening News* (Newburgh, N.Y.), May 8, 1969.

51 ***for Marxist economics***: "Purdue Dropout Is Hijack Suspect," *Tri City Herald* (Pasco, Wash.), Jan. 10, 1969.

51 ***with his bare hands***: "Alleged Hijacker Was Green Berets Veteran," *Times-News* (Hendersonville, N.C.), Jan. 16, 1969. The hijacker in question, Robert "Reds" Helmey, vividly recounts the hijacking in his self-published memoir *The Lemon Dance: Tell Fidel El Rojo Is Coming*.

51 ***who knew the lyrics***: "Many Offer Ways to Foil Plane Hijackers," *Gettysburg Times*, Jan. 30, 1969; "Use Boxing Gloves to Stop Hijackings," *Tuscaloosa News*, Oct. 10, 1970.

51 ***discarded as too expensive***: "What We Can Do to Stop Skyjacking," *Spartanburg* (S.C.) *Herald-Journal*, Jun. 15, 1969. The article's author, John H. Shaffer, was then head of the FAA.

51 ***skies above South Carolina***: "Man Arrested in Hijack Try," *St. Petersburg Times*, Aug. 6, 1969.

51 ***Boeing 707 over Nevada***: "Ex–Panther Head in Skyjack Case," *Lawrence* (Kan.) *Daily Journal-World*, Jun. 21, 1969.

51 ***upon landing in Havana***: "Hijacker Sentenced to Fifteen Years," *Spartanburg* (S.C.) *Herald-Journal*, Oct. 6, 1970.

52 ***along for the ride***: "Greek Family of Four Pull Hijack in 'Name of Democracy and Freedom,'" *Herald-Tribune* (Sarasota, Fla.), Aug. 18, 1969.

52 ***capital of Damascus***: "U.S. Jet with 113 Hijacked to Syria by 2 Young Arabs," *New York Times*, Aug. 30, 1969.

52 ***Zionist Organization of America***: Leila Khaled, *My People Shall Live: The Autobiography of a Revolutionary* (London: Hodder & Stoughton, 1973), 125–28.

52 ***"engaged to the revolution"***: "'I Made the Ring from a Bullet and the Pin of a Hand Grenade,'" *Guardian*, Jan. 26, 2001; "The Arabs' No. 1 Lady Skyjacker," *Victoria* (Tex.) *Advocate*, Nov. 29, 1970.

52 ***for covert operations***: Khaled, *My People Shall Live*, 179–83.

53 ***or prosecute hijackers***: Convention for the Suppression of Unlawful Seizure of Aircraft, http://www1.umn.edu/humanrts/instree/hague1970.html.

53 ***potential "hijacker havens"***: Signatories to the Convention for the Suppression of Unlawful Seizure of Aircraft, http://www.icao.int/secretariat/legal/List%20of%20Parties/Hague_EN.pdf.

53 ***Cuban community***: Mark Feldman, interview by author, Aug. 2010.

53 ***"has just died out"***: "Hijacking

'Fad' May Have Died, FAA Says," *Evening Herald* (Rock Hill, S.C.), May 7, 1969.

54 "*'Send the wop,' they say*": Rich, *Flying Scared*, 128.

54 *250 rounds of ammunition*: "Anatomy of a Skyjacker," *Time*, Dec. 5, 1969.

54 *shots of Canadian Club*: "Hijacker Termed Gentlemanly, Mad," *Spokane Daily Chronicle*, Nov. 1, 1969.

55 *and Shannon, Ireland*: "Pilot Criticizes FBI's Action Here," *New York Times*, Nov. 2, 1969.

55 "*why are you arresting me?*": "Nuova Versione Sul Clamoroso Atto di Pirateria," *Il Corriere di Napoli*, Nov. 9, 1969.

55 "*like to marry him!*": "Minichiello Hero to Countrymen," *Times-News* (Hendersonville, N.C.), Nov. 8, 1969.

55 *perchè m'arresti?*: "Hijacker Subject of Italian Film," *Tuscaloosa News*, Dec. 6, 1969.

56 "*flew across the skies*": "Lex Romana," *Time*, May 3, 1971.

56 *a spaghetti Western*: Rich, *Flying Scared*, 138.

56 *cross the Atlantic*: "Would-Be Hijacker's Apology Too Late," Associated Press, Jul. 5, 2009.

57 *voicing opposition*: "Plane Hijacking Assailed by U.N.," *News and Courier* (Charleston, S.C.), Dec. 13, 1969.

57 *around the world*: Arey, *Sky Pirates*, 330–31.

4. Sweet Black Angel

58 *on Newport Avenue*: Willie Roger Holder, interview by author, Aug. 2011.

58 *whiff of the taboo*: Elizabeth Olson (formerly Newhouse), interview by author, May 2011; "Hijackers Traced to San Diego Area," *New York Times*, Jun. 5, 1972.

58 *girl from Coos Bay*: Holder interview.

59 *reedy Vietnam vet*: Elizabeth Newhouse (later Olson), interview by FBI, Coos Bay, Ore., Jun. 9, 1972 (obtained through FOIA request).

59 *con man at heart*: Olson interview.

59 *Holder as an Oreo*: Ibid.; Newhouse, FBI interview.

60 *his son's surrender*: Holder interview.

60 *its enlistees deserted*: "Vietnam War Produces Highest U.S. Desertion Rate," *Evening News* (Newburgh, N.Y.), Nov. 11, 1972.

60 *accept "bad papers"*: "Black Veterans: The Forgotten Victims of Vietnam," *Ebony*, Sept. 1974, 33–40.

61 *any further medical care*: Holder interview.

61 *visit his twin daughters*: Seavenes and Marie Holder, interview by FBI, San Diego, Calif., Jun. 3, 1972 (FOIA).

61 *place of their own*: Olson interview.

61 *who she was dating*: Patricia Kerkow, interview by FBI, Coos Bay, Ore., Jun. 4, 1972 (FOIA).

62 *much of her supply*: Olson interview.

62 *understanding of the Zodiac*: Newhouse, FBI interview; Holder interview.

63 *trial of Angela Davis*: Holder interview.

63 *Communist Party members*: "UCLA Teacher Is Ousted as Red," *New York Times*, Sept. 20, 1969.

63 *and Frederick Douglass*: Angela Davis, *Lectures on Liberation* (New York: New York Committee to Free Angela Davis, 1971), http://archive.org/details/LecturesOnLiberation.

63 "*and are proud of*": Catherine

Ellis and Stephen Drury Smith, eds., *Say It Loud: Great Speeches on Civil Rights and African-American Identity* (New York: New Press, 2010), 189.

64 ***multiple gunshot wounds***: "Abductors, Judge Slain in Shootout," *Palm Beach Post*, Aug. 8, 1970; "The Facts Behind the Angela Davis Case," *Human Events*, Jun. 17, 1972, 9–15.

64 ***tight-fitting wig***: "FBI Seizes Angela Davis in Motel Here," *New York Times*, Oct. 14, 1970.

65 ***in January 1971***: Bettina Aptheker, *The Morning Breaks: The Trial of Angela Davis* (Ithaca, N.Y.: Cornell University Press, 1999), 26.

65 ***the Ku Klux Klan***: "Defendant Kicks Attorney in Face," *Bangor* (Me.) *Daily News*, May 28, 1971.

65 ***the courtroom theatrics***: "Few Spectators at Magee's Trial," *New York Times*, Dec. 31 1972.

65 ***concept of force***: "Angela Davis Trial to Put San Jose on Map for Sure," *Tuscaloosa News*, Jan. 4, 1972.

65 ***"release Miss Davis"***: "The Kremlin See Angela Davis as an Angela of Communism," *Afro-American* (Washington, D.C.), Apr. 13, 1971.

65 ***teachings of Jesus Christ***: "The Communist Dairy Farmer Who Bailed Out Angela Davis," *Life*, March 10, 1972, 73.

66 ***"my life-long husband"***: "The Facts Behind the Angela Davis Case," 12.

66 ***directed only at him***: Holder interview.

5. "I'm Here and I Exist"

67 ***"the usual air traveler"***: James Arey, *The Sky Pirates* (New York: Charles Scribner's Sons, 1972), 241.

68 ***concern about one's luggage***: H. L. Reighard and John T. Dailey, *Task Force on Deterrence of Air Piracy: Final Report* (Washington, D.C.: FAA Office of Aviation Medicine, 1978), 58–60; "Airlines Screen for Skyjackers," *Washington Post*, Feb. 8, 1972.

68 ***or incendiary devices***: David H. Brown with John T. Dailey, *Nine/Eleven: Could the Federal Aviation Administration Alone Have Deterred the Terrorist Skyjackers?* (Bloomington, Ind.: AuthorHouse, 2004), 15–19.

68 ***offense at the intrusion***: Ibid., 20–21.

68 ***or narcotics charges***: Reighard and Dailey, *Task Force on Deterrence of Air Piracy*, 5.

68 ***done to prevent hijackings***: Brown and Dailey, *Nine/Eleven*, 28.

69 ***screening was in force***: Ibid., 23.

70 ***pay for their insolence***: "Jet Hijacker, Lured by Ransom, Captured in Capital," *New York Times*, Jun. 5, 1970.

70 ***kissed her goodbye***: "The $100 Million Skyjack," *Time*, Jun. 15, 1970.

70 ***National Airport***: "Skyjacker Beat Detector Test," *Gazette* (Montreal), Jun. 6, 1970.

71 ***light a match***: "Jet Hijacker, Lured by Ransom, Captured in Capital."

71 ***shot by the flight's captain***: "Airliner Copilot Killed," *St. Petersburg Independent*, Mar. 18, 1970.

71 ***"unfit to rule"***: "Jet Hijacker, Lured by Ransom, Captured in Capital."

72 ***"Never go alone"***: "The $100 Million Skyjack."

72 ***a populated area***: "Hijacked Jet Shadowed by Fighters," *Boston Globe*, Jun. 6, 1970.

72 ***shot out its landing gear***: "Jet Hijacker, Lured by Ransom, Captured in Capital."

72 ***since the hijacking began***: Roger Buchanan, "The Joy of Being Hijacked," *North American Review* 256, no. 4 (Winter 1971), 2–4.
73 ***his gun to fire***: Ibid.
73 ***from his busted nose***: "$100 Million Hijacker Lured to Capture by Phony Cash," *Boston Globe*, Jun. 5, 1970.
73 ***"he made it worse"***: "Hijacker's Discontent Is Traced to the Loss of His Job in 1963," *New York Times*, Jun. 5, 1970; "He Battled the 'System,'" *Windsor Star*, Jun. 5, 1970.
73 ***by his final hostage***: "Pictures on Board a Hijacked Plane," *Life*, Jun. 19, 1970, 30–31.
74 ***questions about its design***: "Castro Looks at the First Boeing 747 to Be Hijacked," *Ludington* (Mich.) *Daily News*, Aug. 1, 1970.
74 ***accomplice on board***: "Plane Diverted to Cuba by Hijacker Who 'Fooled' Pilot," *Warsaw* (Ind.) *Times Union*, Aug. 25, 1970.
74 ***calling him "nigger"***: "Hijacker Sentenced," *Lawrence Daily Journal-World*, Oct. 25, 1975.
74 ***with Pentagon ties***: "Nixon Jabs Congress," *St. Petersburg Times*, Sept. 12, 1970.
74 ***stretched back her cheekbones***: "'I Made the Ring from a Bullet and the Pin of a Hand Grenade,'" *Guardian*, Jan. 26, 2001.
75 ***planes' blackened wreckage***: News footage of Dawson's Field hijackings, http://www.youtube.com/watch?v=AVIj_RF-lp0 and http://www.youtube.com/watch?v=5de6fYWKDWU.
75 ***by executive order***: "Plea on Hostages Is Made by Rogers," *New York Times*, Sept. 9, 1970.
76 ***"assembled and trained"***: "The Nixon Announcement," *New York Times*, Sept. 12, 1970.
76 ***$80 million per year***: "Sky Marshals to Be Costly," *Gettysburg Times*, Sept. 16, 1970.
76 ***from forty-five feet away***: "For Sky Marshals, No Mace or Chemicals, It's Just Shoot to Kill," *Tuscaloosa News*, May 16, 1971.
76 ***first skyjacking czar***: "Nixon Names Gen. Davis to Head Hijacking Fight," *New York Times*, Sept. 22, 1970.
76 ***skyjacker before boarding***: "Use of Armed U.S. Guards Expected as FAA Sets Up Task Force on Hijacking," *New York Times*, Sept. 10, 1970.
77 ***probably wouldn't enjoy***: *Skyjacking: Hearing Before the Committee on Finance, U.S. Senate, Ninety-First Congress, Second Session, on H.R. 19444* (Washington, D.C.: U.S. Government Printing Office, 1970), 14–18.
77 ***drive instead of fly***: Ibid., 24–26.
77 ***lobbyist meddling***: "Air Tax Proposal Shelved," *St. Joseph* (Mo.) *News-Press*, Dec. 12, 1970.
77 ***favor of paying customers***: "Sky Marshal Program Falls Short of Expectations," *St. Petersburg Independent*, Jan. 21, 1972; "Sky Marshals Force May Be Trimmed," *Nashua* (N.H.) *Telegraph*, Jun. 17, 1971.
78 ***his adolescent angst***: "Youth Blames Parents, School for Hijacking," *Windsor Star*, Mar. 9, 1971.
78 ***in the Bahamas***: "Hijacker Flies to Bahamas via Miami, New York," *Palm Beach Post-Times*, May 29, 1971.
78 ***working on a kibbutz***: "Miner Seized in Hijacking," *Miami News*, Jun. 5, 1971.
78 ***death or dismemberment***: "Hijacked Victims Insurance," *Ocala* (Fla.) *Star-Banner*, Oct. 9, 1970.
80 ***cared about the war***: The account of the Gregory White hijacking is primarily based on four sources: "More Counts Planned in Skyjack-

ing," *Lubbock* (Tex.) *Avalanche-Journal*, Jun. 14, 1971; "Jet Hijacker Held Here on $200,000 Bail," *New York Times*, Jun. 13, 1971; "Passenger Slain in Hijack Effort," *Star-News* (Wilmington, N.C.), Jun. 13, 1971; and "U.S. Hijacker on Murder Charge," *Sydney Morning Herald*, Jun. 14, 1971.

80 ***"who have a ticket?"***: "Puzzling Problem," *Southeast Missourian*, Jun. 14, 1971.

81 ***thirty minutes later***: The account of the Richard Obergfell hijacking is primarily based on two sources: "Hijacker Killed by FBI Agent at Kennedy," *New York Times*, Jul. 24, 1971; and "Slain Hijacker Believed Trying to Fly to Girl," *Press-Courier* (Oxnard, Calif.), Jul. 25, 1971.

82 ***"and crews of aircraft"***: "Air Pirate Shot and Killed," *Spartanburg* (S.C.) *Herald-Journal*, Jul. 24, 1971.

84 ***but as a fool***: The account of the Paul Joseph Cini hijacking is primarily based on four sources: "Anatomy of a Skyjacker," *Gazette* (Montreal), Oct. 21, 1978; "Pilot Kayos Hijacker with Fire Ax," *Telegraph-Herald* (Dubuque, Ia.); "Convicted Hijacker Fighting One-Way Trip to Scotland," *Vancouver Sun*, Jun. 24, 1982; and "Canada Jet Crew Subdues Hijacker After 6 Hours," *New York Times*, Nov. 13, 1971.

84 ***of the Columbia River***: The FBI's records pertaining to the D. B. Cooper case are archived online at http://vault.fbi.gov/D-B-Cooper%20.

85 ***all the way through***: *Parachutist*, the official magazine of the U.S. Parachute Association, ran a detailed three-part series on the Cooper case in its May–July 2010 issues. The series is archived online at http://parachutistonline.com/category/tags/db-cooper.

85 ***"the System"***: "Skyjacker Made into Folk Hero," *Deseret News* (Salt Lake City, Ut.), Nov. 30, 1971.

85 ***"blow some minds"***: "Song, T-Shirt Mark $200,000 Hijacking," *Press-Courier* (Oxnard, Calif.), Jan. 7, 1972.

6. Operation Sisyphus

87 ***tickets to friends***: Willie Roger Holder, interview by author, Aug. 2011.

87 ***cheaper accommodations***: Elizabeth Olson (formerly Newhouse), interview by author, May 2011.

87 ***an alkaline battery***: *Guide to Selected Viet Cong Equipment and Explosive Devices* (Washington, D.C.: Department of the Army, 1966), 63.

87 ***Marie and Seavenes***: Seavenes and Marie Holder, interview by FBI, San Diego, Calif., Jun. 3, 1972 (obtained through FOIA request).

87 ***trying to forget***: Holder interview.

89 ***relatively mundane affair***: The account of the Allen Sims and Ida Robinson hijacking is primarily based on three sources: unpublished disposition in *Ida Patrice Robinson v. United States of America*, Ninth Circuit Court of Appeals, Jun. 17, 1991; "Boy Turns In Mother in Hijacking," *Los Angeles Times*, Mar. 25, 1987; and "Negro Couple Skyjack West Coast Jet to Cuba," *Gazette* (Montreal), Jan. 8, 1972.

89 ***with radio transmitters***: "Skyjacker a Colorado Oddity," *Denver Post*, Jan. 21, 2001.

89 ***"mental assistance instead?"***: "Ex-Paratrooper Is Held in Hijacking," *New York Times*, Jan. 22, 1972.

90 ***as a relief pilot***: "Trapnell Guilty

of Jet Hijacking," *New York Times*, May 17, 1973.

90 ***open-heart surgery***: "Skyjacker Owed Much in Medical Bills," *Gazette* (Montreal), Jan. 28, 1972.

90 ***"take off from my gate"***: "Airlines Screen for Skyjackers," *Washington Post*, Feb. 8, 1972.

90 ***been screened at all***: "Screen Passengers, Airlines Ordered," *Milwaukee Journal*, Feb. 1, 1972.

90 ***detectors among them***: Research and Innovative Technology Administration, Bureau of Transportation Statistics, "Historical Air Traffic Statistics, Annual 1954–1980," http://www.bts.gov/programs/airline_information/air_carrier_traffic_statistics/airtraffic/annual/1954_1980.html; "Funds Approved to Foil Hijackers," *Eugene* (Ore.) *Register-Guard*, May 22, 1972.

90 ***skipped screening altogether***: "Airlines Screen for Skyjackers."

91 ***valid photo identification***: "Still Holes in the Screening System," *New York Times*, Apr. 16, 1972.

91 ***at 12:55 p.m.***: "Bomb Found on Jet Here After $2 Million Demand," *New York Times*, Mar. 8, 1972.

92 ***searched the plane twice***: "A Threat to the Entire Airline System," *New York Times*, Mar. 12, 1972.

92 ***routinely been overlooked***: "Airline Threats Said Winding Down," *St. Petersburg Independent*, Mar. 11, 1972.

92 ***"met piracy in the air"***: "Nixon Vows Air Terrorism War," *Palm Beach Post*, Mar. 10, 1972.

92 ***let its customers die***: "U.S. Mobilizes Forces Against Air Terrorism," *Deseret News* (Salt Lake City, Ut.), Mar. 9, 1972; "President Orders Tighter Security by U.S. Airlines," *New York Times*, Mar. 10, 1972.

92 ***bomb plots and skyjackings***: "Airlines Offering $250,000 Reward," *Lawrence* (Kans.) *Daily Journal-World*, Mar. 17, 1972.

93 ***an unoccupied lavatory***: Elizabeth Rich, *Flying Scared* (New York: Stein and Day, 1972), 161–62.

93 ***"he wouldn't do it"***: "Airplane Hijackers, Why Do They Do It," *Afro-American* (Washington, D.C.), Feb. 4, 1969.

93 ***"480 times a day"***: William D. Davidson and Louise Fitzsimmons, "The Power of the Powerless," *Los Angeles Times*, May 28, 1972. This op-ed was reprinted from *Washington Post*.

94 ***"falling and being destroyed"***: David G. Hubbard, *The Skyjacker: His Flights of Fantasy* (New York: Collier Books, 1973), 31–37.

94 ***"aggressive act of their lives"***: "Psychiatrist Makes Study of Hijackers," *Ocala* (Fla.) *Star-Banner*, Aug. 13, 1970.

94 ***"psychology of the hijacker"***: "Perilous War on the Skyjacker," *Life*, Aug. 11, 1972.

95 ***flight with machismo***: Hubbard, *Skyjacker*, 230–31, 277–78.

95 ***their poor equilibrium***: Rich, *Flying Scared*, 68–69.

95 ***epidemics in the bud***: A. J. Riopelle, et al., "Vestibular Disorder and Space Utilization by Monkeys," *Orthomolecular Psychiatry* 9, no. 3 (Autumn 1980), 188–93.

95 ***sexually immature hijackers***: David H. Brown with John T. Dailey, *Nine/Eleven: Could the Federal Aviation Administration Alone Have Deterred the Terrorist Skyjackers?* (AuthorHouse, 2004), 27.

95 ***"bastards off the planes"***: "Perilous War on the Skyjacker."

96 ***air traffic controllers***: "Psychiatrist-Expert Says Media Fosters Hijackings," *St. Petersburg Times*, Jan. 31, 1972.

96 ***"skyjacker in all of us"***: Rich, *Flying Scared*, 79.

97 ***speak with the pilot***: David Shaw, "The Americanization of Ricardo Chavez-Ortiz," *Oui*, Dec. 1972.

98 ***would inspire copycats***: "Skyjacker: The Richard McCoy Jr. Story," *Parachutist*, Mar. 2011; "FBI Recovers $499,970," *New York Times*, Apr. 11, 1972.

99 ***world-weary face***: Shaw, "Americanization of Ricardo Chavez-Ortiz."

99 ***waterbed and little else***: "Hijackers Traced to San Diego Area," *New York Times*, Jun. 5, 1972.

100 ***to look for work***: Bruce Kerkow, interview by FBI, Seattle, Jun. 7, 1972.

100 ***aligned in their favor***: Holder interview.

100 ***"people of Indochina"***: "War Foe Arrives in Havana," *Pittsburgh Press*, May 6, 1972.

100 ***Marxist insurgents***: "A-B-E Hijacker Who Parachuted into Jungle Is Free from Prison," *Sunday Call-Chronicle* (Allentown, Pa.), Jun. 30, 1985; "Hijack Ransom Missing," *Boca Raton News*, Jun. 6, 1972.

101 ***boulder up a hill***: Holder interview.

101 ***"impressionable minds"***: "*Skyjacked* Ad Held Up," *Washington Post*, May 20, 1972.

101 ***aboard a hijacked jet***: "*Skyjacked* Continues Fast Box-Office Pace in Nation," *Afro-American* (Baltimore, Md.), Jul. 29, 1972.

102 ***masqueraded as an officer***: [Name redacted], passenger on Western Airlines Flight 701, interview by FBI, Queens, N.Y., Jun. 3, 1972 (FOIA).

103 ***"wear to a hijacking?"***: Holder interview; Seavenes and Marie Holder, FBI interview

103 ***was coldly rebuffed***: Olson interview.

103 ***Los Angeles to Hawaii***: [Name redacted], United Airlines ticket agent, interview by FBI, San Diego, Calif., Jun. 5, 1972 (FOIA).

103 ***sneaking through the exits***: Roger Holder, *Eli and the 13th Confession* (unpublished memoir), 146, private collection of Joy Holder.

104 ***killed by a booby trap***: Holder interview; Diane Edrington, interview by FBI, San Francisco, Jun. 2, 1971 (FOIA).

104 ***the very next morning***: [Name redacted], United Airlines station manager, interview by FBI, San Diego, Calif., Jun. 14, 1972 (FOIA).

104 ***the following morning***: Seavenes and Marie Holder, FBI interview.

104 ***blue Beachmates bikini***: [Name redacted], United Airlines baggage supervisor, interview by FBI, Honolulu, Hi., Jun. 4, 1972 (FOIA).

7. "There Are Weathermen Among You"

106 ***less than three hours***: Roger Holder, *Eli and the 13th Confession* (unpublished memoir), 57, private collection of Joy Holder.

107 ***her personal effects***: [Name redacted], United Airlines passenger services supervisor, interview by FBI, Los Angeles, Calif., Jun. 4, 1972 (obtained through FOIA request).

107 ***what to do next***: Holder, *Eli and 13th Confession*, n.p. Based on the book's sequence of events, this page should probably have been numbered 94.

107 ***that very day***: "Angela Davis' Trial Nears Jury," *Rome* (Ga.) *News-Tribune*, Jun. 2, 1972.

107 ***for additional screening***: [Name redacted], Western Airlines ticket agent, interview by FBI, Los Angeles, Calif., Jun. 2, 1972 (FOIA).

108 *their racial mismatch*: Holder, *Eli and 13th Confession*, 95.

108 *Sisyphus was a go*: Regina Cutcher (later Youngren), interview by FBI, San Francisco International Airport, Jun. 2, 1972 (FOIA).

108 *attracting unwanted attention*: Holder, *Eli and 13th Confession*, 131.

108 *"No harm done"*: Regina Cutcher (later Youngren), written statement to FBI, Jun. 2, 1972, private collection of William Newell.

108 *deviate from the plan*: Willie Roger Holder, interview by author, Aug. 2011.

109 *evasive maneuvering*: [Name redacted] of Bellevue, Wash., passenger on Western Airlines Flight 701, interview by FBI, John F. Kennedy International Airport, N.Y., Jun. 3, 1972 (FOIA).

109 *medical receptionist in San Diego*: FBI interview with [name redacted] of North Hollywood, Calif., passenger on Western Airlines Flight 701, John F. Kennedy International Airport, Jun. 3. 1972. Obtained through FOIA request.

109 *played quite shrewdly*: [Name redacted] of [city redacted], Calif., passenger on Western Airlines Flight 701, interview by FBI, John F. Kennedy International Airport, N.Y., Jun. 3, 1972 (FOIA).

109 *slipping away from him*: [Name redacted] of Bellevue, Wash., FBI interview.

109 *bullet on May 15*: FBI Identification Division, Latent Fingerprint Section, report to Special Agent in Charge, New York, N.Y., Jun. 9, 1972 (FOIA).

110 *rear of the plane*: [Name redacted] of Bellevue, Wash., FBI interview.

110 *"Read these"*: Regina Cutcher, written statement.

110 *for a few years*: Carlyn Juergens, interview by author, May 2010.

110 *pick the Boeing 727*: Thomas Crawford, interview by author, Oct. 2010.

111 *"need to read these!"*: Donna Jones, written statement to FBI, Jun. 2, 1972, private collection of William Newell.

111 *bare fists, if necessary*: Crawford interview.

111 *121.5 megahertz*: *Western Airlines Flight Operations Manual*, Section 7-16D through 7-19. Special thanks to former Western Airlines captain Louis DeWitt for sharing this resource.

112 *"someone get my luggage?"*: Edward Richardson, interview by author, Jun. 2010.

112 *nursing school instead*: Regina Youngren (formerly Cutcher), interview by author, Jun. 2010.

112 *destroy the plane*: Cutcher statement.

112 *"Peace"*: [Name redacted] of [city redacted], Wash., nineteen-year-old passenger on Western Airlines Flight 701, interview by FBI, San Francisco, Jun. 2, 1972 (FOIA).

113 *"I'm divorced"*: Crawford interview.

113 *"eight slabs of C-4"*: Communications between Western Airlines Flight 701 and Western Dispatch, transcript, private collection of William Newell. This transcript, which consists of cut-out snippets stapled to yellow graph paper, was given to Newell by Norman Rose, Western's director of flight control at the time of the hijacking.

113 *"Jerry Juergens"*: Thomas Crawford, interview by FBI, San Francisco International Airport, Jun. 3, 1972 (FOIA).

113 *trickling down his brow*: Crawford interview.

114 *"they're sitting at now"*: Crawford, FBI interview; Richardson interview.

114 *or they all died:* Richardson interview.
114 *"Roger":* Western Airlines Flight 701 communications, transcript.
115 *"find half a million":* Crawford interview.
115 *"We want five parachutes":* Norman Rose, Western Airlines director of flight control, handwritten note, Jun. 2, 1972, private collection of William Newell.
115 *"details when I have them":* Ronald Dellinger, interview by author, Aug. 2010.
115 *pockets for rosary beads:* Ibid.
116 *quickly passed out:* Donna Jones, interview by author, Jun. 2010.
116 *"anyone steps out of line":* Dellinger interview; Crawford interview; Steven Leatherwood, interview by FBI, San Francisco International Airport, Jun. 2, 1972 (FOIA).
116 *"Don't do anything funny":* Donna Jones, written statement.
117 *"Get it moving now":* [Name redacted], branch sales manager for Varian Data Machines, interview by FBI, San Francisco International Airport, Jun. 2, 1972 (FOIA).
117 *like rag dolls:* Dellinger interview.
117 *"getting what they want":* Crawford interview.
117 *check on her condition?:* Jones statement.
118 *"Can't possibly do it":* Crawford interview.
118 *"I want another airplane":* Ibid.
118 *"further instructions and info":* Western Airlines Flight 701 communications, transcript.
119 *"name of American justice":* "Angela Davis Case Goes to Jury Today," *Bryan* (Oh.) *Times*, Jun. 2, 1972.
119 *now finally under way:* "Jurors Weigh Davis Case," *Milwaukee Journal*, Jun. 3, 1972.
119 *see her immediately:* "Hijackers Demand Cash, Release of Angela Davis," *St. Petersburg Times*, Jun. 3, 1972.
120 *whisking her away:* "U.S. Kidnap Plan Said Foiled," *Gazette* (Montreal), Nov. 14, 1970.
120 *her shaken expression:* "Angela's Case Is in Jury's Hands," *Spartanburg* (S.C.) *Herald-Journal*, Jun. 3, 1972.
120 *even over the telephone:* "Kathleen Cleaver and Angela Davis: Rekindling the Flame," *Essence*, May 1996.
120 *"Angela Y. Davis' freedom":* "Hijackers Demand Cash, Release of Angela Davis."
121 *for a military operation:* Dellinger interview.
121 *to decline a glass:* Cutcher, FBI interview.
121 *singled out for murder:* Jones interview.
122 *Alka-Seltzer tablets:* [Name redacted], Navy ensign serving aboard the USS *Lynde McCormack*, interview by FBI, San Francisco, Jun. 2, 1972 (FOIA); [name redacted] of Bellevue, Wash., passenger aboard Western Airlines Flight 701, handwritten observational notes, Jun. 2, 1972 (FOIA).
122 *"to be review ASAP":* Willie Roger Holder, handwritten note, Jun. 2, 1972 (FOIA).
123 *find that information useful:* Cutcher, FBI interview; Cutcher statement.
123 *"gets me right":* Holder, *Eli and 13th Confession*, 131; Donald Thompson, interview by FBI, Queens, N.Y., Jun. 4, 1972 (FOIA).
123 *public address system:* Cutcher, FBI interview.
123 *"Roger, stand by":* Western Airlines Flight 701 communications, transcript.
124 *lack of parachutes:* Crawford interview.

124 *"a couple of minutes"*: Western Airlines Flight 701 communications, transcript.

124 *"she got acquitted today"*: Crawford interview.

124 *done on her behalf?*: Holder interview.

125 *"Roger"*: Western Airlines Flight 701 communications, transcript.

8. "Can't You Get a Chopper?"

126 *hung above his desk*: Thomas Crawford, interview by author, Oct. 2010.

126 *his young bride's hair*: William Newell, interview by author, Sept. 2010.

127 *in suburban San Mateo*: Ibid.

127 *main terminal's fourth floor*: FBI, "Critique of Hijack of Western Airlines 727, Jun. 2, 1972," Jun. 9, 1972 (obtained through FOIA request).

127 *items on a folding table*: Ibid., Newell interview.

127 *he declined to reveal*: "Hijack Ransom Missing," *Boca Raton* (Fla.) *News*, Jun. 6, 1972.

127 *comply with the hijackers*: FBI, "Willie Roger Holder, aka; Catherine Kerkow; Crime Aboard Aircraft—Air Piracy; Kidnapping," San Francisco, Jun. 5, 1972 (FOIA).

128 *at least two more hours*: [Name redacted], vice president of Centralized Services Office, Bank of America, interview by FBI, San Francisco, Jun. 2, 1972 (FOIA).

128 *to make some calls*: Newell interview.

128 *between Honolulu and Hanoi*: Airliners.net, data section, aircraft range information.

129 *to be his co-pilot*: Jan Thompson, interview by author, Sept. 2010.

129 *would be his flight engineer*: "Pilot Opposes Force Against Hijackers," *San Diego Evening Tribune*, Jun. 19, 1972.

129 *"going on a trip"*: Donald Thompson, interview by FBI, Queens, N.Y., Jun. 4, 1972 (FOIA).

129 *"in a couple of minutes"*: Communications between Western Airlines Flight 701 and Western Dispatch, transcript, private collection of William Newell.

130 *"regards to this country"*: Ibid.

130 *evidence of a kidnapping*: Edward Richardson, interview by author, Jun. 2010.

130 *jet had been delivered*: Jerome Juergens, interview by FBI, Millbrae, Calif., Jun. 2, 1972 (FOIA).

131 *enable an FBI ambush*: Regina Youngren (formerly Cutcher), interview by author, Jun. 2010.

131 *aboard a full flight*: Newell interview.

132 *"They mean business"*: Western Airlines Flight 701 communications, transcript.

132 *bomb in their midst*: Ronald Dellinger, interview by author, Aug. 2010; Donna Jones interview by FBI, San Francisco International Airport, Jun. 2, 1972 (FOIA).

132 *at 8:05 p.m.*: Western Airlines Flight 701 communications, transcript.

132 *he so desperately craved*: Regina Cutcher (later Youngren), written statement to FBI, Jun. 2, 1972, private collection of William Newell.

133 *would be free to go*: Western Airlines Flight 701 communications, transcript.

133 *"Right"*: Crawford interview.

134 *more than thirty pounds*: [Name redacted], vice president at Centralized Services Office, Bank of America, FBI interview. The weight estimate is based on the fact that each bill, regardless of denomina-

tion, weighs approximately one gram.

134 *into a war zone*: Glenna MacAlpine, interview by FBI, at JFK International Airport, Jun. 3, 1972 (FOIA).

135 *aimed to use violence*: FBI, "Willie Roger Holder, aka; Catherine Kerkow; Crime Aboard Aircraft—Air Piracy; Kidnapping"; Newell interview.

135 *its way to San Francisco*: FBI, "Critique of Hijack of Western Airlines 727, Jun. 2, 1972."

9. "It's All a Lie"

136 *in order to land safely*: Ronald Dellinger, interview by author, Aug. 2010.

136 *flying in from Las Vegas*: Ibid.

136 *as he had instructed*: Communications between Western Airlines Flight 701 and Western Dispatch, transcript, private collection of William Newell.

137 *Holder agreed*: Donna Jones, written statement to FBI, Jun. 2, 1972, private collection of William Newell.

137 *the whole plane's attention*: Thomas Crawford, interview by author, Oct. 2010.

137 *three-quarters of the ransom*: "D. B. Cooper Case Inspired Copycat Hijackings in Reno," *Reno* (Nev.) *Gazette-Journal*, Nov. 22, 2011.

138 *to make the switch*: Western Airlines Flight 701 communications, transcript; FBI, "Willie Roger Holder, aka; Catherine Kerkow; Crime Aboard Aircraft—Air Piracy; Kidnapping," San Francisco, Jun. 5, 1972 (obtained through FOIA request).

138 *"it's almost run out"*: Crawford interview.

138 *"Roger"*: Western Airlines Flight 701 communications, transcript.

139 *with two colleagues*: FBI, "Willie Roger Holder, aka; Catherine Kerkow; Crime Aboard Aircraft—Air Piracy; Kidnapping."

139 *runway 19R immediately*: Western Airlines Flight 701 communications, transcript.

139 *endanger his passengers' lives*: William Newell, interview by author, Sept. 2010.

139 *"It isn't over"*: Donna Jones, interview by author, Jun. 2010.

140 *were about to depart*: Dellinger interview.

140 *hands atop their heads*: Newell interview.

140 *orders to the cabin*: Crawford interview.

140 *"Walk fast"*: Regina Cutcher (later Youngren), written statement to FBI, Jun. 2, 1972, private collection of William Newell.

140 *an appreciative smile*: Regina Youngren (formerly Cutcher), interview by author, Jun. 2010.

141 *urge to be a hero*: Jones interview.

141 *onto the tarmac*: Cutcher statement.

141 *Just go*: Willie Roger Holder, interview by author, Aug. 2011.

141 *a fellow military pilot*: FBI, "Willie Roger Holder, aka; Catherine Kerkow; Crime Aboard Aircraft—Air Piracy; Kidnapping."

141 *back to the 727*: Cutcher statement.

141 *over the left wing*: [Name redacted] of Phoenix, Ariz., passenger on Western Airlines Flight 701, interview by FBI, Queens, N.Y., Jun. 3, 1972 (FOIA).

141 *was free to go*: Crawford interview.

142 *"It's over"*: Cutcher statement.

142 *the universe's majestic plan*: Richard Luker, interview by FBI, Queens, N.Y., Jun. 4, 1972 (FOIA).

142 *"I'll let you know"*: William Newell, interview by FBI, JFK International Airport, Jun. 4, 1972 (FOIA).
142 *jet with cannon fire*: Roger Holder, *Eli and the 13th Confession* (unpublished memoir), 59, private collection of Joy Holder.
143 *"Algiers"*: Newell interview.

10. The Choice

144 *the capital of Algeria*: William Newell, interview by author, Sept. 2010.
145 *transatlantic travel*: Ibid.
145 *any hint of deception*: Richard Luker, interview by FBI, Queens, N.Y., Jun. 4, 1972 (obtained through FOIA request).
145 *expecting them for supper*: Western Airlines Flight 364 cockpit communications, audio recording, private collection of Jan Thompson.
145 *any further FBI meddling*: FBI, "Willie Roger Holder, aka; Catherine Kerkow; Crime Aboard Aircraft—Air Piracy; Kidnapping," San Francisco, Jun. 5, 1972 (FOIA).
145 *end on American soil*: Ronald Dellinger, interview by author, Aug. 2010.
146 *until sleep overcame her*: [Name redacted] of Phoenix, Ariz., passenger on Western Airlines Flight 701, interview by FBI, Queens, N.Y., Jun. 3, 1972 (FOIA).
147 *Holder was acting alone*: Luker, FBI interview.
147 *sit there all alone*: Ibid.
148 *into the scrub*: "D. B. Cooper Case Inspired Copycat Hijackings in Reno," *Reno* (Nev.) *Gazette-Journal*, Nov. 22, 2011.
148 *for their FBI debriefings*: Regina Youngren (formerly Cutcher), interview by author, Jun. 2010.
148 *named Willie Roger Holder*: [Name redacted], passenger on Western Airlines Flight 701, handwritten observational notes, Jun. 2, 1972 (FOIA).
148 *in the Army dress uniform*: Numerous FBI interviews I obtained consisted of only a paragraph or two, in which the agent noted that the interview subject was either intoxicated or hadn't witnessed anything of value.
148 *as four black radicals*: "Four Hijack Jet in West," *Bangor* (Me.) *Daily News*, Jun. 2, 1972.
149 *"a five-year-old's vocabulary"*: "Hijacker of Seattle Plane Is Algiers Bound in Another Jet," *Seattle Times*, Jun. 3, 1972.
149 *with open arms*: Newell interview.
149 *to avoid basic training*: Carol Nizzi, interview by author, October 2010.
149 *the idea of Algiers*: William Newell, interview by FBI, at JFK International Airport, Jun. 4, 1972 (FOIA).
149 *"they want me to do"*: Luker, FBI interview.
149 *rather than New York*: Newell, FBI interview.
150 *"I'll let you know"*: Dellinger interview.
150 *the pitch-black sky*: [Name redacted] of Phoenix, Ariz., FBI interview.
150 *Brown readily agreed*: Newell, FBI interview.
150 *killed Richard Obergfell*: Luker, FBI interview.
151 *"Let's go!"*: Communication between Western Airlines Flight 364 and JFK International Airport control tower, Jun. 3, 1972, transcript, private collection of William Newell.
151 *equipment for the operation*: FBI, memorandum regarding contact between agents and Capt. William

Newell, JFK International Airport, Jun. 6, 1972 (FOIA).

152 *to no avail*: Luker, FBI interview.

152 *"you understand?"*: Western Airlines Flight 364 communications with Kennedy tower, transcript.

152 *the disguised FBI agent*: FBI memorandum regarding contact between agents and Captain Newell.

152 *orders weren't obeyed*: Luker, FBI interview.

153 *exit was still sealed*: [Name redacted], passenger on Western Airlines Flight 701/364, interview by FBI, Downey, Calif., Jun. 6, 1972 (FOIA).

154 *made her choice*: Dellinger interview; Glenna MacAlpine, interview by FBI, JFK International Airport, Jun. 3, 1972 (FOIA).

154 *released thirty hostages*: Newell interview.

154 *Flight 364's captain*: FBI memorandum regarding contact between agents and Captain Newell.

154 *toward Jones Beach*: Western Airlines Flight 364 communications with Kennedy tower, transcript.

155 *"two armed bombs aboard"*: Luker, FBI interview.

155 *caring about the cold*: Willie Roger Holder, interview by author, Aug. 2010; Willie Roger Holder, *Eli and the 13th Confession* (unpublished memoir), 171, private collection of Joy Holder.

156 *had escaped their notice*: Newell interview; Luker, FBI interview.

156 *stock of Kerkow's figure*: Richard Banks, interview by author, Jun. 2010.

156 *Coca-Cola from a can*: Holder, *Eli and 13th Confession*, 151.

156 *"turn him on"*: Richard Wood, interview by author, Jul. 2010.

156 *destination than Algiers*: Newell interview.

156 *"go to Geneva?"*: Ibid.

156 *"give me amnesty?"*: Luker, FBI interview.

157 *Flight 364's every move*: The KC-135 is mentioned twice in the folder of documents that Western Airlines director of flight control Norman Rose gave to William Newell: once in the transcript of a communication between the Western dispatch center in Los Angeles and an unspecified party, and once in a handwritten note evidently made by a member of TWA's flight operations staff. Newell was not told of the shadow aircraft until his return to the United States.

157 *Cuba of the Alps*: Newell interview; unknown Western Airlines official, handwritten note, private collection of William Newell.

157 *Airport at once*: FBI Legat Madrid to acting FBI director, Jun. 7, 1972 (FOIA).

158 *botching Operation Sisyphus*: Newell interview.

159 *"I want Eldridge Cleaver"*: Ibid.; Luker, FBI interview.

11. "We Are Going to Be Friends"

160 *on the first ballot*: "Cleaver of Black Panthers Is Nominee of Leftists," *New York Times*, Aug. 19, 1968.

160 *win the presidency*: Lee Lockwood, *Conversation with Eldridge Cleaver* (New York: Dell, 1970), 117.

160 *"innate gift of language"*: David Evanier, "Painting Black Cardboard Figures," *New Leader* 51, no. 7 (March 1968), 23–24.

160 *"formidably analytic mind"*: Julian Mayfield, "The New Mainstream," *Nation*, May 13, 1968.

161 *something from* King Lear: Eldridge Cleaver, *Soul on Fire* (Waco, Tex.: Word Books, 1978), 93–98.

161 ***"I talk too much"***: Lockwood, *Conversation with Cleaver*, 129.

161 ***another day in prison***: Kathleen Neal Cleaver and Susie Linfield, "The Education of Kathleen Neal Cleaver," *Transition* 77 (1998), 187–88.

161 ***of the presidential vote***: "1968 Presidential General Election Results," *Dave Leip's Atlas of U.S. Presidential Elections*, http://us electionatlas.org/.

161 ***the Ministry of Interior***: Cleaver, *Soul on Fire*, 142–43.

162 ***the Reuters story***: Henry Louis Gates, "Cuban Experience: Eldridge Cleaver on Ice," *Transition* 49 (1975), 32–44.

162 ***nickname for America***: Lockwood, *Conversation with Cleaver*, 54, 67.

162 ***five-hundred-dollar monthly stipend***: Taki Theodoracopulos, "Visiting with Eldridge Cleaver in the Casbah," *National Review*, Jul. 21, 1972, 793.

163 ***fans of Cleaver's work***: Cleaver, *Soul on Fire*, 143–44.

163 ***"under their jeeps"***: "Radio Hanoi Broadcasts Seale Talk," *Reading Eagle*, Sept. 9, 1970.

163 ***across state lines***: "Former Black Panther Patches Together Purpose in Exile," *Los Angeles Times*, Jan. 29, 2012.

163 ***a police informant***: "D. L. Cox, a Leader of Radicals During 1960s, Dies at 74," *New York Times*, Mar. 13, 2011.

163 ***refuge in Switzerland***: Telephone conversation between Eldridge Cleaver and Radio KFRC, Feb. 2, 1971, transcript, Eldridge Cleaver Papers, Bancroft Library, University of California at Berkeley.

164 ***"black in the sun"***: Cleaver, *Soul on Fire*, 149.

164 ***"genius command"***: Eldridge Cleaver, "Revolutionary New Year's Greetings to the 40 Million Heroic Korean People," n.d., Eldridge Cleaver Papers, Bancroft Library, University of California at Berkeley.

164 ***collection of Kim's speeches***: Kim Il-sung, *Juche! The Speeches and Writings of Kim Il-sung* (New York: Grossman, 1972).

164 ***"imagine what it costs"***: "The Exiles: Stokely Eased the Way to Kathleen Cleaver," *Afro-American* (Baltimore, Md.), May 20, 1972.

164 ***down from Marseilles***: Cleaver, *Soul on Fire*, 152–53.

164 ***the party's leadership***: U.S. Senate, Select Committee to Study Governmental Operations with Respect to Intelligence Activities, *The FBI's Covert Action Program to Destroy the Black Panther Party*, Apr. 23, 1976.

165 ***a half-million dollars***: Eldridge Cleaver to Michael Cetewayo Tabor, Sept. 24, 1972, Eldridge Cleaver Papers, Bancroft Library, University of California at Berkeley.

165 ***guiding him to Algiers***: Richard Luker, interview by FBI, Queens, N.Y., Jun. 4, 1972 (obtained through FOIA request).

165 ***"I can be free"***: "Pilot Says Hijacker Spoke of Freedom," *Milwaukee Journal*, Jun. 5, 1972.

165 ***"my own airline someday"***: Luker, FBI interview.

165 ***each crammed with soldiers***: Ibid.

165 ***interpreter by his side***: Willie Roger Holder, interview by author, Aug. 2011.

166 ***back into the cabin***: Luker, FBI interview.

166 ***settle for nothing less***: Willie Roger Holder, *Eli and the 13th Confession* (unpublished memoir), 176, private collection of Joy Holder.

166 **Like a runaway slave**: Ibid., n.p.

166 ***on the copper wire***: Holder interview.

166 ***search for additional bombs***: Wil-

liam Newell, interview by author, Sept. 2010.
166 *crew's excellent service*: Luker, FBI interview.
167 *return from Senegal*: Holder interview.
167 *Boumédiène's favorite assassin*: Robert Irwin, *Memoirs of a Dervish: Sufis, Mystics, and the Sixties* (New York: Profile Books, 2011), chap. 3.
167 *one of Hidjeb's aides*: Cleaver to Tabor.
167 *white hippie girlfriend*: Ibid.
168 *"where's the bread?"*: Ibid.
168 *off to a rocky start*: Holder interview.
168 *his phone number*: Cleaver to Tabor.
168 *"Nothing at all"*: "Algiers Hijackers Arrive," Associated Press Television, Jun. 3, 1972, http://www.aparchive.com/.
168 *disposable-razors box*: "Hijacker Directs Jetliner to Algeria," *Prescott* (Ariz.) *Courier*, Jun. 4, 1972; Holder, *Eli and 13th Confession*, 171.
169 *food since New York*: "Algeria Hijackers Arrive."
169 *the country at once*: Newell interview.
169 *the War of Independence*: Holder interview.
169 *stressful circumstances*: Holder, *Eli and 13th Confession*, n.p. The two pages that cover the Hotel Aletti casino episode are both marked "+4."
170 *room's lace curtains*: Ibid.; Holder interview.

12. "My Only Bomb Is My Human Heart"

172 *prison for decades*: Elizabeth Olson (formerly Newhouse), interview by author, May 2011.
173 *hijacker's hair as blond*: "Skyjack Suspect an All-American Girl," *Oregonian* (Portland, Ore.), Jun. 6, 1972.
173 *"something like this"*: "Hijackers in Algiers with $500,000 Ransom," *World* (Coos Bay, Ore.), Jun. 5, 1972.
173 *"three years ago"*: "Coos Bay Residents Stunned by Girl's Role in Hijacking," *Oregonian* (Portland, Ore.), Jun. 7, 1972.
173 *pleasures of marijuana*: "Miss Kerkow Recalled as 'Hippie Type,'" *Bulletin* (Bend, Ore.), Jun. 8, 1972.
173 *"want to be alert"*: "Coos Girl's Hijack 'Unbelievable,'" *Oregon Journal*, Jun. 6, 1972.
173 *"enough to be a hijacker"*: "Coos Bay Residents Stunned by Girl's Role in Hijacking."
173 *"crazy son would do"*: Rosemarie Wilson, interview by author, Apr. 2012.
174 *hijackers' political agenda*: Seavenes and Marie Holder, interview by FBI, San Diego, Jun. 3, 1972 (obtained through FOIA request).
174 *knew Holder from Vietnam*: "D. B. Cooper Case Inspired Copycat Hijackings in Reno," *Reno* (Nev.) *Gazette-Journal*, Nov. 22, 2011. The information regarding Heady's unit in Vietnam comes from an Internet forum posting that he made in February 2009. That posting has since been deleted.
174 *the hijacking of Flight 701*: "Angela Davis Acquitted," *Deseret News* (Salt Lake City, Ut.), Jun. 5, 1972.
175 *granted a private audience*: Willie Roger Holder, interview by author, Aug. 2010.
175 *phone line was dead*: Eldridge Cleaver to Michael Cetewayo Tabor, Sept. 24, 1972, Eldridge Cleaver Papers, Bancroft Library, University of California at Berkeley.
175 *had to be "processed"*: Ibid.

175 ***"Zionism or American imperialism"***: "Cash Hijacked for Causes," *Oregon Journal*, Jun. 9, 1972.

175 ***and his gorgeous wife***: Kathleen Cleaver and Canadian Broadcasting Company, acceptance contract, Apr. 14, 1969, Eldridge Cleaver Papers, Bancroft Library, University of California at Berkeley.

176 ***"billions from the people"***: "Hijacks Hailed by Panthers," *Spokane* (Wash.) *Daily Chronicle*, Jun. 14, 1972.

176 ***based on a single glance***: Holder interview. My description of the Algerian presidential palace, popularly known as El Mouradia, was aided by photographs found online at http://www.skyscrapercity.com/showthread.php?t=1181085.

176 ***"want to see your eyes"***: William Newell, interview by author, Sept. 2010.

177 ***"would be genuinely free"***: "Jet Crew Hijacked to Algiers Flies to L.A.," *Los Angeles Times*, Jun. 5, 1972.

177 ***avoid wounding passengers***: "U.S. Bids Airlines Stiffen Resistance to Hijackers," *New York Times*, Jun. 8, 1972.

178 ***North African country***: "Pilots' Union Plans Boycott of Nations That Provide Sanctuary for Hijackers," *New York Times*, Jun. 7, 1972.

178 ***the United States for prosecution***: "U.S. Bids Airlines Stiffen Resistance to Hijackers."

178 ***because of Holder and Kerkow***: "Pilots Call Strike in Hijack Protest," *Los Angeles Times*, Jun. 17, 1972.

178 ***"have to do something"***: "Pilots Halt Flights Abroad, but Strike Falters in U.S.," *New York Times*, Jun. 20, 1972.

179 ***as initially feared***: "International Flights Severely Hampered by Pilots' Strike to Protest Skyjacking," *Wall Street Journal*, Jun. 20, 1972.

179 ***"cooperative international efforts"***: Ibid.

179 ***"100 percent for motherhood"***: "U.N. Must Toughen Stand on Hijacking," *Deseret News* (Salt Lake City, Ut.), Jun. 22, 1972.

179 ***his parachute's rip cord***: "Sky Piracy Episode Smacks of Danger, Futility," *Chicago Tribune*, Jul. 2, 1972.

179 ***for the union's taste***: "Pilots' Group May Boycott Airports," *Los Angeles Times*, Jul. 2, 1972.

179 ***fundamental American right***: "Airline Pilots Set to Strike," *Spartanburg* (S.C.) *Herald*, Jun. 19, 1972.

180 ***leave their sight***: Holder interview.

180 ***the two young Americans***: Cleaver to Tabor.

180 ***"Students of Revolution"***: Holder interview.

181 ***the Algerian government***: Cleaver to Tabor.

181 ***the gentle waves***: Holder interview.

181 ***and his American wife***: Jean-Michel Caroit, interview by author, Jul. 2012.

181 ***the money was gone***: Cleaver to Tabor.

181 ***natural gas to the United States***: Holder interview; "Curbs Rescinded in Gas-Import Bid," *New York Times*, Oct. 5, 1972.

181 ***better than to complain***: FBI Legat Paris to acting FBI director, Jul. 14, 1972 (FOIA).

182 ***statue in Coos Bay***: Ibid.

182 ***was rightfully theirs***: Cleaver to Tabor.

182 ***badass revolutionary***: "Coos Bay Woman Would Sell Hijack Story," *Eugene Register-Guard*, Jul. 21, 1972.

182 ***Black Panthers to shoot***: Holder interview.

182 ***probably an FBI informant***: Jean McNair to Roger Holder, Mar. 24,

1972, private collection of Joy Holder.

182 ***John Dellenback***: "Dellenback Works on Kerkow Telephone Call," *World* (Coos Bay, Ore.), Jun. 7, 1972.

182 ***helped hijack Flight 701***: "Coos Bay Woman Would Sell Hijack Story."

183 ***access to skyjackers***: "Coos Girl Hijacker Seeks to Sell Story," *Oregon Journal*, Jul. 20, 1972.

183 ***"into darkness here"***: Olson interview.

185 ***all the world to see***: The account of the Nguyen Thai Binh hijacking is primarily based on four sources: "Plane's Captain Explain Thwarting Hijack," *Lewiston* (Id.) *Morning Tribune*, Jul. 3, 1972; "When Is Deadly Force Justifiable Against Hijackers," *Eugene* (Ore.) *Register-Guard*, Jul. 12, 1972; "Hijacker Killed in Saigon; Tried to Divert Jet to Hanoi," *New York Times*, Jul. 3, 1972; and "'My Only Bomb Is My Human Heart,'" *Peace Newsletter* (Syracuse, N.Y.), Aug. 1972, 9.

185 ***"without loopholes"***: "Pilot Urges Death Penalty to Curb Air Hijackings," *Bulletin* (Bend, Ore.), Jul. 7, 1972.

187 ***sitting next to his wife***: The account of the Michael Azmanoff and Dimitr Alexiev hijacking is taken from three sources: Tom Emch, "Anatomy of a Hijack," *California Living Magazine*, Sept. 17, 1972; "Skyjacking Foiled; 3 Slain," *Chicago Tribune*, Jul. 6, 1972; and "Three Die in Shootout," *St. Petersburg Independent*, Jul. 6, 1972. Special thanks to Becky Emch for sharing the excellent *California Living* story, which was written by her father.

187 ***"out there at the airport"***: "Fast and Harsh Justice Urged for Air Hijackers," *New York Times*, Jul. 10, 1972.

188 ***bullet on the brain***: "Lawman Gets Hijacker to Give Up," *Palm Beach Post-Times*, Jul. 8, 1972; "Hijacker Frightened Into Surrender by CHP Officer," *Los Angeles Times*, Jul. 7, 1972.

188 ***Western White House***: "Hijack Checks Extended to All Domestic Flights," *Afro-American* (Baltimore, Md.), Jul. 15, 1972.

188 ***loophole at once***: "Security Checks Ordered for Busy Shuttle Flights," *New York Times*, Jul. 8, 1972.

188 ***ended in surrender***: "Two Airliners Hijacked," *Ledger* (Lakeland, Fla.), Jul. 13, 1972.

188 ***"if my bill is adopted"***: "Senator Seeks Hijack Rein," *Pittsburgh Post-Gazette*, Jul. 21, 1972.

188 ***a vote of 75–1***: "Senate Backs Broad Curbs on Hijacking by 75–1 Vote," *New York Times*, Sept. 22, 1972.

188 ***a quiet death***: "Conferees Snag on Hijacking Bill," *New York Times*, Oct. 12, 1972.

13. "How Do You Resign from a Revolution?"

189 ***find other accommodations***: Eldridge Cleaver to Michael Cetewayo Tabor, Sept. 24, 1972, Eldridge Cleaver Papers, Bancroft Library, University of California at Berkeley.

189 ***dress shop owner***: "Mildred Klein, Fashion Shop Owner," *Ridgefield* (Conn.) *Press*, Dec. 8, 1994.

189 ***the Algerian government***: Frank J. Rafalko, *MH/Chaos: The CIA's Campaign Against the Radical New Left and the Black Panthers* (Annapolis, Md.: Naval Institute Press, 2011), 103.

190 ***on the Rue Viviani***: Cleaver to Tabor.

190 ***personal stash of weapons:*** Willie Roger Holder, interview by author, Aug. 2011.
190 ***with the Black Panthers:*** Ibid.
190 ***Trotskyite revisionism:*** Eldridge Cleaver, tape recorder notes, March 26–28, 1971, transcript, Eldridge Cleaver Papers, Bancroft Library, University of California at Berkeley.
190 ***America's inner cities:*** Eldridge Cleaver, Korea trip notebooks, 1970, Eldridge Cleaver Papers, Bancroft Library, University of California at Berkeley.
190 ***Watts Riots:*** Eldridge Cleaver, draft of speech to be delivered on Aug. 18, 1972, Eldridge Cleaver Papers, Bancroft Library, University of California at Berkeley.
191 ***admiring Zairian politician:*** Cleaver, Korea trip notebooks; Eldridge Cleaver, record of second meeting with Salah, Aug. 16, 1972, Eldridge Cleaver Papers, Bancroft Library, University of California at Berkeley.
191 ***"with $1 million":*** Cleaver to Tabor.
191 ***stuck in its chest:*** "Cleaver Calls on Algerian President to Keep Black Skyjackers' $1 Million," *Jet* 42, no. 21 (Aug. 17, 1972), 9.
191 ***a racist America:*** Melvin McNair et al., *Nous, Noirs Américains Évadés du Ghetto* (Paris: Editions de Seuil, 1978), 101.
191 ***"Fly Delta's Big Jet":*** "Skyjackers Get Million Ransom," *Gazette* (Montreal), Aug. 1, 1972.
192 ***all of them black:*** W. Martin Dunleavy, *Black Police in America* (Bloomington: Indiana University Press, 1996), 99.
193 ***parents were up to:*** McNair et al., *Nous, Noirs Américains Évadés du Ghetto*, 27–101.
193 ***without any interference:*** "Algerians Seize $1 Million Ransom," *New York Times*, Aug. 2, 1972; "Hijackers Told Delta Crew Fleeing 'Decadent America,'" *Sumter* (S.C.) *Daily Item*, Aug. 3, 1972.
193 ***prone to violence:*** Cleaver to Tabor.
194 ***to inspect the money:*** McNair et al., *Nous, Noirs Américains*, 103.
195 ***would win the day:*** Cleaver to Tabor.
196 ***"I couldn't say":*** "Hijack Suspects 'Expect to Be Killed Off,'" *Oregonian* (Portland, Ore.), Aug. 8, 1972.
197 ***additional screening:*** "Once More Into the Breach," *New York Times*, Aug. 6, 1972.
198 ***checked by hand:*** David J. Haas, "Electronic Security Screening: Its Origin with Aviation Security 1968–1973," *Journal of Applied Security Research* 5, no. 4 (Sept. 2010), 508–23.
198 ***$30,000 machines:*** Ibid.
198 ***they could tack on:*** "Once More Into the Breach."
199 ***thirty years in prison:*** The account of the Frank Markoe Sibley hijacking is primarily based on four sources: *United States of America v. Frank Markoe Sibley*, Ninth Circuit Court of Appeals, Apr. 27, 1979; "Stopping Mad Dogs," *Time*, Aug. 28, 1972; Dave Turner, ed., *Society of Former Special Agents of the FBI* (Paducah, Ky.: Turner Publishing, 1998), 51; and "Hijacker to Be Examined," *Spokane* (Wash.) *Daily Chronicle*, Nov. 28, 1972.
200 ***"whole of the American people":*** Eldridge Cleaver, *Soul on Fire* (Waco, Tex.: Word Books, 1978), 159–60. Cleaver's archives at the University of California at Berkeley include an earlier, more confrontational draft of this letter, in which Cleaver offers to donate $500,000 to Palestinian militants should the Panthers be given the Hijacking Family's ransom.
200 ***join the excited crowd:*** Holder interview.

201 ***public relations blunder***: Cleaver to Tabor; "Algerian Police Isolate Panthers' Headquarters," *St. Petersburg Times*, Aug. 12, 1972.

201 ***during the villa raid***: Cleaver, record of second meeting with Salah.

201 ***the headstrong Cleaver***: Cleaver to Tabor.

201 ***he lost all faith***: Holder interview.

202 **Willie Roger Holder**: Cleaver to Tabor; "Panthers in Algeria Pick Hijacker Chief," *Chicago Tribune*, Sept. 28, 1972.

14. "The Olympics Wasn't Anything"

207 ***"in four-by-four-foot boxes"***: The account of the Southern Airways Flight 49 hijacking is primarily based on five sources: Ed Blair with Capt. William R. Haas, *Odyssey of Terror* (self-published, 2006); Garrett M. Graff, *The Threat Matrix: The FBI at War* (Little, Brown, 2011), 31–55; "Convicted Hijacker Shares Story, Details 1972 Threat to Oak Ridge," WBIR.com, May 25, 2011; "Hijacked Plane at McCoy Briefly," *Ledger* (Lakeland, Fla.), Nov. 12, 1972; and "Chronology of a Hijacking," *New York Times*, Nov. 13, 1972. The detail regarding the $5 million Lufthansa payment comes from "Bonn Paid $5M Jet Ransom," *Guardian*, February 26, 1972. The detail regarding the number of STRESS-related fatal shootings comes from W. Marvin Dulaney, *Black Police in America* (Bloomington: Indiana University Press, 1996), 99.

207 ***more than two dozen innocents***: "FBI Hit for Firing at Plane," *Vancouver Sun*, Nov. 14, 1972.

207 ***destination such as Algeria***: "Head of FBI Says He Ordered Hijacked Planes' Tires Shot Out," *New York Times*, Nov. 15, 1972. Six days after defending his decision, Gray was admitted to the hospital for "intestinal obstruction," reportedly brought about by the stress of dealing with the fallout from Flight 49.

208 ***"stop them at the boarding gate"***: "Hijacking Steps Tightened in U.S.," *Calgary Herald*, Dec. 6, 1972.

209 ***"a cloud of fear"***: Jon Hendricks and Jean Toche, oral history interview by Allen Schwartz, Dec. 13, 1972, Smithsonian Archives of American Art, http://www.aaa.si.edu/collections/interviews/oral-history-interview-jon-hendricks-and-mr-jean-toche-11910.

209 ***might meet that test***: "Skyjacking: Constitutional Problems Raised by Anti-Hijacking Systems," *Journal of Criminal Law, Criminology, and Police Science* 63, no. 3 (Sept. 1972), 356–65.

210 ***who flew each day***: "Politics, Economics and Skyjacking," *New York Times*, Dec. 3, 1972.

210 ***without federal assistance***: "Volpe Opposed to Hijack Police Force," *Ellensburg* (Wash.) *Daily Record*, Jan. 11, 1973.

211 ***receptive to that adjustment***: Mark Feldman, interview by author, Aug. 2010.

211 ***on December 12***: Robert A. Hurwitch to U.S. secretary of state, Dec. 12, 1972, U.S. Department of State Archive, http://2001-2009.state.gov/.

212 ***in Bab el-Oued vacant***: Eldridge Cleaver to Michael Cetewayo Tabor, Sept. 24, 1972, Eldridge Cleaver Papers, Bancroft Library, University of California at Berkeley.

212 ***at Pointe Pescade***: Willie Roger Holder, interview by author, Aug. 2011.

212 *"problems will be solved"*: Cleaver to Tabor.

212 *most avid supporters*: Henry Louis Gates, "Eldridge Cleaver on Ice," *Transition* 75/76 (Winter 1997), 308–9.

212 *sticking with the recipes*: Eldridge Cleaver, journal entry, Oct. 29, 1972, Eldridge Cleaver Papers, Bancroft Library, University of California at Berkeley.

213 *lost interest in his duties*: Roger Holder to Lynne Stewart, Oct. 9, 1986, private collection of Joy Holder; "Algeria's Haven for Hijackers Isn't All That They Expected," *Hartford* (Conn.) *Courant*, Dec. 12, 1972.

213 *worry and gloom*: Holder interview.

213 *to face prosecution*: Melvin McNair et al., *Nous, Noirs Américains Évadés du Ghetto* (Paris: Editions de Seuil, 1978), 107–8.

213 *in such delicate tasks*: Kathleen Cleaver to "Comrade T," Dec. 15, 1972, Eldridge Cleaver Papers, Bancroft Library, University of California at Berkeley.

214 *left behind in Algiers*: Gates, "Eldridge Cleaver on Ice," 309–10.

214 *than he already had*: McNair et al., *Nous, Noirs Américains*, 108–9.

214 *Algerian intelligence*: Eldridge Cleaver, personal datebook pages, Jan. 1–16, 1973, Eldridge Cleaver Papers, Bancroft Library, University of California at Berkeley.

214 *about his fate*: Holder interview.

215 *respond to Holder's proposal*: Ibid.

15. "Monsieur Lecanuet, Anyone Can Steal . . ."

216 *"glory be!"*: "Anti-Hijacking Rules Go Into Effect," *Tuscaloosa* (Ala.) *News*, Jan. 6, 1973.

216 *only for weapons*: "Stretching the Fourth Amendment," *New York Times*, Dec. 24, 1972.

217 *in their checked luggage*: "Anti-Hijacking Rules Go Into Effect."

217 *any human inspector*: David J. Haas, "Electronic Security Screening: Its Origin with Aviation Security 1968–1973," *Journal of Applied Security Research* 5, no. 4 (Sept. 2010), 515–24.

217 *amounts of radiation*: Ibid., 492–95.

218 *thirty-four cents per ticket*: "Air Fares to Reflect Anti-Hijacking Costs," *Sarasota* (Fla.) *Journal*, Mar. 29, 1973.

218 *7 percent in 1973*: "Historical Air Traffic Statistics, Annual 1954–1980," Research and Innovative Technology Administration, Bureau of Transportation Statistics, http://www.bts.gov/programs/airline_information/air_carrier_traffic_statistics/airtraffic/anual/1954_1980.html.

218 *sit idle for a day*: "'Rabbi Jacob' Est Sorti Entre Rire et Drame," *Paris Match*, Sept. 30, 2008.

218 *hijacked in 1974*: FAA, Civil Aviation Security Service, "Hijacking Statistics for U.S. Registered Aircraft (1961–Present)," April 1, 1975, https://www.ncjrs.gov/pdffiles1/Digitization/28885NCJRS.pdf.

218 *back to the United States*: "Florida Hijacker in Custody of Cubans," *Lewiston* (Me.) *Daily Sun*, Dec. 16, 1974.

219 *for further questioning*: FBI Legat Paris, report to FBI director, Jan. 7, 1975 (obtained through FOIA request).

219 *precisely how long*: Ibid.

219 *Fifteenth Arrondissement*: Record of the Court of Assize of Paris, Jun. 13, 1980, private collection of Joy Holder.

219 *by week's end*: FBI Legat Paris, report to FBI director, Jan. 7, 1975.

220 ***various states of assembly***: FBI Legat Paris, report to FBI director, Jan. 8, 1975 (FOIA); Willie Roger Holder, interview by author, Aug. 2011; "Two Hijack Suspects Arrested in Paris," *Los Angeles Times*, Jan. 26, 1975.

220 ***Latin Quarter of Paris***: Melvin McNair et al., *Nous, Noirs Américains Évadés du Ghetto* (Paris: Editions de Seuil, 1978), 108–9.

220 ***each other's nerves***: Holder interview.

220 ***Cleaver for help***: Ibid.

220 ***highly placed politicians***: Eldridge Cleaver, *Soul on Fire* (Waco, Tex.: Word Books, 1978), 193–97.

221 ***to the documents***: FBI Special Agent in Charge, Washington field office, memo to FBI director, Jan. 29, 1975 (FOIA).

221 ***near the Rue Beaubourg***: Holder interview; Denis de Kergorlay, interview by author, Jul. 2012.

221 ***traumatized war veterans***: Jean-Michel Caroit, interview by author, Jul. 2012.

221 ***in left-wing politics***: Holder interview.

222 ***during his sabbatical***: Ibid.

222 ***four tranquilizers***: "Black Panther Hit by 'Nervous Crisis,'" *Los Angeles Sentinel*, Jan. 30, 1975.

222 ***a disorienting mess***: Holder interview.

223 ***Cleaver political asylum***: Cleaver, *Soul on Fire*, 189–206.

223 ***on the Left Bank***: Ibid, 186.

223 ***"Babylon"***: Eldridge Cleaver, interview by David Mills, University of Maryland, 1982, http://undercoverblackman.blogspot.com/2007/02/q-eldridge-cleaver-pt-1.html.

223 ***safe house to the next***: FBI Legat Paris, memo to FBI director, Jan. 16, 1975 (FOIA).

223 ***fingerprints from the French***: Seavenes and Marie Holder, interview by FBI, San Diego, Jan. 21, 1975 (FOIA).

223 ***Janice Ann Forte***: "Two Hijack Suspects Arrested in Paris"; FBI director, memo to special agents in charge of Portland, New York, San Diego, and San Francisco field offices, Jan. 24, 1975 (FOIA).

224 ***"their quiet strength"***: Jean-Jacques de Felice, "Memories of the War in Algeria," *Men and Freedom* 116 (Sept.–Nov. 2001).

224 ***discomfort to the powerful***: Geoffrey Adams, *The Call of Conscience: French Protestant Responses to the Algerian War, 1954–1962* (Waterloo, Ont.: Wilfrid Laurier University Press, 1998), 114, 214.

224 ***"concern for human rights"***: Cleaver, *Soul on Fire*, 193–94.

226 ***"going to be all right"***: Holder interview; Aline Mosby, wire report, United Press International, Jan. 28, 1975; "Black Panther Hit by 'Nervous Crisis.'"

226 ***February 18 memo***: U.S. secretary of state to Paris embassy, Feb. 18, 1975 (FOIA).

227 ***"shall be final"***: Extradition Treaty Between the United States and France, signed in Paris on Apr. 5, 1909, http://images.library.wisc.edu/FRUS/EFacs/1911/reference/frus.frus1911.i0017.pdf.

227 ***"so obviously political"***: Paris embassy to U.S. secretary of state, Apr. 29, 1975 (FOIA).

227 ***for Holder and Kerkow***: Mark Feldman, interview by author, Aug. 2010.

227 ***would be trouble-free***: U.S. secretary of state to Paris embassy, Mar. 21, 1975 (FOIA).

228 ***"let us stay in France"***: "Panther Hijacker in Paris Bucks Extradition to the U.S.," *Chicago Defender*, Mar. 4, 1975.

229 ***constituted a genocide***: Paris em-

bassy to U.S. secretary of state, Mar. 12, 1975 (FOIA).

229 *making his decision*: Paris embassy to U.S. secretary of state, Mar. 18 and Mar. 26, 1975 (FOIA).

230 *"and the court"*: U.S. secretary of state to Paris embassy, Mar. 26, 1975 (FOIA).

230 *to take a look*: Paris embassy to U.S. secretary of state, Mar. 26, 1975.

230 *"exactly how many times"*: U.S. secretary of state to Paris embassy, Apr. 1, 1975 (FOIA).

231 *"in this and further cases"*: Paris embassy to U.S. secretary of state, Apr. 2, 1975 (FOIA).

231 *at Fleury-Mérogis*: Paris embassy to U.S. secretary of state, Apr. 14, 1975 (FOIA).

232 *"at bay for ransom"*: Secretary of state to Paris embassy, Apr. 16, 1975 (FOIA).

232 *the "hijacking menace"*: Paris embassy to U.S. secretary of state, Apr. 22, 1975 (FOIA).

233 *"for Anglo-Saxons to understand"*: Paris embassy to U.S. secretary of state, Apr. 29, 1975 (FOIA).

16. Omega

235 *"what I did was patriotic"*: "U.S. Return Is Intended by Hijacker," *Spokesman-Review* (Spokane, Wash.), May 7, 1977.

235 *twice a month*: Paris embassy to U.S. secretary of state, Jun. 2, 1975 (obtained through FOIA request).

235 *appeared quite smitten*: Willie Roger Holder, interview by author, Aug. 2011.

236 *men too much*: Ibid., wire report by Associated Press, Nov. 24, 1978; "Shocking Case of Black American Political Prisoners in France," *Sun Reporter* (San Francisco), Aug. 24, 1978.

236 *time to stop running*: Holder interview.

237 *discuss the matter further*: Paris embassy to U.S. secretary of state, Apr. 30, 1976 (FOIA); U.S. secretary of state to Paris embassy, May 5, 1976 (FOIA).

237 *a phone call away*: Holder interview.

238 *family in Oregon*: "U.S. Return Is Intended by Hijacker."

239 *"trying to get away from"*: "Eldridge Cleaver's New Pants," *Harvard Crimson*, Sept. 26, 1975.

239 *a born-again Christian*: Eldridge Cleaver, *Soul on Fire* (Waco, Tex: Word Books, 1978), 208–212.

240 *"companions to the Lord"*: "Cleaver 'Testifies' as an Evangelical," *New York Times*, Dec. 12, 1976; "Cleaver Got No Help," *Leader-Post* (Regina, Sask.), Jul. 25, 1977.

241 *never followed through*: Paris embassy to U.S. secretary of state, Oct. 5, 1977 (FOIA).

241 *Doctors Without Borders*: Denis de Kergorlay interview by author, Jul. 2012.

242 *discuss the future then*: Holder interview.

17. Tweety Bird

244 *Cutcher was also staying*: Thomas Crawford, interview by author, Oct. 2010.

244 *they slept that night*: Regina Youngren (formerly Cutcher), interview by author, Jun. 2010.

244 *one defendant on trial*: Crawford interview.

244 *or April 17*: Paris embassy to U.S. secretary of state, Apr. 5, 1978 (obtained through FOIA request).

245 *obtain a new passport*: Paris embassy to U.S. secretary of state, Bern embassy, and Zurich consulate, May 11, 1978 (FOIA).

245 *neglected to renew it*: U.S. secretary of state to all European diplomatic posts, May 4, 1979 (FOIA).

246 *fitting Kerkow's description*: Paris embassy to U.S. secretary of state, Bern embassy, and Zurich consulate, May 11, 1978.

246 *within forty-eight hours*: Kerkow's timing was fortuitous: prior to January 1, 1978, replacement passports had been valid only until the expiration date of the one that had been lost. By changing this policy and making replacement passports valid for a full five years, the State Department made Kerkow's ruse much easier to pull off.

246 *absorbed the child*: Willie Roger Holder, interview by author, Aug. 2011.

246 *his hijacking trial*: Paris embassy to U.S. secretary of state and Brussels embassy, Apr. 27, 1979 (FOIA).

246 *prominent French supporters*: Denis de Kergorlay, interview by author, Jul. 2012.

246 *the Marais district*: Joy Holder, interview by author, Apr. 2012.

246 *engineering program*: Roger Holder interview.

246 *psychological crises*: Joy Holder interview.

247 *trial had taken place*: Paris embassy to U.S. secretary of state, Apr. 5, 1978 (FOIA).

247 *the Hijacking Family*: Paris embassy to U.S. secretary of state, Oct. 26, 1976 (FOIA).

248 *settle in France*: "France Convicts 4 Yanks in Hijack," *Pittsburgh Post-Gazette*, Nov. 25, 1978.

248 *exonerating Holder*: Youngren interview.

249 *through the motions*: Crawford interview.

249 *an eye at the cheers*: Youngren interview.

249 *at least 1985*: Paris embassy to U.S. secretary of state, Jun. 25, 1980 (FOIA).

250 *tinge of joy*: Holder interview.

250 *many splendid rooms*: De Kergorlay interview.

250 *resist the draft*: Ibid.; Holder interview.

250 *work on his memoirs*: Ibid.

250 *performed odd jobs*: Ibid.; Henri Boivin, interview by author, Jul. 2012.

250 *eager to learn*: Holder interview.

250 *James Baldwin novels*: De Kergorlay interview.

250 *reach either goal*: Holder interview.

251 *heard from him again*: De Kergorlay interview.

251 *memories of combat*: Medical certificate signed by Dr. C. Louzon, Psychiatric Hospital of Vieille-Église, Apr. 15, 1981, private collection of Joy Holder.

251 *assignment to the next*: Joy Holder interview.

251 *hardware store*: Roger Holder interview.

251 *his car for days*: Joy Holder interview.

251 *possession of hashish*: Supplemental affirmation, *United States v. Willie Roger Holder*, Nov. 18, 1987; and motion for dismissal of indictment, *United States v. Willie Roger Holder*, Jan. 8, 1988, both in private collection of Joy Holder.

252 *on American soil*: U.S. secretary of state to Paris embassy, Aug. 13, 1985 (FOIA).

252 *powerful psychotropic drugs*: Psychiatric evaluation of Willie Roger Holder, conducted at Federal Correctional Institution in Butner,

N.C., Dec. 26, 1991, private collection of Joy Holder.

252 *had finally come true*: "Ex–Black Panther Extradited to U.S.," *New York Times*, Jul. 27, 1986.

252 *the offices of IBM*: "Code Book Connected 7 to NY Bombings," *Lewiston* (Me.) *Daily Sun*, Mar. 14, 1985.

253 *"deaths taking place"*: Willie Roger Holder to Lynne Stewart, Oct. 9, 1986, private collection of Joy Holder.

254 *"a life for himself"*: Judge Eugene H. Nickerson, memorandum and order, *United States of America v. Willie Roger Holder*, May 29, 1992, National Archives and Records Administration, Central Plains Region, St. Louis, Mo.

254 *Torrita as her own*: Holder interview.

254 *act of paternal love*: Correction to DD Form 214 for Willie Roger Holder (service no. 18910865), Jul. 19, 1978, private collection of Joy Holder.

254 *was not to be*: Holder interview.

255 *office that December*: Susan Tipograph, handwritten notes from meeting with Willie Roger Holder at Metropolitan Correctional Center, New York, Jul. 27, 1991, private collection of Joy Holder. I could find no record of a divorce between Holder and his first wife, Betty Bullock, a fact that suggests that this marriage was bigamous.

255 *a freeway junction*: Rosemarie Wilson, interview by author, Apr. 2012; search warrant for 1117 33rd Street, San Diego, signed by Violetta Velkova, Jul. 2, 1991, private collection of Joy Holder.

255 *"his psychological problems"*: Judge Nickerson memorandum and order.

255 *earned in prison*: Holder interview.

255 *after a few weeks*: Seavenes Holder, Jr., interview by FBI, in San Diego, Jul. 10, 1991 (FOIA).

255 *"his part in history"*: Judge Nickerson memorandum and order.

255 *change the world*: San Diego FBI field office to FBI director, Jun. 13, 1991 (FOIA).

256 *adulterous ex-wife, Betty*: Judge Nickerson memorandum and order.

256 *possessing drugs*: Ibid.

256 *Mandela's political party*: California attorney general Daniel E. Lungren to United States Probation Office, Jul. 2, 1991 (FOIA).

256 *for fifteen years*: Judge Nickerson memorandum and order.

256 *think it over*: Ibid.

256 *"caps as you can"*: Susan Tipograph to Willie Roger Holder, May 11, 1992, private collection of Joy Holder.

257 *while living in France*: "Hijacker from '70s Lands in Trouble," *San Diego Union-Tribune*, Jul. 17, 1991.

257 *"want to back out"*: Judge Nickerson memorandum and order.

257 *military-grade explosives*: Holder interview.

257 *he said, the better*: Ibid.

258 *brick of C-4 explosives*: Willie Roger Holder, interrogation by FBI, handwritten notes, Jul. 2, 1991 (FOIA).

258 *project was complete*: Judge Nickerson memorandum and order.

258 *by the following week*: Special Agent David Torres, California Department of Justice, affidavit, Jul. 2, 1991 (FOIA).

258 *"boat putty"*: Judge Nickerson memorandum and order.

258 *given them the slip*: Ibid.; Torres affidavit.

258 *in Santa Barbara*: Torres affidavit.

258 **Terror by Fiat**: FBI, report on execution of search warrant in connection with investigation of Willie Roger Holder, Jul. 9, 1991 (FOIA).

259 *with the Black Panthers*: Susan

Tipograph, interview by author, Feb. 2011.

259 ***competent to stand trial***: Psychiatric evaluation of Willie Roger Holder.

259 **big-time political terrorist?**: Jason Brown, interview by author, Jun. 2010.

260 ***sting operation going***: Judge Nickerson, memorandum and order.

260 ***recapturing past glory***: Ibid.

18. Erased

261 ***"costs appear enormous"***: William M. Landes, "An Economic Study of U.S. Aircraft Hijacking, 1960–1976," National Bureau of Economic Research, Oct. 1977, http://www.nber.org/papers/w0210.

261 ***of Landes's study***: Research and Innovative Technology Administration, Bureau of Transportation Statistics, "Historical Air Traffic Statistics, Annual 1954–1980," http://www.bts.gov/programs/airline_information/air_carrier_traffic_statistics/airtraffic/annual/1954_1980.html.

261 ***jumped from the cockpit***: "The Hijacking: 'The Whole Thing Was Just Some Pathetic Cry for Help,'" *Evening Independent* (St. Petersburg, Fla.), Mar. 14, 1978.

262 ***his outstanding debts***: "Suspect to Face Air Piracy Charge," *Bulletin* (Bend, Ore.), Aug. 24, 1979.

262 ***her mother's lover***: "17-Year-Old Girl Held in Hijacking," *Milwaukee Journal*, Dec. 22, 1978. The girl in question, Robin Oswald, was trying to liberate Garrett Brock Trapnell, who had been wounded by FBI agents while hijacking a TWA flight in January 1972.

262 ***afoul of the law***: "Disheartened Refugees Try Hijacking as a Way Home," *Pittsburgh Post-Gazette*, Aug. 19, 1980.

262 ***country at large***: "12th Hijacking Try and 9th Success," *Deseret News* (Salt Lake City, Ut.), Aug. 5, 1983.

262 ***to face prosecution***: "Castro Returns Two Cuban Hijackers," *Palm Beach Post*, Sept. 19, 1980.

262 ***the mentally unwell***: Laura Dugan et al., "Testing a Rational Choice Model of Airplane Hijackings," *Criminology* 43, no. 4 (2005), 1041, 1043.

263 ***in American airspace***: FAA, Office of Civil Aviation Security, "Criminal Acts Against Civil Aviation 2000," http://www.skyjack.co.il/pdf/Criminal_Acts_Against_Civil_Aviation_2000.pdf.

263 ***instructional videos***: Cletus C. Coughlin et al., "Aviation Security and Terrorism: A Review of the Economic Issues," *Federal Reserve Bank of St. Louis Review*, Sept.–Oct. 2002, 9–24.

263 ***was just $12,000***: Paul W. Parfomak, "Guarding America: Security Guards and U.S. Critical Infrastructure Protection," Congressional Research Service, Nov. 12, 2004, http://www.fas.org/sgp/crs/RL32670.pdf.

269 ***in a military cemetery***: My thanks to Roger Holder, Joy Holder, and Rosemarie Wilson for sharing the memories included in this section. The Angela Davis quote comes from "Kathleen Cleaver and Angela Davis: Rekindling the Flame," *Essence*, May 1996.

270 ***Western Airlines Flight 701***: Hannah Cooney, interview by author, Coos Historical and Maritime Museum, Apr. 2011. Patricia Kerkow declined to be interviewed for this book. For the record, this was her

one statement to me: "I have no intention of meeting with you or putting my family through that ever again."

270 ***let alone her crime:*** Author's visit, May 2011.

271 ***swap in 1972:*** Elizabeth Olson (formerly Newhouse), interview by author, May 2011.

271 ***seems to believe:*** Paris embassy to U.S. secretary of state, Bern embassy, and Zurich consulate, May 11, 1978 (obtained through FOIA request).

Index

I

S

T

U

ABOUT THE AUTHOR

BRENDAN I. KOERNER is a contributing editor at *Wired* and the author of *Now the Hell Will Start*, which was optioned by filmmaker Spike Lee. A former columnist for both the *New York Times* and *Slate* who was named one of *Columbia Journalism Review*'s "Ten Young Writers on the Rise," he has also written for *Harper's*, the *New York Times Magazine*, *ESPN the Magazine*, and many other publications. Visit www.theskiesbelongto.us and follow @brendankoerner on Twitter.